Chicken Soup for the Soul: Step Outside Your Comfort Zone
101 Stories about Trying New Things, Overcoming Fears, and Broadening Your World
Amy Newmark

Published by Chicken Soup for the Soul, LLC www.chickensoup.com
Copyright ©2017 by Chicken Soup for the Soul, LLC. All Rights Reserved.

The publisher gratefully acknowledges the many publishers and individuals who granted Chicken Soup for the Soul permission to reprint the cited material.

Front cover artwork courtesy of iStockphoto.com/oneblink-cj (©oneblink-cj)
Back cover and Interior photo artwork courtesy of iStockphoto.com/hudiemm (©hudiemm)
Photo of Amy Newmark courtesy of Susan Morrow at SwickPix

Cover and Interior by Daniel Zaccari

Distributed to the booktrade by Simon & Schuster. SAN: 200-2442

Publisher's Cataloging-In-Publication Data
(Prepared by The Donohue Group, Inc.)

Names: Newmark, Amy, compiler.
Title: Chicken soup for the soul : step outside your comfort zone :
      101 stories about trying new things, overcoming fears, and
      broadening your world / [compiled by] Amy Newmark.
Other Titles: Step outside your comfort zone : 101 stories about
      trying new things, overcoming fears, and broadening your world
Description: [Cos Cob, Connecticut] : Chicken Soup for the Soul,
      LLC, [2017]
Identifiers: ISBN 978-1-61159-974-9 (print) | ISBN 978-1-61159-274-0
      (ebook)
Subjects: LCSH: Risk-taking (Psychology)--Literary collections. |
      Risk-taking (Psychology)--Anecdotes. | Courage--Literary
      collections. | Courage--Anecdotes. | Change (Psychology)--
      Literary collections. | Change (Psychology)--Anecdotes. | LCGFT:
      Anecdotes.
Classification: LCC BF637.R57 C45 2017 (print) | LCC BF637.R57
      (ebook) | DDC 158.1--dc23

Library of Congress LCCN: 2017947989

PRINTED IN THE UNITED STATES OF AMERICA
on acid∞free paper

25 24 23 22 21 20 19 18 17   01 02 03 04 05 06 07 08 09 10 11

Chicken Soup for the Soul.

STEP OUTSIDE YOUR COMFORT ZONE

101 Stories about Trying New Things, Overcoming Fears, and Broadening Your World

Amy Newmark

CSS

Chicken Soup for the Soul, LLC
Cos Cob, CT

Chicken Soup for the Soul

Changing your life one story at a time ®
www.chickensoup.com

Table of Contents

3

~Connect with Someone~

4

~Reinvent Yourself~

5

~Face Your Fears~

❻

~Be Spontaneous~

❼

~Go Far Away~

❽

~Find Love~

❾

~Take a Risk~

Introduction

A ship in harbor is safe, but that is
not what ships are built for.
~John A. Shedd

've been in this position — editor-in-chief and publisher of Chicken Soup for the Soul — for almost a decade now, and it falls mainly on me to come up with our list of new titles each year. I always say, "I'm out of topics. I'm not going to be able to come up with a dozen new ideas." But invariably, the topics present themselves — because I see them emerging as subthemes in the stories we're sent by the public. No matter what they're writing about, their stories are colored by the other things that are important to them as well.

That's how the "Step Outside Your Comfort Zone" topic came about. We saw so many of our contributors challenging themselves to face their fears and try new things. They reported how that changed them for the better, and led to more new things, and a broader, more meaningful life.

I found myself doing the same thing — trying things that frightened me, or that I just assumed I wouldn't like: rock climbing in a gym, ziplining, riding every roller coaster at Universal Studios Hollywood, appearing on television shows, wearing my bathing suit in front of people, and forcing myself to try avocados again even though I knew I hated them. Now avocado toast is one of my favorite breakfast items!

Whether it's the little things, like new foods, or the big things, like flying to a faraway country, we feel empowered when we do something that challenges us. I talk about that in my story, "Run," about paragliding off a cliff in Oman. I was terrified, but it changed me. Now I know: If I can run off a cliff in Oman, anything is possible.

A big part of stepping outside your comfort zone is learning to trust. You need to trust the experts who say it can be done, or that friend or relative who tells you that you can do it. You also need to trust strangers, and we have many stories about that in this collection. I know that my college semester in a remote part of Brazil almost forty years ago taught me a great deal about the kindness and good intentions of strangers. I talk about that in my story, "The Oddity," and how I still draw on the reserves of strength and trust that I built during that lonely, but exhilarating, experience.

When we post a new topic on our website, we never know exactly how our writers will interpret it, and we don't go into making a book with any preconceived notions. I always say that our books are like mirrors reflecting back to our readers what thousands of them have told us is on their minds. After I've selected the 101 stories for each volume, I sort them into chapters, and that's when all our subthemes develop. I am so excited about the chapters that jumped out of this collection. Look at these great ideas:

1. Just Say Yes
2. Learn to Trust
3. Connect with Someone
4. Reinvent Yourself
5. Face Your Fears
6. Be Spontaneous
7. Go Far Away
8. Find Love
9. Take a Risk
10. Take Back Your Life

Now I'm envying you. You're starting the journey I just completed. I came away changed, and I bet you will, too. I'd love to know what you try after reading these stories. Let me know by e-mailing amy@ chickensoupforthesoul.com. I'll report back on the Chicken Soup for the Soul podcast, and in our next book on this topic, *Chicken Soup for the Soul: The Power of Yes.*

So go forth! Try new things, overcome your fears, and broaden your world. And here's my little secret: If you're about to do something scary, see if there's a video about it on the Internet. Before we went ziplining in Costa Rica, I watched a couple of videos that tourists had posted on YouTube, from the very place we were going. That's why I seemed so cool, calm, and collected when we got there. I already knew what was going to happen.

I put my favorite quote of all time at the top of this introduction: "A ship in harbor is safe, but that is not what ships are built for." I live by that philosophy, and I highly recommend that you, too, set sail from your safe harbor. Feel the wind, see new sights, and make your world bigger.

And thank you for being one of our readers.

~Amy Newmark
August 31, 2017

Chapter 1

STEP OUTSIDE YOUR COMFORT ZONE

☑ Just Say Yes

Run

Continuity gives us roots; change gives us branches,
letting us stretch and grow and reach new heights.
~Pauline R. Kezer

Okay, so I would never jump out of an airplane. How could I ever trust that a piece of fabric with a million strings coming out of it wouldn't get tangled up and fail to work? I have plenty of friends who have done it, but I won't.

But I'm all for doing new and scary things, especially as I get older, because I recognize the value of saying "yes" and ensuring that my world doesn't get narrower and narrower. And I've been inspired by all the Chicken Soup for the Soul stories that I've read by people who were advancing in years and made a special effort to try new things. So last year, when I was facing the prospect of turning sixty, a truly surprising development, I renewed my commitment to trying new things, including the *scary* ones.

And that's how I found myself standing at the top of a 1,000-foot cliff in Oman, on my way to a beautiful beach resort on the Persian Gulf.

You might think that taking a beach vacation on the Persian Gulf was enough of a "step outside your comfort zone" experience, but *that* was easy. It was gorgeous and luxurious and they picked us up at the airport in Dubai and took care of getting us across the border into Oman. Oman is a beautiful country on the Arabian Peninsula, known for its craggy sandstone mountains that plummet right down to the sea. It's very dramatic to see those tall mountains with sheer cliffs right next to the water, occasionally with beaches running along the edge of the sea.

The challenging part was the approach to the resort, which is so remote that you have three choices for the last part of the trip: 1) arrive by speedboat; 2) drive down a narrow, winding mountain road with hairpin turns and no guardrails; or, 3) jump off that 1,000-foot-high mountain cliff and paraglide down to the beach. According to tripadvisor.com, the really cool guests paraglide in.

I decided, that as a very cool fifty-nine-year-old, I would paraglide down to the beach. I imagined some kind of fixed wing thing, like bird wings. That made aerodynamic sense to me. Wings that were already in place would be guaranteed to work — not like parachuting out of an airplane where the fabric might somehow *not* get itself organized into the right shape, or the strings might get tangled up.

So I was shocked when they were putting the harness on me and I turned around and saw a flimsy piece of fabric lying on the ground behind me — with lots of strings attached to it. That was when I realized that *para*gliding is *called* that because you use a *para*chute. For someone who specializes in words and clear language, I had truly been off my game!

But I didn't have much time to think about it because they were already strapping me in. Then they stuck a helmet on me. I don't know *what* they said this was for, but whatever they were saying, what I *heard* was: *to identify the body.* And then they told me that it was critically important that I run toward the cliff and absolutely not stop under any circumstances. Because if I didn't run right off the cliff, the flimsy piece of fabric with the one million strings wouldn't catch the air and I would plummet to my death.

Before I could change my mind the guide and I were running toward the edge of the cliff. And then, miraculously, that parachute filled with air and we were soaring, riding the air currents and flying even higher than where we had started. The guide was thrilled that the air currents were so strong, and that we could stay up an extra long time. Of course, I was only half enjoying it, because the other half of my brain was trying to remember what "wind shear" was and whether that was relevant. If the winds changed, could we just drop like a rock?

Nevertheless, we soared for fifteen minutes and then, finally, we flew lower and lower until we put our legs out and ran to a stop on the beach. *Mission accomplished, time for a stiff drink, and I never have to do that again!*

But it was empowering, and I'm so glad that I did it. I've tried plenty of other less scary things since then, because now I compare everything to paragliding. If I can run off a cliff in Oman, I can certainly ride a roller coaster back here in the States, or be a keynote speaker at a conference, or try a new kind of food. Everything seems possible now. And sixty doesn't feel quite as old as I feared.

~Amy Newmark

Third Time's the Charm

Try, try, and try again. Never stop trying.
~Lailah Gifty Akita

"I can't like it." My toddler made a face and spit her spinach back onto her plate. "I want nuggets."

Exasperated, but bound and determined not to be one of those moms who gave in to her child's picky eating habits, I gathered myself and tried a different approach. I firmly believed that junk food should be for special occasions, not a daily habit.

"Mommy worked hard to make you a nutritious and delicious meal. Please eat it," I begged, almost at my wits' end. This was the fourth time that week I had made dinner, only to have her refuse it.

"No!" she yelled. "I WANT NUGGETS! All my fwiends at school get whatever they want for dinner. I hate you!" She was screaming while tossing her food on the floor. I bowed my head in shame, feeling as if I was failing as a parent.

I took a deep breath and tried to keep my cool. I gave her a stern "don't-mess-with-me" look and said, "Come on, you know the rule."

"Yes, I should try evwething tree times," she replied with a roll of her eyes.

"That's right," I said in my sweetest mom voice. "So two more bites."

When I was a child, my mother refused to make me eat everything on my plate. Her mom had insisted that food never be wasted, and she was convinced that this training was the reason for her being overweight.

My mother had a different approach. She said I had to try every food three times. Her reasoning was this: one time to try it, the second time to get over the fact that you had just tried it, and the third to make sure that you don't like it. After those three attempts, if I still hated the taste, she would never make me eat it again. Her rational and supportive approach worked almost every time — except with liver and bananas (which I still won't eat to this day).

I was raising my daughter with this same — reasonable — rule. A small smile crept onto my face now as I saw her swallow her second bite of spinach and then open her mouth for the third. She slowly chewed her final forced bite, and my thoughts returned to how the "three things rule" had affected my life.

As I grew older, I brought that three-times philosophy into my daily life. I had been terrified of the diving board at the pool, but I had managed to make that first terrifying jump off the board. When I breathed in water, my mother, who was carefully watching me, jumped in to help me. Before she could even reach me, I was up and out of the pool, heading back to that diving board. I barely paused before I jumped off with a flourish the second time. More coughing ensued, but I was steadfast in beating this fear. When I got out of the pool the second time, my mom tried to cover me with a towel and escort me home. Instead, I threw off the towel and finished my mission.

The third time there was no fear and no water in my nose. In fact there were cheers from the others at the pool. At that point, I was hooked. For the next few summers, you couldn't pull me out of the water unless it was to dive into it. I have still never met a pool I didn't want to jump right in.

Every time I am faced with something that is outside my comfort zone, I repeat to myself that I must try everything three times, and it gives me the strength to forge ahead. From public speaking to job interviews, how am I going to know the outcome unless I go for it? Roller coasters, flying, changing careers, dating... all my major fears have somehow been faced by one simple idea that my mom came up with to get me to eat my vegetables. Sure, he may have not been great on the first date, but perhaps the second or third would be better.... This thought process even led to my marriage! My life has been full because my brain repeats this one simple rule: Try everything three times.

"Mommy?" My daughter's voice pulled me out of my memories. "I can like it now," she said as she finished all the spinach on her plate.

We are all afraid of the unknown. But how can we be sure that something won't be enjoyable unless we give it a shot? After all, if I hadn't tried everything three times, you would not be reading this. Instead, I would be stuck at a job that made me miserable, only dreaming of things that I could accomplish. In my mid-thirties, I left a successful job that did not fulfill me in order to pursue my dream of being a writer. After two rejections, I took a deep breath and tried for a third time, all while picturing that diving board. I have been happily living the life of a writer ever since.

And my daughter the picky eater? She's now a sixteen-year-old vegetarian. Spinach is one of her favorites, although she also still likes nuggets if they are soy — but only on special occasions.

~Jodi Renee Thomas

Flying High

Tell me, what is it you plan to do with
your one wild and precious life?
~Mary Oliver

M y husband David had gone through a grueling cancer treatment in 2006 while working hard at his maintenance job so I could be home with our eight children. When he lost his job in 2010, it seemed like one of the worst things that could happen to a cancer survivor. And once he was home, I saw how easily he tired from puttering around the yard, and wondered how he'd kept his job for as long as he had.

"Someday, we'll travel. We'll fly on an airplane, walk on a beach, and see the ocean," David would dream out loud. That "someday" seemed extraordinarily remote, but I wasn't about to deny his dreams.

With David around to help with the children, I was free to turn my writing hobby into part-time work. I freelanced for the local newspaper and David encouraged me to begin writing a book about the subject I'd lived and breathed for thirty years — couponing.

As part of building a platform for my couponing book, I designed an instructive workshop for community colleges. That workshop resulted in being hired by a metro-area newspaper to write a weekly column on the same topic. David drove me to the photo shoot, where I spent two hours posing and throwing coupons in the air. On the way home, we joked about how incredible it was: the very idea of me, who had always been shy, striking poses in front of a camera for a front-page story. It wasn't anything either of us had ever imagined me doing.

"You're flying. You're soaring. This is just the beginning," David predicted. "Someday, you'll be a public speaker. Your book will be published."

I laughed at that. So much of what he believed I could do was entirely outside my comfort zone. But then, libraries and community colleges began requesting classes on writing and couponing. I found a new calling teaching on topics I was passionate about. David drove me everywhere, worried about my night blindness, and claiming the time alone with me in the car was well worth the wait as I made my presentations. Once, I glanced to the back of the room where he sat and saw such adoration on his face that I had to pause to catch my breath. On the way home, he marveled at the difference he saw in me when I was in front of a room full of people.

"I love seeing you like this," he said, and I reminded him that none of it would be possible without his support and encouragement.

"You're the wind beneath my wings," I replied. "I couldn't do it without you."

Then, one day, I had to.

In March 2012, David experienced a heart attack and underwent stent surgery. The weekend he came home from the hospital, I was scheduled to do three workshops. He wouldn't allow me to cancel, assuring me he'd be fine with our children helping him. My teens cleaned the house and cooked for their dad while I was gone most of that Saturday. On Monday night, I left for another presentation. I'll never forget the moment I walked through the door that evening. David sat in the recliner, waiting for me. His eyes lit up when he saw me.

"It went well? You look so happy," he commented with a broad smile. We held hands and talked for a while, but his eyes kept drifting shut. When I realized he planned on staying in the recliner, I offered to sleep on the couch. He insisted I sleep upstairs so I could get a good night's rest. I don't even remember if I kissed him goodnight.

When I came downstairs the next morning, I discovered his heart had stopped beating sometime during the night, and I was certain mine had broken in two. The person who believed in me, the wind beneath my wings, was gone.

How could I go on doing the things he'd been such a part of — the workshops, the driving at night to events, or the completion of a book that had been his idea in the first place?

But how could I not, when he'd so obviously reveled in those endeavors?

The night of David's wake, I learned I'd won a full scholarship to a June writing conference. The idea of leaving my children for a few days so soon after their father's death seemed preposterous. Yet, David had encouraged me to apply for the scholarship, despite the fact the conference concluded on our wedding anniversary.

"Apply for it," David had said when I'd told him about it. "We'll have other anniversaries. This would be a wonderful opportunity for you."

So, three months after my husband died, I left my older children in charge of their younger siblings. Three months later, I flew on an airplane for the first time, headed to another writer's conference, where I would meet the man responsible for the scholarship I'd won, an author who would eventually become my mentor.

Stepping onto that airplane without the husband who'd dreamed of sharing a plane ride with me was one of the hardest things I've ever done. There was only one empty seat on that flight, and it happened to be the one next to me. I lay my hand on it as the plane took off, closing my eyes in fear. Then I abruptly opened them, determined to look at what David had always dreamed of seeing. My heart ached with bittersweet joy as the plane ascended. Bright sunlight streamed through the windows as we rose high above the clouds.

The airplane ride was just one more step in opening up a world I'd never imagined for myself, but my husband had. Seven months after David's death, I signed a contract for the book he'd encouraged me to write. By the time it was released a year later, I'd signed two more. A year after his death, I stood in front of a church congregation to speak about finding hope in grief. As a writer, I'd always known the power of the pen. When I saw people wiping away tears, I realized how equally powerful the spoken word could be. I added inspirational public speaking to the roster of things I'd never imagined doing.

In January 2017, at the age of fifty-seven, nearly five years after my husband's death, I took online courses to become a certified grief counselor. To celebrate the accomplishment, I did something unprecedented, traveling simply for the fun of it. My two youngest daughters accompanied me on a plane trip to Florida, where we stayed with my sister and brother-in-law.

On the day we visited a beach, I wandered away from everyone for a moment, plopping down on the soft, white sand David had always wanted to see. With the sound of the ocean waves lapping against the shore, I closed my eyes and strained to hear what sounded like a gentle whisper in the breeze.

"Someday."

~Mary Potter Kenyon

Go for It!

*Once in a while it really hits people that they
don't have to experience the world in
the way they have been told.*
~Alan Keightley

Without looking up from my desk, I recognized the man's voice. "I want to thank you for changing my life," he said.

"You're welcome," I chuckled, assuming he was referring to the addition of a second bathroom, made possible by the home-improvement loan I had processed for him.

He nodded. "Having a second bathroom is great, but I'm referring to your article in the Sunday magazine of *The Mercury*," he said. "You've made me see the error of my ways. Growing up, I loved baseball and aspired to be a professional baseball player. I expected my son to love the sport and have the same aspirations, but he dreads going to practice and playing the game. After reading your story, I knew what had to be done. This morning, my son hung up his cleats. He's going to follow in your son's footsteps. He wants to dance. I will no longer hinder his dream. I borrowed your words, 'Son, go for it!'"

"Yes, this guilt-ridden mom felt compelled to share her story," I gulped, fighting back the tears. "Your son is fortunate to have such an understanding and supportive dad. I'm grateful society has become more accepting of male dancers, and that there's an excellent local dance academy your son can attend."

After all these years, there's still a tug at my heart strings when I remember how mesmerized my five-year-old son was by the beauty and agility of the dancers performing the classic Christmas story, *The Nutcracker*, presented by the San Francisco Ballet company. But afterwards, when he expressed an interest in learning to dance, the classmate who lived next door laughed. "Don't be silly," she scoffed. "There are no boys in my dance classes."

One afternoon when my son waved from the front window to this leotard-clad classmate as she left for dance class, his eyes welled with tears. "Mom, boys dance too."

The neighborhood friend wasn't the only person who didn't support his interest in dance. Many family members and friends tried to discourage him by making disparaging remarks. "You can't wear dance shoes on the pitcher's mound." "Boys don't dance." "Dancing is for sissies."

My son disliked playing baseball and begged to hang up his cleats to pursue dance. But I hindered his dreams and succumbed to the views of my peers. Dance lessons were put on hold. To stop the taunting and criticism after he opted out of baseball, I enrolled him in swim lessons, science camp, art classes, bicycling, and summer school enrichment classes. But he never lost interest in learning to dance, and it intensified when he watched dancers on television, and in Broadway shows and movies.

Finally, he got to have his dance and voice lessons during his sophomore year of high school. His goal was to try out for the school's madrigal choral troupe, a group of twenty-eight students that performed at various California community events, political functions and holiday festivities from San Francisco to Santa Cruz during the senior year. Two weeks before graduation, the troupe tours and performs in Renaissance costumes in London, England. The competition to become a madrigal is fierce, and madrigal selections are made and posted at the end of the junior year by the Musical Director.

I marveled at my son's ability to cram in voice and piano lessons between ballet, tap, and jazz classes at a dance academy that welcomed male dancers. The hard work paid off — he made the cut. He thrived as a member of the madrigal troupe, and it paved the way to his dance career.

The summer after my son graduated from high school, he choreographed a group of junior high students in a production of *South Pacific*. How proud I was on the final night of the play when the cast thanked my son and presented him with a signed group photo in a silver frame. Seconds later, the students moved in for a group hug in the middle of the stage, and my son held the photo above his head and shouted, "You've been great to work with. I want all of you to pursue your dreams. Go for it!"

During his first year of college, he was offered a role in a national touring company of *A Chorus Line*. When my son asked if he should dance or finish college, I didn't hesitate to give him my blessing. "No more dashed dreams. Go for it!"

Several years later, he moved to New York City and was offered a chance to join his idol — the legendary dancer, choreographer and Tony Award-winning director, Bob Fosse — in his tour of *Sweet Charity*. Over the years, my son has danced in dinner theatre, summer stock, television and other musicals, such as *Evita*, *La Cage aux Folles*, *Pippin*, *Cabaret*, *Chicago* and *Fiddler on the Roof*. Indeed, boys dance, too.

Even though I wrote the article about diversity twenty years ago, I still recall the sense of pride I felt when that father dropped by my office and thanked me for changing his life… and his son's. My message holds true today: "It's okay to be different. Go for it!"

~Georgia A. Hubley

The Challenge

When we say yes, we do more, create more, live more.
~Author Unknown

The challenge came from my empty nester's group — the Happy Empty Nesters (Hens). Now that our chicks had flown from the coop, it was time to focus on our roosters. We gave each other two assignments for the next month. First: Say nothing negative or critical to our husbands. Second: When our husbands initiated an activity, say "Yes!" This could be something simple like taking a walk around the block after dinner or something more involved, like taking a cruise around the world.

I approached the challenge with trepidation; it is scary to give up control. What if I was tired or bored or afraid? But I was resolved to do it; I'd have to report back to the Hens the next month. To the best of my ability, I would agree to my husband's requests.

My first opportunity occurred that evening as I was making dinner. My husband asked tentatively, "How about if we eat out on the deck?" I had to admit it was a lovely day — puffy white clouds with sunshine — but his suggestion added work to my already long day. We'd need to clean off the patio furniture and shuttle all the food and utensils out there. We might be plagued by any number of annoyances — insects, gusts of wind, sun in our eyes.

I didn't say any of that. In the spirit of the challenge, I said, "Sure." My husband's eyebrows went up in mild surprise, and he wasted no time pulling out a tray and loading it up.

The clouds shielded us from the glaring sun for most of our spring dinner out on the deck. I could feel the warmth on my face and smelled a faint hint of jasmine from the yard. We heard the honks of Canadian geese at the pond in the distance. As we discussed our day, a Nuthatch landed on the deck rail just feet from where we sat. We froze in place. The tiny bird was joined by another (a mate?), and then they frolicked off. My husband caught my eye and smiled. At that moment, the clouds parted to reveal the sun setting low in the sky in a riot of color. We had front row seats to the delights of nature and a spectacular view.

We made a romantic memory that evening, and I would have missed it had I not consented to join my husband on a new mini-adventure.

A couple days later, my husband came home from work and said, "The latest action-adventure movie got good reviews, and it starts in half an hour. Wanna go?" Though not my favorite genre, I could do this. I said "Yes" again. The movie wasn't bad, and my husband appreciated my willingness to join him. He mentioned it multiple times.

That Saturday, we had planned to jog together, but the weather turned threatening. This time, I took the lead and asked my husband if he would run with me anyway. He agreed. We reached our farthest point before turning back when the clouds opened up and swamped us in a deluge of water. We laughed so hard it was difficult to keep running, and we returned home soaking wet and utterly happy.

When the month was up, the Hens met again. The reports were generally positive. But for one woman, the challenge sparked a complete turnaround in her marriage. I suggested we continue the challenge indefinitely, and everyone clucked in approval.

Throughout the next few years, my husband and I sought out adventure with each other. We flew kites on the National Mall during the National Cherry Blossom Festival; we tramped through newly fallen snow to capture photos; we drove Jeeps on the beach in the Outer Banks; we smelled the fragrant flowers of Longwood Gardens; we flew in a hot air balloon at the Albuquerque International Balloon Fiesta; we hunted down all the Fabergé Imperial Eggs in the country; and we built our own spa in the sand at Hot Water Beach in New Zealand.

The challenge changed my mindset from doing what is easy to thinking of ways to say "Yes" to my husband, "Yes" to adventure, and "Yes" to life. Of course, it would be easier to say "No." But this is a better way. This is living life and feeling truly alive — not just marking time, but living life to the fullest. Did this ever make me feel uncomfortable? It certainly did. But it has also been one of the best things I've ever said "Yes" to.

~Monica Cardiff

Jump

Do one thing every day that scares you.
~Eleanor Roosevelt

"One, two, three, jump!" I watched from the deck as one of my cousins jumped off the nearby cliff into the cool, clear water of the lake below. I heard the cheers and laughter from the rest of my cousins who were lined up waiting for their turns to jump.

The Fourth of July had always been a holiday full of happy memories for me, enjoying swimming, sand castles, sunburns and fireworks with family and friends. Each year, we would drive two hours to the Missouri River to swim, boat, picnic, and water ski for the day.

But this year was different. It was the first Fourth of July without my dad.

My dad had passed away from a massive heart attack just six weeks before. He was only fifty-six, but he had been fighting heart disease since his early thirties.

My mother, my two sisters and I were trying to figure out how to move forward without him. We decided to start a new tradition this Fourth of July. Instead of going to our normal spot on the Missouri River, we went to my cousin's house. She and her husband lived on a beautiful lake, one with cliffs rising on one side of it. Kids had been jumping off those cliffs for years, and it was a tradition for my cousin's family.

Now I was watching as one cousin after another took the plunge. "Hey! Come join us!"

I shook my head with a smile as a bead of sweat made its way down my brow.

I had always been more cautious than adventurous—the proverbial "good girl." I was the one who watched from the sidelines. But as I sat on my cousin's deck, I couldn't help but think about how my dad had lived his short life. He had always tried new things. He took on new challenges without worrying about failing. He ate octopus in Mexico and golfed in Scotland. He would parasail or water ski or go tubing without a second thought. He would try anything once. Even though he never mentioned having a bucket list to me, he lived as if every day he was quietly checking off one more item.

I wondered what it would be like if I packed up my fear for a moment, walked up the hill and jumped off that cliff. What would it be like? How would it feel?

That is ridiculous, I thought. *I am a grown woman. I have a two-month-old baby. People will laugh at me. I don't want to look silly. And besides, I just don't do this type of thing.*

And then I looked up at the cliff again. I was going to do it. I made a vow in that moment to not let fear control me anymore. I was going to start living with no regrets. I stood up slowly and removed the towel that was draped around my shoulders and stepped off the deck.

I followed the dusty dirt path up the hill. When I got to the top, it took everything I had not to turn around and run back down the hill. I stood in line, my heart pounding as the line in front of me shrunk from three to one.

Suddenly, it was just me and the cliff. I stepped up to the rocky point. I wiggled my toes over the edge as I looked down into the water below. The sun sparkled off the gentle waves created by the constant breeze. The hard stones dug into my feet. I continued to breathe. A bird chirped in the distance as I took one last deep breath.

"Okay, Daddy. This is for you."

I bent my legs and jumped out as far as I could. As the wind blew through my hair while I fell, I felt so free and alive.

As my body met the cold water below, I heard my dad's voice: "No, sweet daughter, this is for you."

~Janet L. Christensen

The Redemption Project

Courage is a love affair with the unknown.
~Rajneesh

My roommate Deana pointed up at the metal giant on the Santa Cruz boardwalk. I had suggested we each pick our favorite ride, and my choice was the carousel. Not only did I love horses, but it was the slowest, mellowest ride. Deana — a world traveler — was much more adventurous.

This was a bad idea. What was I thinking?

I could count on one hand the number of times I'd ridden a roller coaster. I'd certainly never been on any ride as gravity-defying as the one that loomed in front of us. But I'd made a deal, and it was time to keep my end of the bargain.

I left my keys in a cubby, trying not to think about what I was doing, and let myself get locked down in the seat next to Deana. As the harness clicked into place, the finality of my decision — the abdication of control — made my heart pound before the ride even began. Slowly, the ground swept farther and farther from my feet, until the horizon inverted in a dizzying whip of speed and motion. I clung to the seat, trying to repress the scream in my throat.

When the ride paused for a heart-stopping second, I saw the ocean waves crashing onto the shore. In that moment another emotion overwhelmed the fear. It was more than adrenaline. It was exhilaration — cracks of joy breaking the shield of fear I had worn my whole life. I let the shout leave my lips.

After two minutes of high-flying freedom, I wobbled down toward the beach, reeling from this altered reality. The fear of trying new things had robbed me of so many experiences. I hadn't realized how much regret I had accumulated for each opportunity missed. Ever since I was a little girl, I had been a cautious planner, a perfectionist driven by a fear of failure, a control freak. I earned straight A's because I didn't want to make mistakes. It took me months to decide to cut my hair. I always ordered the same thing at my favorite restaurants (heaven forbid I order something new and not like it!).

I had a magnet on my fridge that said: "Only those who risk going too far will ever know how far they can go," but that was the opposite of how I lived my life. It should have said, "Failure is not an option. Don't risk it!" As I sat on the Santa Cruz sand, I realized how stagnant my world had become.

That scary ride opened up a freedom I hadn't experienced before. That week, I made a list of all the times fear had kept me from trying something new. They were small things — not wanting to make a pot on the pottery wheel in sixth grade because I might be bad at it, never going fishing again after a two-hour disappointment, and never eating clam chowder with my family on the wharf because any type of seafood had to be disgusting. The list grew. As a young adult, I stood on the sidelines and watched my friends shoot clay pigeons. What if the kickback of the gun hurt? I chickened out of climbing the ropes course after an agonizing emotional battle with myself. What if I froze halfway up the tree? I turned down dates because I wasn't 100 percent sure of how I felt. What if there was someone better?

After that day at the boardwalk, I embarked on the "Redemption Project." One by one, I started going back and redeeming each of those experiences, replacing the old regret with a new memory. Sometimes I learned that, nope, I didn't really like that new food at the restaurant. I was entitled to that opinion because I'd tried it. But most of the time, my world expanded. I discovered that I loved clam chowder and fish wasn't so bad. I could actually hit a target with a gun. I climbed every element in the ropes course and even learned how to belay others. Each new experience was a practice of bravery, which evolved into boldness. With this newfound confidence, I took on the biggest risk yet: online dating.

That's how I met Michael. He was entrepreneurial. He saw trying something new as an opportunity to grow and an act of faith. He embraced change. This budding relationship with him was far riskier than a roller coaster. It meant taking risks emotionally, being vulnerable in the face of uncertainty. Because of the Redemption Project, I discovered that I had the capacity and the courage to walk into this new adventure one step at a time. Ironically, Michael was from Santa Cruz, where my journey in freedom had begun. On one of our dates, we strolled down the boardwalk. After a little sunburn, a shy kiss in the photo booth, and a carousel ride on my favorite horse, he pulled me through the throngs of people toward the wooden roller coaster.

"I'd like to take you on the Giant Dipper. You up for it?"

Someday, I would tell him about the Redemption Project, but for now I just smiled. "Great idea!"

~Sarah Barnum

A Woman with a Secret

To all girls with butts, boobs, hips and a waist, put on a
bikini — put it on and stay strong.
~Jennifer Love Hewitt

Around me, everyone had stripped down to their bathing suits: men, women, children. The young, the old. It didn't matter. They smiled. Splashed. Played.

I stood stiffly beneath a shady umbrella, taking in my surroundings as my two kids disrobed.

"Walk!" I called as they giggled, pulling on goggles, hurrying to the pool.

Behind my sunglasses, I gazed at barely clothed neighbors. Bare-shouldered. Bare-bellied. Women sunbathing on lounge chairs and dragging children through the water. I touched the knot tied tightly behind my neck. I wore a tankini. A practical, two-piece ensemble that provided the comfort a one-piece suit lacked. Loose and flowing over the middle. Like a T-shirt. Nothing said "not sexy" like a tankini.

But despite the tankini's appeal, I did not long for the endless summer afternoons that now loomed before us at the town pool. I didn't walk around in my house this bare, and I couldn't figure out how I'd get used to doing it in public.

But the benefits outweighed my discomfort: fresh air and exercise. And no one could beg for Netflix or video games.

It was too hot to sit modestly on the pool's edge. Plus, my kids had no skills. I didn't want them to drown. I had no choice.

I took a deep breath and stepped out of my cover-up. Then I race-walked across the hot pavement and slid into the water.

That first summer in our new neighborhood, as I played with my kids at the pool, I couldn't help staring at the other women, especially the ones brave enough to wear bikinis. Other moms had abandoned the tankini and gone for bandeau tops, halter tops, and even push-up tops. And not everyone had a perfect figure! Yet they weren't afraid to show what they had. Tanned, toned, pudgy, pregnant. None seemed as uncomfortable as I felt. Rather, they glowed with more than sun-kissed skin. They exuded confidence, which, in turn, made them beautiful.

With my two kids in tow, I did not look or feel beautiful. I didn't even know if I wanted to. I just wanted to survive and not endure some version of a wardrobe malfunction.

"Give me a ride!" My daughter Audrey enjoyed the water but liked using me as a water taxi. I feared the strap of my tankini would somehow come loose as she gripped and hugged me. Meanwhile, my son Aidan circled like a shark, trying to "get" Audrey as I'd heave her this way or that. He'd leap toward her, and she'd shriek as we barely escaped his grasp.

Occasionally, he'd hook his finger in my bathing suit bottom, and I'd yelp, releasing Audrey on my back as my hands flew to my bum, ever-conscious of the dozens of goggle-eyed children swimming around us.

Needless to say, the anxiety of stripping at the pool to clothing the size of my undergarments, coupled with the frantic efforts to keep said clothing from falling off in the water, kept me on edge. Only Labor Day, and the pool's closing, brought relief.

And, as the seasons changed, and our first winter gave way to blossoming flowers and warmer air, the thought of endless days at the pool filled me with dread.

The tankini waited for me.

Two summers passed in our new home. Two summers of summer living at the pool, wearing my faded, flowery tankini, and racing in and out of the pool. As my kids grew taller and more confident, they played more with friends and less with me. I found myself chatting with other moms in the water as we watched our little ones. I still had to be careful not to risk a full-frontal if one of my children came splashing toward me or a full-moon if one surprised me from behind. But those risks somehow dwindled. I still watched the bikini moms perched on the pool's edge, or standing in the shallow end, shoulders back, smiling. I marveled at the way they took charge of their kids, but enjoyed themselves in a swimsuit that looked so daring.

The bikini seemed to be a bridge between the old life and the new: If I'm going to be a mom in the pool with my kids, it said, I'm going to look good doing it.

It hinted at the possibility that the bikini wearer had her own secrets. I mulled over the idea that, despite revealing more skin, a bikini made the woman wearing it more of a mystery.

Around this time, I also turned forty. Something happened. I came to detest the dated, dowdy tankini I wore each day. I couldn't help noticing other women my age or older wearing bikinis, looking happy and not the least bit self-conscious. They rocked their bikinis, and I started to think, *Why shouldn't I?*

In my bedroom, I pulled out a bikini I'd bought almost a dozen years earlier for a trip to Hawaii, before my children even existed. I tied the strings behind my neck and turned to face my reflection.

Yikes.

Too tight here, digging into me there. Childbirth had changed my body, and this suit didn't fit the current me. Plus, the trim looked dated. Not the look I was going for.

So I did some shopping and found a cute blue-and-white-striped bikini with a halter top. It fit well. No pinching in the wrong spots. Not too skimpy. Just enough support and elasticity to make me believe I wasn't going to fall out of it if my son decided to attack me *Jaws*-style.

Still, the cut had similar dimensions to my bra and underwear.

I stared at myself in the full-length mirror in my bedroom. I inhaled slowly, pushing back my shoulders, reminding myself of the other women I'd seen.

I could do this.

The first time I dropped my cover-up and dashed to the water in my bikini to join the kids, I imagined myself under a spotlight — everyone watching. But when I glanced around, searching for smirks, I didn't make eye contact with a single person. I was just another mom at the pool — in a bikini.

But once I slipped into that pool, the cool, blue water rushing over my bare belly, I felt different — not more fit or toned or tan, but somehow stronger. I had crossed a hurdle that I didn't imagine I ever could. As I stood with a friend in the shallow end, our kids playing nearby, I remembered that I was a mom, but a woman, too. I stood tall, the sun beating on my shoulders, feeling beautiful — even if the only person who noticed was me.

Long after leaving the pool, even as the leaves turned color and fell from the branches, I held onto that feeling.

I wore that bikini all summer and the next. And though the dash to the water didn't decrease much with time, I never went back to the tankini. I'd outgrown it. A blue-and-white-striped bikini helped me enjoy the body I had. So I rocked it as best I could.

As if I had a secret of my own.

~Mary Jo Marcellus Wyse

Trying Something Different

*I would rather have a mind opened by
wonder than one closed by belief.*
~Gerry Spence

June 2016. I am driving on Highway 75 west of Atlanta. My wife Carolyn and I (both sixty-eight) are on our way to check out Tellico Village, a retirement community south of Knoxville. I am worried. I'm fine with our plans to move from our home in Florida. That's not the problem. The problem is that we booked two nights in a private home through one of those Internet home-sharing services.

"Why not stay at a motel like we usually do?" I had asked Carolyn when she first brought up the idea a month ago.

"This place is located right in Tellico Village," she said. "We'll be staying with someone who lives there and can give us an insider's view."

"A stranger. What if we don't get along with her?"

"We will. Her name is Jo Ann, and she's got great reviews."

"Wouldn't a motel be cheaper?"

"No. This place costs less, and we have kitchen privileges, so we'll save on meals too. Besides wouldn't it be nice to try something different for a change?"

I diplomatically chose not to answer her question. If I did, the answer would have been *No. I value my privacy and the idea of staying in a stranger's home does not appeal to me at all.* But I knew I had already lost the argument.

Our GPS leads us more efficiently than I would have liked to the front door of our host's home. If I could drag my feet outside the car to slow us down, I would. But here we are in a neighborhood of beautiful homes. Jo Ann has a lovely single-story house, well landscaped and with two large white rockers waiting on a porch festooned with flowers. The house is dark inside. It is 4:00 p.m., the exact time we said we would arrive.

"So where is she?" I ask. I have a hint of "I told you so" in my voice. "Didn't she confirm our arrival time?"

"Yes," says Carolyn. She rings the doorbell. No answer.

As I dial Jo Ann's number I think: This wouldn't have happened if we had booked a motel like we usually do. Jo Ann answers. She apologizes for not being here to greet us. She says she has been trying to reach us to let us know she is attending a church activity this evening. She tells me to look under the cushion of one of the porch rockers for the house key and garage door opener.

"Just park your car in the garage and make yourselves at home," she says. "Your bedroom and bathroom are located behind the kitchen, but feel free to use the living room, television, and back porch." She tells me that she cleared a shelf in the refrigerator for us and that she will be coming home late.

I am relieved. For the next several hours, we have a home away from home. The house is gorgeous, modern, immaculate, and tastefully furnished. We unpack and go for a walk around the neighborhood. The neighbors we meet outside their homes greet us and are happy to tell us their experience living in the Village. One gentleman tells us how smart we are for staying at Jo Ann's house so we can experience the neighborhood firsthand.

After a home cooked dinner, we watch the news and go for a drive to the lake to explore. In the evening we relax on the screened-in back porch. At 10:00 p.m. I hear a key turn in the door. Jo Ann is back.

Jo Ann is a gracious and welcoming host. She apologizes again for not meeting us when we arrived. She pours herself a glass of wine and offers some to us. We have a forty-five minute conversation about how she came to the Village several years ago, the growing pains of the

Village, and her experience selecting a lot and building her house. She offers to put us in touch with a neighbor who is a Realtor if we decide to build or rent a home. We learn things about the Village from her that we would never have learned had we stayed at a motel. When she says good night, she informs us that she will not be home the next day. She says she likes to give guests as much privacy as possible.

"Just put the keys and garage door opener under the rocker cushion when you leave," she says. "Come back for another stay any time."

What little anxiety I have left vanishes. I couldn't have imagined a better stay. We make ourselves at home for the rest of our time. I kick myself for being so reluctant to try this. I worried so needlessly.

That summer we book several more stays in people's homes in three states: Tennessee, Wisconsin, and New York. Every stay works out wonderfully. Now whenever we travel, this is one of the options we consider. But if I hadn't endured the anxiety of "trying something different for a change," we would still be staying at impersonal motels. And we may not have moved to Tellico Village, where we are now living, pleased with our decision.

~D.E. Brigham

You Never Know

Before anything great is really achieved,
your comfort zone must be disturbed.
~Ray Lewis

The evening started out innocently enough. A member of our local theater company asked my wife to audition for their upcoming play. Melissa had never acted before. She wasn't entirely sure she wanted a speaking part, but she decided to go to the auditions anyway. I take my role as a supportive husband very seriously, so when Melissa asked me to drive her to the tryouts, I agreed. It didn't hurt that she told me she would take me out for a steak dinner afterward.

I thought I would wait outside in the truck, but my wife insisted I accompany her inside for moral support. I followed her into a room full of hopeful amateur actors all gathered around a large conference table. "I'll wait for you over there," I whispered to Melissa while pointing to a lone chair in the corner. "Good luck." She nodded as she grabbed a script and began studying.

It didn't take long for one of the veteran community troupe members to notice me. We live in a small town, La Vernia, Texas, where I grew up. I knew most of the people in that room. "Well, looky here! It's Joey Wootan! Please tell me you are auditioning for our play." The woman speaking pulled up a chair and plopped down next to me. I assured her I was not. She was persistent, but so was I.

And then I heard it… a familiar voice coming from the direction of the conference table. "He'd be good. Talk him into it." It was my wife! She was looking over at us with a big grin on her face.

My cheeks grew hot, and I began to feel trapped. No way was I going to act in a play. I hunt and fish and drink beer. I oversee a bunch of construction workers, and I raise cattle in my spare time. I drive a truck and eat my steaks rare. I do not act in plays.

Before I knew what was happening, someone handed me a script. I walked out to the truck in a daze as my wife chatted away. "I can't believe you just auditioned for the play! It was so much fun reading with you. Thank you for doing that! I really can't believe you just did that! Can you believe you just did that?"

No, I really couldn't. And I convinced myself there was no way I was going to get the part because I had never acted. I was wrong. Two weeks later, Melissa called me with the news — I was LV Shoestring Stage Productions' newest actor.

Melissa vowed to help me with my lines. We would be performing the comedy at a Mother's Day dinner theater event. I only had four weeks to prepare for my acting debut.

We read the script aloud several times before we were able to get through it without Melissa laughing hysterically. "I'm laughing with you, not at you," my wife managed to squeak out as she gasped for air. For the sake of my pride, I chose to believe her. It was a comedy, after all. She was supposed to be laughing, right?

"Louder!" the director shouted as I delivered my lines at my first play rehearsal. I started again.

"Louder, babe." Now my wife was directing me. I took a deep breath and practically shouted my next line. Melissa gave me the thumbs-up as she smiled at me proudly. I felt an unexpected sense of accomplishment.

On the drive home, Melissa held my hand as she told me what a good job I'd done. "I know you're only doing this for me, and I want you to know I really appreciate it."

She was right, of course. I had auditioned for the play to make her happy, and while I was certainly enjoying the extra time we were spending together, I was quite vocal about the fact that I would never do it again. She just smiled and nodded.

On Mother's Day, Melissa sat next to me on the front seat of my pickup truck as we drove to the theater. "I have a confession," I began sheepishly. "I wasn't sure about this acting thing at first, but I've actually had a lot of fun doing this with you."

Melissa smiled broadly. "Oh, really? So does that mean you'd do it again?" she asked.

If I've learned anything from this experience, it's to never say never. I might end up eating my words. Or delivering them to an audience from the stage.

~Joey Wootan

Chapter 2

STEP OUTSIDE YOUR COMFORT ZONE

☑ Learn to Trust

A Night in Philly

*Whenever you feel uncomfortable, instead of retreating
back into your old comfort zone, pat yourself on the
back and say, "I must be growing," and
continue moving forward.*
~T. Harv Eker

was in Philadelphia for a work conference when I saw an ad in
the hotel lobby. A nearby theater was showing a documentary
about several local animal shelters that were helping to save
dogs from high-kill shelters in the South. I love animals, and this
fundraising event sounded right up my alley. However, none of my
co-workers would go with me, and I was worried about navigating
the streets by myself, at night, alone.

I resigned myself to spending the evening in my hotel room, but
as soon as I got back to my room I felt restless and bored. The theater
where the event was taking place was only about five blocks from the
hotel — how lost could I get? And the area around the hotel didn't
seem particularly dangerous. So I decided to brave it. I gathered up
my wallet and room key and set off.

It was already getting dark as I made my way down the street.
The hotel was located in the business district, and the streets were
nearly deserted. I managed to find the street the theater was on, but
when I turned the corner, I stopped in shock. The street in front of
the theater was chock full of bikers — lots and lots of very big, tough-
looking bikers.

Now, I've known lots of motorcycle enthusiasts in my life, and most are the nicest people you'll ever meet. I don't buy into "biker" stereotypes in general, but in this case, I was a woman all alone, in a strange neighborhood, at night, and there were twenty or so very large men — all wearing insignia that denoted they were in some sort of club or gang — standing before me. And, like most women in that situation, warning bells began to sound in my head, and my heart jumped into my throat. Was I at the right theater? Had I misread the date of the animal shelter event? Had I inadvertently wandered into a bad neighborhood after all?

A sign outside the theater assured me that I was in the right place on the right evening. Nevertheless, I wondered if I should hasten back to my hotel instead of walking through that crowd of bikers. I finally decided that I would be safer inside the theater where there was, presumably, a crowd of people. Hopefully, the bikers would have dispersed by the time the documentary was over.

I scurried into the theater, which turned out to contain even more bikers than the street outside. What was going on? I paid the suggested donation and moved inside where I anxiously took a seat, chiding myself over and over for going on this little adventure in the first place.

I tried to put my anxieties — about the bikers and about getting back to the hotel without getting lost — out of my mind. A local blues-rock band was the opening act, and within a few minutes, their performance drew my attention. They were good — really good. So good, in fact, they had me dancing in my seat, and I later went online and bought all of their albums. (To this day, they remain one of my favorite bands.) Enthusiasm for the band's performance soon drove all of the worries from my mind, and I began to relax and have a good time.

After the band was done, the emcee for the event took the stage, introducing us to the tiny Chihuahua that he had adopted through the effort detailed in the documentary. Then the film began to play, and I understood the presence of the bikers: They had been part of the caravan that escorted the adoption vehicles from New Jersey to Georgia and back. They were all part of an animal rescue group. Many ended up adopting dogs from the caravan as well. In that moment, I was struck by the bonds that had drawn so many disparate folks to the theater that night. We had been brought together by our shared love of animals.

I stayed until the very end and made it back to my hotel without incident. To my surprise, in the hotel lobby I spotted the evening's emcee with his Chihuahua! I was delighted to see them there as I hadn't had a chance to speak to him at the event. I told him I had been at the event and had enjoyed it immensely. It turned out he was the concierge at my hotel.

I think of that night often. The film detailed many monumentally moving acts of kindness, and it was a privilege to attend the event and meet the people who had been involved. I made new friends, discovered a band that I love, and supported an important cause. Something gave me the courage that night to venture into the unknown, and the result was one of the best nights of my life.

~Terri Bruce

More Kindness than Danger

Travel doesn't become adventure
until you leave yourself behind.
~Marty Rubin

Another spring had arrived and, with it, my familiar and frustrated wanderlust. I had waited years for my friends to go to Europe with me, but there was always some reason they couldn't. I proposed the trip once again to the same friends and received the same excuses.

I wasn't going to let another year go by without making this dream come true, so I decided to take the trip alone. I bought a one-way ticket to Copenhagen and told my friends I would send them a postcard.

On the day of my departure, I was excited but also surprised at how worried I felt — not just about being lonely, but also about the dangers I might encounter. My parents also questioned the wisdom of walking around Europe alone for months. They warned me not to be too trusting, to stay out of bad neighborhoods, and to avoid going out by myself at night. In retrospect, it was cruel to subject them to such torment, but they eventually understood that I just wanted to see the beauty of the world while I was still young.

My own worry was more difficult to assuage. Maybe I had watched too many movies that showed the darker side of man's nature. Conflict is the essence of drama, after all. All those movies about naïve vacationers being attacked, kidnapped or thrown into abusive prisons had taken their toll on my trust in people. Watching the bad news at six o'clock didn't help, either. But there was no turning back, so I hugged my parents goodbye, got a ride to the airport from a friend, and flew into the big, blue sky and complete uncertainty.

It was early April, but snow was still on the ground in Copenhagen when I landed. Determined to be frugal, I chose the cheapest youth hostel in my travel guide. As I slept that first night on an ancient, unpleasant-smelling mattress beside a cracked, graffiti-covered wall, homesickness began to overwhelm me. I thought, *What am I doing? I could be home in my clean, comfortable bed.* But even that wasn't there anymore because I had vacated my apartment and sold most of my belongings to finance this trip. I sat up, took out a miniature flashlight and found a note in my pocket that a friend back home had given me. He had written down the name and number of someone he knew in Copenhagen named Lisbeth. He said she would be happy to take me in for a few days. I decided to call her the next morning, and then fell asleep from exhaustion.

When I arrived at her door, she welcomed me like family and showed me the sights of Copenhagen for several days. I felt so accepted by her and her friends and had so much fun that I forgot to feel homesick.

One night, they took me to a karaoke bar. Word got around that I was from California, so someone asked me to sing a Beach Boys song. I chose "California Girls" but changed "California" to "Copenhagen." The syllable count was a perfect match. The first time I sang "I wish they all could be Copenhagen girls," everyone cheered, and I made a hundred friends instantly.

That's another thing about movies. Nobody can sit in a bar in a movie without some group of drunken nincompoops harassing them. But this bar was filled with the nicest people imaginable. It was just another example of the skewed reality of cinema. Travel was working its magic. My faith in human beings was being restored.

I stayed in Copenhagen for a week before moving on. I was alone again, but invigorated by a great first week away from home. My solitude didn't last long, however. I found travel companions everywhere I went, especially on the trains. My backpack was a silent invitation to other wayfarers to join forces and see something new together.

With only four thousand dollars, I didn't know how long I would be able to travel. I ended up stretching it out for six months. When I wasn't sleeping at youth hostels or the homes of new friends, I saved money by sleeping in train stations or on moving trains between one destination and another, roughing it for the sake of extending the adventure. Besides, with so many new people to get to know and so much world to see, sleep wasn't much of a priority. It wasn't just that, though. I wasn't tired anymore. The continuous excitement of exploration freed me from the weariness that often plagued me at home.

While my friends back home repeated another typical summer, I awoke to the view of cotton clouds drifting through a pastel blue sky above Venice, Italy, as opera students practiced arias in the square below my hotel window. I dipped my feet in the cool water of the Trevi Fountain in Rome and imagined I had discovered the fountain of youth. I watched the sun rise over the red tile roofs of Florence. I held hands with a Parisian beauty at the top of the Eiffel Tower. I sat silently in the cool air of a mountainside prairie in Switzerland as spring exploded around me. I parasailed over Swiss Alps so fertile that the lake below them was bright yellow with floating pollen. I watched a rainbow form over the Irish Sea. I held my hand against the cold monoliths of Stonehenge and felt their mystery flood through me. I read poetry by candlelight in a cave at the base of the mountain the Acropolis stands upon while colorful hot-air balloons filled the night sky in the distance. I recited a monologue under a full moon at the Theatre of Dionysus. I walked the ancient cobblestone streets of Athens. I danced all night in a Greek disco pulsating with life. I watched a golden sunfish sail past my rowboat in the Aegean Sea and imagined it was Zeus taking the shape of a fish to observe me more closely.

I walked through ancient ruins and felt with an ache how brief my existence is, but how sacred and powerful it is for that same reason. And through it all, I had time — that most precious commodity — to read, write, watch and really see, listen and really hear, and savor my life while gazing through the moving church of a train window. I discovered what Joseph Campbell meant when he said people aren't as interested in the meaning of life as they are in the experience of being alive.

I arrived home with less than a dollar in my pocket, but with a heart and soul overflowing with riches and dozens of new stories to tell. Traveling alone can seem intimidating at first, but the world is full of kindness and generosity, and they are both showered upon us for prices anyone can afford — respect, friendliness, and an open heart.

I'm twenty-five years older now, and those same friends who didn't come with me on that adventure can't recall what was important enough to make them stay home back then. My problem these days is not fear of travel or distrust of humanity; it's being content at home. The desire for adventure only grows stronger with age. How can one have enough fun? Amazement? Romance? A world full of wonders, ever-pulsating outside my window, still calls me to new adventures, but now I accept the invitations fearlessly, knowing the rewards far outweigh the risks, and there is much more kindness in this world than danger.

~Mark Rickerby

Lord Knows

Grandmother-grandchild relationships are simple.
Grandmas are short on criticism and long on love.
~Author Unknown

In a way, my grandmother Victoria knew me better than myself. She recalls when I was around seven years old and wanted to be a pastor. A lifelong Pentecostal, my grandmother fully supported this career move. She even bought me a tiny blue suit so I could look good while reciting Bible verses in the living room. We called it my "pastor suit."

I loved and honored my grandma. I couldn't imagine disappointing her. When I came out at sixteen, the one person I knew I'd never tell was my grandmother. One, because she couldn't handle it, and two, because I couldn't handle losing her.

Victoria's righteous passion was well-known throughout Palmer, a small town in Alaska. You never quite knew what would stir her rage. Someone once asked why she kept playing the tambourine during slow songs at church, and she refused to look at the person again. When friends angered her, she cut them off. It didn't matter if the friendship had lasted ten or twenty years. I learned about these breakups through casual conversation, usually long after the rupture.

"Grandma," I'd ask her, "how's Philip doing these days?"

"Lord knows," she'd state.

This was code that their relationship was over, and so was the conversation.

During my first year of college, I knew I had to tell my grandmother. We couldn't have a real relationship unless she knew about me being gay and how instrumental it was in shaping me.

Spring was starting, and I was walking around the campus green, thinking of ways to tell her. I took a rest beneath a large oak tree. I thought of calling her landline on the mountain, but my heart started racing, and I felt like throwing up. If I couldn't think of the phone conversation without feeling dizzy, how would I act when it was time for me to tell her in real-time?

It hit me all at once that I'd send her a letter. My grandma was a prolific letter writer. In my first semester of college, she had already sent me seven letters. She preferred bulky, wide-ruled legal paper. She'd only write on one side of the paper and always with a red pen. She would fold the pages at least three times, shove the thick wad into an envelope, and seal it all up with tape.

I enjoyed these letters although I didn't finish all of them. Her cursive was wildly ornate. It took her a long time to write like this, and by page three she got impatient, and the words looped together in a blur I couldn't read. It didn't matter. I already knew her great themes: love of God, family, and being good to your teachers. She supported each theme with a new Bible verse.

I tore out three pages from a journal and started to write. On the first page, I told her about the motivated kids I was meeting and all the smart professors. On the second page, I said I loved her, and I was grateful for her help in raising me. And on the final page, I wrote, "It's because I love you that I feel the need to tell you I am gay. I've known this for a long time, and I want to tell you because I want to be honest and have no lies between us. I hope this doesn't change anything between us."

I tried to make everything light again by mentioning the spring weather and upcoming tennis try-outs. Then I folded the three pages like she did, three times, and squashed the pages into the back of my journal and walked to my next class.

I couldn't think clearly the next two days. I imagined Victoria sending me to a conversion camp. She might write back with all the Bible verses that supposedly hated gay people. Or knowing my preference for science, she might send me magazine clippings saying homosexuality made no evolutionary sense. The most probable reaction was also the worst: She would refuse to speak with me. When people asked how I was doing, she'd state drily, "Lord knows."

Eventually, I dropped the letter into a mailbox right outside my dorm. It was early in the morning, and with nothing else in the mailbox, I heard the letter hit the metal floor. For a brief moment, I wanted the letter back. But then I decided — I would rather have true rejection than false acceptance.

A few weeks later, I received a brown, flat envelope from Victoria. I weighed the package in my palms; it was light. The envelope had her familiar red script. *It couldn't be a bomb,* I thought. *And I'm pretty sure they still scan for anthrax. Right?*

I walked around the campus green again and sat beneath the oak tree where I had written the letter. My heart was pounding.

I ripped off the top binding like a Band-Aid. I tilted out the contents. My heart sank.

It was filled with photos. There I was on my fifth birthday with a bunch of cake on my face, smiling like crazy. There I was hitting a forehand at sixteen. There I was playing the trombone at thirteen. There were two dozen pictures with no explanation.

She no longer wanted to remember me. This was the first of a series of "Lord knows" statements regarding me.

I stuck my hand in the envelope again. My fingertips brushed a scrap of paper. I pulled it out. It was the size of a fortune-cookie scroll. In red coiled letters, it read: *"Yo te amo mucho, mucho."* I love you very, very much.

I laughed.

Under the oak tree, I flipped through more pictures. She saw me in each moment: spelling bees, band concerts, tennis tournaments. I shuffled them and felt her say, *I loved you in this moment, and this moment, and this moment, and I love you now.*

Tears swelled in my eyes. I had expected her to choose politics or religion, to find any reason to justify her disgust. But of all the things she could have said, she had chosen love.

~Matt Caprioli

A Foothold in Life

*One of the greatest discoveries a man makes, one
of his great surprises, is to find he can do
what he was afraid he couldn't do.*
~Henry Ford

A dozen children ran around laughing and playing in my friend's yard, while we parents sat chatting and sipping cool summer drinks. It was Memorial Day. The barbecue had been cleared away when our host announced a surprise. A huge truck backed up the long, narrow driveway, capturing everyone's attention. Adults and children watched with curiosity as the driver got out, adjusted some mechanical gadgets, and slowly raised a huge, portable rock wall.

It was about twelve feet wide, made of gray molded plastic with indented footholds that stretched straight up for what looked like at least a hundred feet. The enthusiastic kids swiftly lined up to give it a try, and with the complete fearlessness most children possess, scrambled to the top and rang the bell that hung at the highest point. There wasn't really anything to be afraid of since they were belted into place. Three people could climb side by side and talk to each other, so gradually the adults tried it, too.

"Come on; let's go get in line," my husband Neil urged.

"No, you go ahead without me." I had all sorts of good excuses: I don't have the right shoes; I forgot my sunglasses; I have to help the hostess. I have a unique talent for seeing unthinkable danger in almost every situation, and this scene seemed perilous to me. I watched everyone else having fun, though, and finally convinced myself to try it.

With all the nerve I could muster, I started the climb. The belt wrapped around me like a diaper so there was no way to fall. *Yes, I thought, this is fun and safe!* Concentrating on each foothold, I slowly made my way up. I avoided looking down to prevent any sudden panic, and within a few minutes I made it to the top and proudly rang the bell.

"Woo hoo!" my daughters called up to me.

"Way to go, Col!" Neil yelled.

I enjoyed my success and the fabulous view of fields and farmland until I realized there was a line below me waiting for a turn. It was time to go down.

It was one thing to look out at the world in the distance, but it was a whole other thing to look straight down. I was paralyzed with fear. I willed my hands to let go of the ripples in the wall, but I couldn't move them. I slowed my breathing and decided to work on my feet first. I wiggled my right foot, trying to find a safe hold without having to look. I couldn't find one. I started to sweat so much the belt chafed my belly and thighs, and I wondered if my clammy hands would lose their grip.

This is ridiculous, I thought. *You climbed up. Now just reverse the whole process and go down.* It sounded so easy in my head. Taking another deep breath, I looked ever so slightly to the right. This time, I spotted a foothold about three feet away and slid my foot into it. Unfortunately, now I was splayed out like a starfish across the wall. The children below recognized my fear and called up all sorts of recommendations.

"Move your right hand down three inches!"

"No, move your left foot first!"

"Just hold the rope and jump. You can't fall!"

All well-intentioned advice, but the fact remained that I couldn't move.

I heard some commotion below, and then my husband was suddenly next to me on the wall.

"Hi," he said. "Need some help?"

"I don't see how you can help. You can't carry me down, and I can't move."

"Of course you can. You just need to stop thinking about how high we are."

"I know that. I just can't do it," I whined.

"Okay, then let's just sit here and chat for a while," he said. "Did you have any of Dawn's barbecue beans? They were delicious."

"They were good, but my favorite was the honeyed melon balls."

We chatted about the party for a few minutes, and then he said, "Col, brush that fly away from your head." Without thinking, I did, and then instinctively reached out for a different ledge to grab. I smiled, realizing that, of course, I could move. Over the next fifteen minutes, Neil talked me all the way down, step by step. "Move your left foot a little to your left and then look over your shoulder. You'll be able to see the apple tree." "Reach about six inches to the right, and you'll be able to see the kids in the yard blowing bubbles." So it went, and with each step he pointed out something lovely to distract me.

By the time we got to the bottom, I felt great. I wasn't anxious or stressed; in fact, I was calmer and more peaceful than when I started out. It was a great lesson in mindfulness. Fixating on being stuck on the top of the wall paralyzed me from being able to move on. Focusing instead on all the good things I could see along the way down connected me back to the moment and distracted me from my fear. Who would have thought that an adventure on a rock wall would teach me such a good lesson about life? Don't fret about what lies behind you or fear what lies ahead. Just take one step at a time and concentrate on the beauty in the moment!

~Colleen M. Arnold

A Stepping Stone to Joy

*Change is the law of life. And those who look only to
the past or present are certain to miss the future.*
~John F. Kennedy

Returning home from our honeymoon, my husband and I were
overflowing with happiness and filled with joyous memories
of our recent elopement in Mendocino. We were completely
unprepared for the news that he would be losing his job
within thirty days. It was especially devastating because not only
were we newlyweds, but I had quit my job shortly before due to a
long commute. Now we would have no income.

I stifled my fear and cheerfully declared, "It's okay. We've discussed relocating before. This is just God nudging us along in a new
direction." Inside, I could feel my stomach knot up as panic over our
uncertain future arose, but on the surface I struggled to remain the
image of serenity and calm. I was determined to be strong and not let
my husband sense my panic.

Then, we did what we always do during times of trouble: We
prayed. A lot! "Please, dear Lord, please guide our steps," I'd repeat
throughout the day. Each night, we'd consider our options, unable to
make a decision, yet knowing that our lives were about to be changed
in unexpected and unfamiliar ways.

First, we did nothing. Why not stay in Los Angeles? We had our
apartment, friends, and family, and it was our home. However, with
no job and a stagnant economy, that didn't sound like a promising

option. Next, we toyed with heading to Seattle where the possibility of a job and the deep green pines could heal our soul. Nothing was off the table. We found ourselves considering Utah, Georgia, Illinois... The possibilities were endless, all the while not feeling like any were the right fit. Unexpectedly, my husband said, "How about Boston?" He knew that since I had left Boston in 2002, I had always had a deep longing to return.

"Boston? But we don't have a job there! And it'll be expensive to move cross-country," I reasoned. Yet somehow his suggestion felt right. I had always dreamed of settling back East to be closer to my family and have a change of seasons, but had been scared to take a chance. Having lived there, I knew how brutal the winters could be and how expensive the heating costs were, and I was hesitant to attempt that long cross-country drive in the cold of November.

Still unsure, yet feeling undeniably excited about his suggestion, I found myself enthusiastically shouting "Yes!" before he could change his mind. I masked my inner fear to give my husband the confidence he'd need for such a huge change. After all, he was a California boy who had never even driven in snow!

Once the decision was made, the next few weeks became a whirlwind. Spare time disappeared, replaced with packing, searching for apartments online, applying for jobs (not easy when you live 3,000 miles away), and more packing. It's incredible how many belongings we accumulate throughout the years.

Enthusiastic in our decision, we were surprised to meet resistance from family and friends who questioned our sanity and didn't share our vision. That only pulled us closer together. We became a two-person team united in the faith that God would somehow work out our situation; we were excited about the possibilities of a new chapter ahead.

Slowly, yet miraculously, things started coming together. My husband's job was extended another couple of weeks, allowing us the financial means and time off to fly to Boston and secure an apartment. My husband had a phone interview for a promising job. That turned into a second interview and then a third. Who cares that the third interview took place by Skype at 5:00 a.m. on the day that the movers were coming, adding stress to an already stressful situation? As my husband breathed a sigh of relief after surviving the grueling, two-hour, seven-person interview, I barely had time to congratulate him. I was tearing the last picture off the wall and nudging him to change from his suit into something more appropriate before the movers arrived. I promised him we'd have plenty of time to talk about the interview as well as many other things on our drive across America.

Although we originally planned to take the northern driving route across the United States to explore Salt Lake City, Mount Rushmore, Chicago, and Niagara Falls, a polar vortex surprised everyone by dumping snow across the nation and causing us to change to the southern route. Worse yet, upon loading the car, we discovered that we had packed the car so full of belongings that our cat's oversized kennel wouldn't fit into the back seat. Suddenly, I found myself squished into the sliver of space in the back seat surrounded by clothes, pots and pans, snacks, etc., while our cat, Boss, enjoyed the panoramic view from the front seat, unaware of how lucky he was.

But something magical happened as we were driving cross-country. As the countryside passed, and the miles between us and Massachusetts dwindled, we found our stress slowly fading away. Watching the changing scenery of desert to farmland to mountains as we drove through the diverse landscapes, we found ourselves laughing and enjoying ourselves. The long drive became a way to bond, process our thoughts and resume feeling like newlyweds.

Being forced to spend hours in the car without a television or computer, we found ourselves having long discussions and talking for hours, much like we had when we had first started dating. And we loved it! Instead of grumbling about the cost of the move, we looked at the cost as a vacation of sorts. Not only were we off to start a new life, but we were also crossing states off our bucket list! We made it a point to try local cuisine along the journey, and although we weren't able to explore the tourist sites due to traveling with our cat, we found we didn't mind. We were a tight-knit family of three, and sometimes families have to make sacrifices. Our confidence grew with each mile we drove.

The day after our arrival, my husband received "the call." Yeah, that's right. That job he'd interviewed for three times was now his. And it came with a pay raise. Even better, they had just changed locations and were now accessible off the "T," allowing my California husband to take the subway and thus have a snow-free drive.

Had we not taken a chance, and had the job loss never occurred, we would have missed out on the joyful life we have now. Sometimes, what starts out as a roadblock blossoms into a stepping stone if we allow it to. We just have to keep the faith and believe.

~Joanna Dylan

16

Black Diamonds Aren't Forever

It is only in adventure that some people
succeed in knowing themselves.
~André Gide

'd always thought of myself as a timid skier. But until recently, I'd also thought of myself as happily married. Now, in that limbo between separating and signing the divorce papers, I wanted to prove something to myself. I signed up for four days of ski lessons in Aspen, Colorado.

There were four of us in the class — all women in our mid-thirties — each with our own goals. Sandy, from Los Angeles, raised her ski pole exuberantly, shouting into the frigid air, "I hope we tackle some tough runs!"

I gulped, clutching my own ski poles tighter and responded, "I don't ski black diamonds. They're too tough for me."

"Not to worry," said a reassuring voice, and we turned to meet Trish, our red-haired ski instructor. "This is an intermediate class."

We skied our first run past a video camera, snow crunching like popcorn as we made S-turns. Watching the tape later, Trish urged, "Find something you like about your skiing." I tried, but all I saw was my fanny sticking out and my arms flailing like windmills.

Still, Sandy, Patti, Roxanne and I murmured encouragement to each other, and as the day progressed, so did our skiing. Patti skied baby moguls without falling. Roxanne improved her turns. Sandy showed real grace as she hurtled down a run. Snow showered from our skis as we followed Trish like obedient ducklings down one run after another.

Then came a slope that dropped more precipitously than any other we had skied. "Just remember to crouch," said Trish. She pushed off so quickly that no one had time to think. Our poles flicked the snow as we slid down after her. Crouch, turn! Crouch, turn! Down, down — until I cried, "I did it!" Trish beamed. "Yes, and you just skied a black diamond."

My grin could have lit up New York. I felt like that Helen Reddy song, "I Am Woman!"

But then Trish headed for another black diamond run. The first one had been steep but wide. This one was a narrow chute with trees on one side and a sheer drop on the other.

"I — I can't do this one," I stammered.

"Sure you can. Two turns, maybe three, and you'll be down," said Trish, as she slid over the edge. The others followed. I stayed frozen at the top. Finally, Trish called up, "Side-step it, Barb!" And, ignominiously, I half-stepped, half-fell down the run.

The group made comforting noises. "We all freak out on something." "Don't give up." And from Trish, "You have the skill to ski any run on Aspen Mountain, Barb. It's simply a matter of up here." She tapped her head. "At a certain point, you have to let go and trust yourself. Don't let fear hold you back."

In my remaining days of vacation, I stayed on the safe blue runs and worked on technique. On my last afternoon, though, something drew me to the run that had scared me. I peered down the chute. My stomach churned. The trees rose like a fir barrier. The cliff dropped off into nothingness. A storm was predicted, and the light had flattened, making it hard to see.

"I don't ski black diamonds," I said. I whispered it, ghostlike, an echo of all my old beliefs. "I don't do divorce either," I said, but here it was in my life.

I hurled myself forward. Shrieking in fear — "I'm going to crash!"

Turn. "The cliff! I'm going over the edge." Crouch. Turn. I ended in an awkward snowplow position, but Trish was right. Two turns, and I'd made it.

I caught my breath and looked back up the run at the narrow ledge, the plunging edge. The air crystalized in my lungs.

Then I smiled.

They've got it pegged, those ski instructors. I'd gone over the precipice and survived. I hadn't done it gracefully, but I'd done it. I hadn't even fallen. If I could get down a black diamond run, I could maneuver my way through this divorce.

I'd just have to let go and trust in myself—and maybe in a force I couldn't see. And I'd have to allow myself more than one run.

~Barbara Bartocci

17

The View from the Ground

Leap and the net will appear.
~John Burroughs

I stood sixty feet off the ground, grasping the trapeze bar and willing myself to leap off the platform and swing over the abyss. Beneath me, some flimsy netting was the only barrier between the floor and me. My eighth grade students waited on the gymnasium floor, cheering me on. "Come on, Ms. Long! You can do it!" But my body refused to believe them. Step by step, I climbed back down the ladder and wriggled sheepishly out of my harness, embarrassment burning my cheeks.

Two months after the Circus Arts Field Trip Fiasco, my students and I were gearing up for an even greater challenge: a trip to Costa Rica. As we waited in the airport before I chaperoned them onto that plane, we talked about our hopes and fears for our ten-day trip.

My students worried about homesickness, Spanish slip-ups and feeling uneasy with their homestay families. But strange foods or meeting new people didn't concern me. What terrified me was the "highlight" of the trip: a ziplining flight over the jungle valley bordering Arenal Volcano. Just the thought of it left my mouth dry. I made a secret pact with myself to find an excuse to get out of it at the last minute. The last daredevil physical challenge I had taken on was in the fourth grade when my sister convinced me to share a toboggan ride with her down an ice chute in Ohio. I assure you, she never made such a request again.

When the fateful day arrived, I stood shoulder to shoulder with my students while the guides tugged on our harnesses to test them for tightness. I had braved the cable tram ride up the mountain to our launch point, the anticipatory butterflies feeling more like a stirred-up hornet's nest in the pit of my belly.

We arrived at the peak to a breathtaking vista of the volcano and the valley. "Awesome!" I heard one of my students shout. I wished I felt her excitement rather than a sudden urge to lie down on the cement platform and curl up in the fetal position. I wasn't afraid of heights. My panic stemmed from my fear of that stomach-sinking sensation, like on a roller coaster or on those torturous pirate-boat rides at amusement parks.

The guide instructed, "Spread your legs apart to slow yourself down when you brake." I wondered how I would possibly keep my wits about me to remember to do so. We practiced proper positions on a short, mini-zip: tucking our knees into our chests and braking by swiveling the handlebar and using the other, gloved hand to tug on the guide wire. I was trembling, and we were only three feet off the ground. The guide added, "After this trial run, there are seven zip lines heading down the mountains. Once you set off on the first, there is no going back."

My student Eileen sidled up next to me. Her face was pale, and she fiddled with the buckles on her harness. "I'm scared," she whispered. "Will you stay back with me?"

Here was my chance! I could get out of ziplining and still save face!

"I'm scared, too," I confided.

"Yeah. You're really white, and you're sweating," she said. "I thought you'd be the right person to ask 'cause I remember when you couldn't do the trapeze."

Her words woke me up, and something clicked in me. If I couldn't step outside of my comfort zone, how could these kids be expected to do so? "Maybe we should give it a try," I said, my voice shaky. I felt a little sick, and I couldn't believe that my body was actually moving toward the launch point. "Come on."

"Okay," she agreed. "But I'm going before you 'cause otherwise I'll chicken out."

Eileen zipped off, shrieking with fear or glee, I wasn't sure which. Her scream persisted as she flew along the entire first cable. Once she was across, I mounted the platform, shaking with nerves as the guide clipped the carabineer to the trolley. "You okay?" he asked. He really sounded concerned.

"Just push me off before I change my mind."

A half-second later, I was flying. I squeezed my eyes shut and tamped down the violent urge to lose my lunch — but the awful sensation of falling never happened. There was a slight dip as the cable tautened, but otherwise I sailed smoothly through the air. Still, my stomach was in a knot and my heart raced. I could hear someone shouting at me from the far platform. Eventually, I squinted between my pressed eyelids and realized that I was nearing the end of the cable. I had forgotten to brake! I came in fast, nearly slamming into the safety mat, caught in the rescuing arms of the guide, who had been calling, "Brake! Brake!"

Eileen had waited for me. "You forgot to brake," she said, as if I might not have noticed. She beamed from ear to ear. "It was great, right?" I nodded numbly. "Are you okay?"

"I'm okay," I managed. "You go ahead without me. I'll just be a little behind the group." I sat down on the metal grate of the platform. Then, after Eileen took off, I lay on my side, trying to still the swirling sky.

The platform guide put a hand on my shoulder. "You can rest here as long as you want, but you know there's really no other way down."

"Okay. I can keep going." I stood with fresh resolve. "I can do this."

This time, as I zipped over the valley, I dared to open my eyes for a few seconds, and I even remembered to split my legs to brake before the opposite platform. Then, with each of the following five zips, my confidence grew. By "Big Daddy," the final mile-long cable, I gazed in wonder as I flew hundreds of feet over the jungle floor, wide-eyed as the tip of Arenal Volcano pushed its peak through the cloud cover. In the distance, I spotted the yellow beak of a flying toucan, and a thought flashed through my mind: *I'm just like you!*

By the time I caught up with the group, I felt exhilarated. "Good job, Ms. Long! You did it!" Eileen couldn't stop smiling. "It was really fun, right? I'm so glad I did it."

"Yeah. Me, too," I said honestly. Having mastered my fear, I wished I could have repeated the entire course and just enjoyed the relaxing sensation of flying above that mystical paradise.

I had no idea then that four years later I would move with my family to teach in Costa Rica. The first long weekend that we had a break from school, I suggested we try the Arenal zip line. My brave, teenage twins were thrilled and excited, but as we traveled up the mountain on the gently swaying tram, beads of sweat trickled from beneath my husband's helmet and slid over his pale, furrowed forehead.

"Are you okay?" I asked. Steve nodded, but his bobbing Adam's apple gave away his nerves. "It's only scary at first. Hang in there."

That was three years ago. Since then, we've returned to the same zip line twice more to enjoy the birdlike freedom of zipping above the distant treetops.

~Ilana Long

18

Kryptonite

Fear is only as deep as the mind allows.
~Japanese Proverb

Tucked in between farmland and rivers in upstate New York is a small "ranch" consisting of one shack-like building, a lot of grass, three airplanes and dozens of insane people who jump out of planes every day for a living. On a busy Saturday, up to twenty flights carrying eager twenty-somethings and bored fifty-somethings fly 13,500 feet above the ground, only to promptly throw said customers out of the plane while attached to an instructor.

"You are a student," one of the instructors informs us. "Your job is to listen to your instructor, follow his directions, and have fun."

I'm standing in line with five of my co-workers as this cigarette-smoking skydiving expert tightens my harness, makes a joke about the placement of my genitals, and explains how to stand at the edge of the plane once the door is open right before we jump. He tells me to keep my feet together and my head back, putting emphasis on looking up when I jump. A friend of mine told me this was to protect us from snapping our head back, knocking out our instructor and having to land with our parachute by ourselves.

It was about the scariest thing I'd ever heard.

I'm a fairly confident guy in most situations, but put me a few hundred feet above the ground, and my equilibrium gets thrown off. Heights are my kryptonite. My knees feel weak, I get clammy hands, and my heart races. I can't focus on anything except how high up I am.

Yet, somehow, my co-worker Rafa convinced me to drive two hours north of New York City, pay $200, and spend a day living out my worst nightmare.

A few weeks before, Rafa — who happens to be a Stanford graduate, engineer and pilot from Mexico — took me on a flight in a four-seater Cessna airplane as a little warm-up for skydiving.

We did a "skyline tour" of New York, where we flew south down the Hudson River, did a U-turn, passed the World Trade Center within a few hundred feet on our right, avoided helicopters flying at 1,500 feet, and got one of the coolest views of New York City I'd ever seen. But throughout the whole flight, my legs numbed with anxiety at every bump or turn.

I never really imagined I'd go through with skydiving.

And then, there I was, shaking hands with a guy named Danish to whom I was entrusting my life.

"Once we're in the sky, the order of priorities goes: 1) my comfort 2) your safety," he says with a Hungarian accent, smirking. I laugh, knowing this big-brother, trash-talking instructor is exactly who I need.

As a group, we board the plane, which is about four times the size of the Cessna I rode in weeks before but still much smaller than a commercial airliner. Inside are two long benches that we straddle, with our instructors behind us and the jumpers who would go alone sitting on the floor near the door.

"What are you scared of?" Danish asks seriously.

"I don't know," I say, pausing for thought. "Dying? Being scared of heights?"

"It's not about a fear of heights," he says curtly. "It's only about the altitude."

With that, Danish straps his harness to mine as the plane takes off and climbs toward the clouds.

"I know, I know… I should have bought you dinner first," he quips as he hooks himself to my harness inside the plane. "This is part of my job, alright?"

"I think I'm going to puke," I tell him honestly.

"If you puke on me, I'll pee on you," he says, and I don't get the sense he is joking this time.

On this trip, we'll be climbing 13,500 feet into the air, where the temperature is about 40 degrees Fahrenheit, a nice relief on a hot 93-degree summer day. As the plane continues to rise, Danish checks in by showing me his altitude watch. 3,000 feet… 5,000 feet…. 8,000 feet…

"We'll be at altitude in about five minutes," Danish tells me.

This is about the point where my phobia starts to kick in. I feel my eyes widen and my chest tighten. My knees get weak.

"No matter how scared you are," another instructor had told me, "one thing is for certain: Your body loves adrenaline and dopamine. And when you jump out of that plane, you're going to get a shot of both of them."

At 13,500 feet, a light goes on in the plane. One of the skydivers yells something, and seemingly everyone else in the plane chants something back. I didn't get the memo. Instead, I am burying my head into the back of the instructor in front of me, begging every god I know to help me get out of this plane and make it to the ground in one piece.

"DOOR!" someone shouts.

And just like that, a five-foot-tall side door on the plane swings open, and I am staring down at the clouds, at New York, and at my imminent death.

"You ready, *mijo*?!" Rafa shouts to me.

"F---, yeah!" I scream back, pretending to be ready.

The scariest part of skydiving is seeing the person in front of you jump out of the plane. Imagine driving on the highway, rolling down the window, and then reaching out and letting a piece of balled-up paper go flying down the road. It's just like that, except the piece of paper was my boss. One second, he's there giving me a thumbs-up, and the next second he's a speck in the clouds, flying away at what looks like light-speed. Suddenly, I realize I am in a plane going hundreds of miles per hour with the door open and, oh my god, he's pushing me out!

Before I know it, I'm belly down trying to scream, but I can't really scream because the wind is so strong it fills up my mouth and lungs. For a brief moment, all I feel is the distinct sensation I'm probably not going to survive, but then I acclimate. I find the horizon, see the trees, and remember that a dude who does this for a living is attached to me. And then he taps my shoulders, the sign to put out my arms. I think for a second and then remember where I am, willing myself to take my hands off my harness.

And in that moment, I feel it. I'm freefalling from a plane, I'm safe, I can breathe, and it is one of the most gorgeous things I've ever seen. There is no stomach-dropping, roller-coaster feeling in my stomach, just the sensation of flying, of control. The clouds pass by quickly, and now I have a clear, 360-degree view of everything around me. Freefall speed is about 55 meters per second, so in ten seconds I've covered 1,800 feet, five hundred feet more than the Empire State Building. By the time I'm oriented, I'm about 12,000 feet off the ground. Flying.

The instructor reaches around and gives me a thumbs-up.

I give him the thumbs-up back and nod furiously with joy.

Danish shows me his watch, which says we are at about 11,000 feet and gives me another thumbs-up. I give it back, remembering what my friend Casey — a frequent skydiver — said before I jumped. "Don't just look down. Make sure you look up and down and all around." I do. I look at the horizon and up to the clouds, which seem only feet away, closer than I've ever seen them without a thick airplane window between us. It is a beautiful, sunny, blue-and-green day, and I look to my left and see the massive Wallkill River. I can see the first of the parachutes below me and know that Rafa's freefall is up; he was about twenty-five seconds before me.

Before I know it, Danish is guiding my hand to the golf-ball-sized attachment that he told me I could pull to release the chute. I rip it, and suddenly there is the loud thunder of nylon catching air, harnesses doing their jobs, and the force of the parachute slowing us down in what is now the scariest part of skydiving.

And then there is quiet.

"Holy crap!" I scream, elated at the incredible rush that is the last fifty seconds.

"Welcome to my office," Danish says with a laugh behind me.

And what an office it is. Lush green trees and farmland are all around. Cities are on the horizon, and I see small-town suburbia built along the rivers. Danish pulls at the steering controls, or brakes, and starts to rotate us in a circle as we descend, giving me a view of everything around us.

I am out of breath now and quiet, but the beauty of everything around is stunning. It is so much better than flying over a city in an airplane. I can see both sides, and down and up and straight out in front of me.

As we work our way closer to the ground, I am already feeling the urge to go again. The fear, the rush, the panic, the camaraderie — it all feels so addictive. In that moment, I realize: *I want to go back up in that plane and jump out... again!*

I can't believe that in a matter of minutes what was once my biggest fear became something I would do over and over again if it weren't such an expensive hobby.

As we get closer to the ground, Danish reminds me to lift my feet up in the air as we come in so we can land on our butts.

One by one, my co-workers and I slide into the grass field, safely and smoothly on our behinds, ending five of the most exhilarating minutes of my life.

The jump reminded me that our fears are usually built around what we don't know, as opposed to what is actually dangerous or worrisome. In the span of a few hours, I went from being someone who couldn't look over a balcony without feeling queasy to thinking about how I could save money to jump from a plane for a second time.

But more than anything else, conquering my fear didn't just feel good because skydiving is fun; it felt good because I had overcome my kryptonite. In the legend of Superman, kryptonite is his weakness but gives regular humans super powers. That day, flying like Superman 13,000 feet above ground, I realized that my kryptonite had indeed turned into a power source for me, one that encourages me to face my fears to this day.

~Isaac Saul

Learning to Breathe

The cave you fear to enter holds the treasure you seek.
~Joseph Campbell

"Let's take a Caribbean cruise." I couldn't believe the words coming out of my husband's mouth. Phil and I had never done anything so adventurous. I felt giddy at the idea of gazing from ocean to shore rather than the other way around. I thrilled at the idea of new experiences by way of shore excursions.

Then I realized the obvious. Shore excursions involve water. Scuba diving, snorkeling, swimming with sea creatures. Each activity revived a childhood memory.

At the age of twelve, I nearly drowned in a muddy creek near my house. Thrashing about, I thought, *I can't breathe! Which way is up? I'm going to die in this blackness!*

Just as the horror threatened to crush me, I felt the strong arms of my brother Leonard. He lifted me into the sunlight. I sucked in air and vowed to stay out of water.

My poor husband loved water. Phil's happiest memories included swimming and boating. He even worked as a lifeguard a few summers. "Wait," he said. "Listen to this description of snorkeling. 'A two-hour excursion to Villa Blanca Reef where you will experience beautiful soft coral as well as an amazing variety of tropical fish in knee-deep water. Bilingual guides available to assist those who need a little help.' What do you think of that?"

"Knee-deep?" I sat up taller in my chair. "I can stand up any time I want?"

My husband smiled. "Sounds like it."

"I can do that."

After reading the description again, we booked a cruise to Cozumel, Mexico, and signed up for snorkeling.

My husband and I wandered the decks, watching waves as wind blew our hair. There were spas and ice sculptures, pools and hot tubs, shows and dancing. So much to see and do.

Two days later, we docked at Cozumel. An employee of the snorkeling crew held a sign aloft for participants to follow. After a bouncy boat ride, we landed at Villa Blanca Reef.

A lady fitted me with a mask, fins, and a yellow life jacket resembling a giant baby bib. The snorkel was attached to the right side of my mask. I only half-listened to the instructions about the paraphernalia. After all, the water would only be knee-deep.

I pulled my hair into a ponytail and stepped into 80-degree water. The gentle slope of the ocean floor allowed the water to inch up my ankles, knees, and thighs. When it approached my waist, I began to back up.

A whistle sounded. An instructor motioned for everyone to follow her to the deep water.

"Hurry up," my husband called over his shoulder.

I shook my head. "I thought the water stopped at our knees."

"I thought so, too," he said apologetically, "but we can do this."

"You go," I told him. "I'm going back to knee-deep water."

"Don't you want to see coral formations?" Phil's voice was thick with disappointment.

My tears threatened to spill over and make the Caribbean an inch deeper. "Let me practice."

I slid the mask over my eyes and nose. Trying to remember the instructor's words, I stuck one end of the snorkel in my mouth and pointed the other toward the back of my head. Leaning forward, I pushed into the water and looked beneath the surface.

Water seeped into my mask before I could even focus my eyes. I forgot to breathe through the snorkel and breathed through my nose instead, which fogged up the mask. Unable to see or breathe, I tried to stand, but couldn't find the bottom. I choked on a mouthful of ocean before my husband planted me on my feet again.

Phil wanted to catch up to the others, but I was too afraid. I insisted he go without me.

A young man with curly black hair and a thick accent glided toward us. He said in broken English, "You go, señor. She with me. You go."

The man, an instructor, took my hand. I echoed his words. "Yes, please go."

As Phil swam away, I wanted to kick myself for being so fearful, but I didn't have time. The instructor led me to the safety of knee-deep water. "My name Diego. Your name?"

"Arlene," I answered.

Diego pulled the ponytail holder from my hair. "This no good, Arlene. Water get in mask." He ran dark fingers through my hair, smoothing each bulge, and then re-positioned my mask. "Breathe through mouth," he said, and then explained how to use the gear.

This time, I listened.

Diego seemed to have all the time in the world. He helped me practice breathing through the snorkel, floating on my stomach, peering through the mask at the ocean floor two feet below, and propelling myself forward with the flippers.

I stood up. "I saw a little black fish!"

He smiled, and then we did it all over again. Just as I began to enjoy myself, he announced, "We go deep now."

"No!" I pulled away.

Diego called to another instructor. The guy hurried over with an orange oval flotation device about two feet in diameter. Diego wrapped my fingers around handles on each side of the device and then pointed toward the deep water. "You want to see out there. You ready."

Diego smoothed my hair and replaced my mask. I grabbed the handles in a death grip. He crooked his arm through a cord on the side of the device, swam toward the deep, and pulled me along with him. He paused twice to remind me to breathe through my mouth, kick my feet, and look beneath the water.

Beams of light shot through the water and revealed coral formations teeming with activity. My eyes darted back and forth at rock formations, damselfish, sponges, eels, sea fans, anemones, and creatures I couldn't identify.

The fish darting around me were not a simple orange, blue, or yellow. They were fluorescent orange, cobalt blue, and canary yellow. Small, medium, large. Solid, striped, dappled, and gorgeous.

Diego touched my shoulder. His brown eyes found mine, and he pointed at a silver barracuda, three feet long with a severe underbite.

Something gently brushed my entire body. I was in a school of silvery fish with black stripes and touches of yellow. Scurrying after bits of food deposited by Diego's co-workers, the fish flitted and fluttered. Just beyond the fish, someone took my picture. Even with a snorkel in his mouth, I could tell my husband was smiling. So was I.

Later, on shore, I thanked and hugged Diego. We said our farewells, and then I paused for a last glimpse of Villa Blanca Reef.

The shallow water was full of instructors working with would-be snorkelers. The guides resembled Diego, but not one of the students looked like me — they were all less than seven years old!

Diego had led me like a child without treating me like one. Side by side, we ventured into a beautiful underwater world teaming with life. For a brief moment, I became a part of that world and beheld all its treasures.

~Arlene Ledbetter

20

Reaching New Heights

It does not matter how slowly you go
as long as you do not stop.
~Confucius

ooking down from the top of a tall building didn't bother me years ago. Or climbing up the metal-grid stairs to the top of a lighthouse. Or sitting by the window on an airplane. But they all seem to bother me now.

As I've gotten older, my opinion has changed. I've developed a case of acrophobia, and now I do everything I can to avoid heights.

When my daughter-in-law Kathy and I went on a trip to the West Rim of the Grand Canyon, discussing our plan didn't bother me at all. I envisioned myself standing back and admiring the sight from a safe distance.

During our three-hour bus ride to our destination, the guide played a video giving us background information and explaining the process of building the Skywalk, the West Rim's premiere attraction. The horseshoe-shaped glass bridge juts seventy feet over the Grand Canyon, and the walkway has a clear glass floor. Between the floor and the shoulder-high, safety glassed wall, nothing obstructs getting a unique view of the canyon while standing four thousand feet over the bottom. Watching the video made my palms start to sweat.

When we finally arrived at the West Rim, the first thing I noticed was the absence of any safety rails at the canyon's edges.

"Just don't go too close," said our tour guide cheerfully. "It's a long way down."

The bravest among our tour group, including Kathy, went right to the edge and peeked over in awe. I kept at least two feet between me and the brink, but still couldn't make myself look anywhere but straight ahead. Thankfully, I didn't feel dizzy or lightheaded as long as I concentrated on keeping my eyes up.

The beautiful layers of red, orange, brown, and gray were so enormous and jaw-droppingly majestic that there really wasn't any need to walk closer. Speechless, I stared at the stunning display provided by the canyon, with a view that seemed to go on forever. I couldn't tear my gaze away from the beauty that had been carved by nature's own hand over many thousands of years.

While I admired the scene, Kathy appeared beside me and said, "Let's go on the Skywalk."

Despite the sun's heat, a shiver rippled down my back. "I don't know. Maybe you should go without me."

Being a good sport, Kathy smiled and said that would be fine. Then I took another look at the spectacular view. "You know what?" I told her. "I'm going to try."

We walked to the end of a long line waiting to buy tickets, and I tried not to think about what I'd agreed to do. The line moved a lot more quickly than I wished it would. Before I knew it, we were instructed to put disposable paper booties over our shoes — an alarming reminder of a hospital operating room — and put our belongings in a locker. Then a uniformed employee waved our group through to the Skywalk. Kathy moved forward with the others while I stood at the entrance and let everyone else go around me. My sense of balance seemed off, and my skin prickled. Looking at the large crowd on the bridge, I envisioned the entire structure crumbling under the weight of so many people. Yet hadn't the video explained how carefully the Skywalk had been constructed?

Inhaling deeply, I took one step, and then another and another. My blouse grew damp with perspiration, but I continued to walk. A brisk breeze tousled my hair, drying my forehead and cooling my face.

Just as I reached the halfway point, I stopped and looked to the side. The same gloriously sculpted vistas met my eyes. As others walked past me, the glass floor creaked and groaned. Taking another deep breath, I looked down.

Far below, I could see what appeared to be an endlessly deep ravine surrounded by the steep crags and ledges of the canyon's walls. An eerie mixture of anxiety and dizziness hit me, but I didn't close my eyes. After more than a full minute, I finally lifted my chin and inched my way back from where I'd started.

Peeling off the booties, a shaky smile lifted the corners of my mouth. Even though I didn't make it all the way around, I made it halfway. A sense of triumph replaced my jittery nerves. I'd just done something I wouldn't have dreamed possible, and I knew the experience had changed me.

Although I can't claim going on the Skywalk turned me into a reckless daredevil, it did teach me something. When I find an activity frightening, there's no reason to run away from it. Focusing on small steps can be just as valuable as taking large ones. I didn't forget the lesson on our airplane ride home.

For the first time in a long time, I chose the window seat.

~Pat Wahler

Chapter 3

STEP OUTSIDE YOUR COMFORT ZONE

☑ Connect with Someone

21

I Was There

I've learned that people will forget what you said,
people will forget what you did, but people will
never forget how you made them feel.
~Maya Angelou

was heading to the gym one evening in late autumn. It was cold and windy. I was hurrying along, happy that the trip to the gym would accomplish the last 3,000 steps needed for my daily total.

As I walked through a parking lot, I saw a homeless man out of the corner of my eye. He was settling in to sleep against the wall surrounding a trash bin. As I zoomed by, my heart sank.

I was about half a block past him when I turned and walked back. I knew it was not a good idea to bother this man. Many people in the streets suffer from mental illness. As a woman, it was unwise for me to ask a strange man if he needed help. And it was getting dark. I was shivering as I stood before the man. "Sir," I began, "I live over there." I pointed to my complex and explained that a liaison to our community, a police officer, said they would try to help the homeless find housing if we called. She further assured us that they had placed several families in the past year.

I braced myself for a possible rebuke, but what I heard was a gentle voice from a thoughtful man. "I *would* like a place to stay," he answered.

I asked if it was okay to call the police, and he said that it was. Since I do not carry a cell phone, I made a call at a nearby business.

When I returned, I told him I had made the call and asked if it was okay for me to wait with him. I was afraid the police would pass by and not see him. I did not want him to be invisible. Again, he calmly agreed. He then asked, "Do you think they'll find me an apartment?"

I did not know and felt even more unease with stopping. A person should know the answer to these questions, and I did not. But I answered, "I think they will get you shelter tonight and get your information. Then, over time, I think they will be able to locate something for you." As he was digesting that, I added in earnest, "Sir, it's too cold to sleep out here."

I did not have any money or food with me — just two water bottles. I smiled, pulled out one of the water bottles and offered it to him. He took the bottle and then sat up, as if he wanted to respect the effort I made. He thought for a moment and then began drinking small sips of the water.

When the officers arrived, one immediately strapped on rubber gloves. I cringed. I understood the precaution, but still hoped the man would not be offended. The officers assured me that he would have shelter and even thanked me. To my surprise, I was reluctant to leave the man. I realized an unexpected connection was born.

I have sometimes wondered why I stopped that night. Though I have since become involved with the homeless through my church, I knew very little about them that cold night. But that calm man, whose name I never knew, reminded me that though there will always be people who are better able to do something, sometimes you must stop because you are the one who is there.

~CL Nash

Elevator Challenge

Since there is nothing so well worth having as
friends, never lose a chance to make them.
~Francesco Guicciardini

Five years ago, after celebrating our sixty-third wedding anniversary, I reluctantly agreed with my husband that it was time to sell the house we'd lived in for forty-eight years.

He looked forward to the ease of apartment living. *I* was concerned about closet space.

More importantly, I had always been blessed with warm neighborly relationships. Would I be able to make new friendships at eighty-three?

We chose a twenty-one-story condominium complex in our Queens, New York, neighborhood, with 1,100 apartments, 1,800 residents and a health club. For the first time, I became dependent upon an elevator every time I left home, and again when I returned. There I was, confined to a 4x6-foot cubicle, along with one, two, sometimes as many as seven strangers. I hadn't given any thought to this aspect of high-rise living, and I was uncomfortable with it.

I never used the elevator in the five-story apartment house where I grew up. My family lived one floor up, and it was faster for me to run up the stairs. When I married Arthur, my high school sweetheart, we rented a studio apartment on the ground floor. We raised our children in a garden apartment, and finally in a Cape Cod on a quiet suburban street. Neighbors were always part of my daily life. Elevators were not.

When I'm in an office building elevator, I look straight ahead, and like everyone else, make no eye contact with anyone. Riding up or down, surrounded by neighbors in my new home, I realized that almost everyone was duplicating office building behavior—no eye contact, no interaction. Creepy! Every second in that small enclosure felt like five minutes to me.

At first, I conformed to what I imagined was elevator etiquette, occasionally nodding or smiling at my fellow neighbors, sometimes receiving a nod or a smile in return. Not a totally satisfying experience. We live in the most ethnically diverse county in the country. Our condo is a reflection of that diversity. Its residents come from all over the world. For a few fleeting moments, we find ourselves enclosed in a cage-like conveyance. Still, I decided to challenge myself, to transform our serendipitous encounters into social interactions.

I began by assuming the role of elevator operator, my thumb poised, ready to push buttons. "What floor?" I ask each person who enters. For a high floor, I may follow up with a question about the view up there. For a seventh or eleventh floor, I might comment on it being a lucky number. Sometimes I get a detailed response. I've also gotten riders who insist on pushing their own buttons.

With practice, it has become easier to communicate. Weather conditions, clothing, hair, shopping—all offer up possibilities. "How's it out there?" "Has the rain stopped?" "Is that sweatshirt warm enough?" I admire their outfits—from a funky straw hat to spike-heeled red shoes. A chic haircut often leads to inquiries about the stylist. Packages people carry identify the supermarket or department store they've shopped in. A relevant comment almost always elicits a friendly reply. Sometimes, the response is "No English," or "I don't understand." I'm not much of a linguist, but body language is often sufficient. Still, there are times when I am no competition for an occupant's enchantment with a smartphone. At other times, I am simply at a loss for a creative prompt.

Sharing an elevator with youngsters presents its own challenges. "What school do you go to?" I ask the kids toting backpacks as heavy as themselves. "Is that a violin case you're carrying?" "Do you go to college?" I joked, pointing to a six-year-old's university-branded T-shirt. We both laughed. Children respond to my questions, but I've learned not to expect personal questions in return. With the exception of one toddler who called me Grandma, I've found that children, my own grandchildren included, are focused on themselves.

"Are you a new resident?" is a question I often ask people I've never seen before. Sometimes, the answer is "Yes," in which case I may ask where they moved from and how they like living here. Often, I discover that they've been here for many years longer than I have, and they inquire about me. Where did I move from? How do I like living here?

It took more than two years before I thought of requesting a condo-sponsored tenant discussion group, and many months before it was approved. About fifty residents attend our weekly meetings. Wide-ranging conversations have led to new friendships and an ongoing elevator camaraderie campaign. I no longer feel like a lone crusader. I enjoy going down for the mail or up to water a vacationing neighbor's plants. Every excursion is an adventure. Who will I meet this time?

Entering our building one evening, my husband confided that he wasn't feeling well, then slumped to the ground and fainted in the elevator just as we got to our floor. I quickly pushed the down button and shouted for help when we got to the lobby. People assembled quickly, lifting him out and onto a nearby couch. At that instant, the door to one of the building's four elevators opened, and a visiting nurse emerged. Florence Nightingale to the rescue — a serendipitous encounter of another kind! Arthur was okay when she left, with a recommendation to visit his doctor the next day. The elevator, once a chamber of discomfort and dependence, has become a place of reassurance and connection.

My husband marvels at how a couple of strangers can engage in the short time each elevator trip occurs. He participates in a men's morning coffee klatch and a condo board committee, but unless someone approaches him, he is not prone to acknowledge those he does not know. My interactions have encouraged him to give it a shot. I see people stopping to speak with him when we are on the premises.

"Who's that?" I ask.

"An elevator friend," he answers, smiling.

~Ruth Lehrer

23

Friendship in Translation

The great thing about new friends is that
they bring new energy to your soul.
~Shanna Rodriguez

"Mom," my daughter told me, "that felt so strange. I didn't fit in there at all!" I laughed to hear her say so. We were leaving a Korean grocery store after stopping by to pick up some ingredients for a recipe.

For context, my daughter and I both speak English as our first language. And even though she attends a public school in Southern California, with a very diverse student body, she's not used to being surrounded by people who don't speak her language.

The reason she got the chance to step outside her comfort zone is because, several months ago, I stepped outside of mine.

I have four children, and they love playing outside — especially if there are other neighborhood children outside who want to play, too. When a new family moved in next door, my children started to play with their children, and I got to meet the mother of the family, Lydia.

Lydia is Korean, and her family moved to our city so her husband could go to graduate school. We started talking, and she was apologetic about how bad her English was, but I didn't care. After all, her English was so much better than my Korean (which, of course, was nonexistent). I knew how hard it was to learn a second language, and I knew English was particularly difficult, given how it constantly broke its own rules of grammar and pronunciation. I enjoyed chatting with Lydia as we watched our kids play.

It was what came next that challenged me: Lydia asked if I'd be willing to help her with her English.

Now, I am not a teacher. I admire teachers, and I'm grateful for teachers, and it's because I admire what they do so much that I was very, very sure that I couldn't do it myself.

But Lydia was sure that she wanted my help. I was doubtful. I wasn't sure my "help" was even worth being called by that name.

But because she asked me, I said "yes."

And that was the beginning of a friendship. Lydia and I spent afternoons sitting together and reading the newspaper, and as we did, she asked me questions when she had them — questions about language, yes, but also questions about the new culture she found herself in.

In turn, I asked my own questions, growing curious about her home country and culture. We bonded over our shared faith and our struggles as mothers of kids with special needs. When I complimented her cooking, she began to teach me about Korean food, eventually leading to a shared trip to explore the Korean grocery stores in our city.

Because of Lydia, I learned more about my own hometown than I ever could have learned by myself.

I'm still not sure that I'm any good as a teacher. But I'm grateful I said "yes" when my neighbor asked me to help her with her English. That meant spending extra time with my neighbor, and that extra time meant she didn't remain just my neighbor.

She became my friend.

~Jessica Snell

24

Knocking on a Stranger's Door

The kindest way of helping yourself is to find a friend.
~Ann Kaiser Stearns

come from a long line of quiet and shy people. My mother, grandmother, and I are what you would describe as introverts. My mother can spend hours on end reading. I can sit in absolute silence and write. My grandmother listened to music. Thinking about going to a social event gives me a twinge of anxiety. I always admire those who can bounce around the room talking to anyone and everyone, easily making friends. That would never be me, and I accepted that fact.

But that changed twelve years ago. I was a busy mom of four and had just been diagnosed with breast cancer. My husband and I were overwhelmed with our kids and jobs already. The kids were fairly young — ages four, six, seven, and eight — and we had just begun baseball season. As we sat at the game, another parent came and sat with us.

I usually just watched the kids play while my husband did the talking, but this man struck up a conversation with me. He told me he was newly divorced, and his ex-wife and I would make good friends. He said we had a lot in common, and since we both had four kids practically the same ages, they could play together. But it was his last point that really convinced me: He said she was having a hard time with the divorce, and since I had cancer, he thought maybe we could support each other.

I went home and thought about what he said. I really did want someone to talk to. My husband tried his best, but there are things about breast cancer that only another woman would understand. Then I thought about what she must be going through. She was starting a new life and raising four kids, which is a lot to have on one's plate. I had never just gone up and introduced myself to anyone before and wasn't sure I could, but I had a strong feeling I should try.

It took me two weeks to talk myself into doing it. One day, I woke up, put on a brave face and decided to make a new friend. The kids were in school except for my youngest, so I grabbed her and we headed over to the woman's house. I knocked on the door and figured she would think I was some sort of lunatic standing at her door, but I was quite surprised when she answered.

I introduced myself and explained I had met her ex-husband at baseball, and I understood our kids were close in age. We stood there talking about our kids, the town and baseball. Before I knew it, an hour and a half had gone by. Talking to her was like talking to an old friend. There was no awkward silence, just a great conversation. We made plans to take the kids to the park after school. This was the first of hundreds of trips to that park. The red park bench at the playground became our therapy bench.

Season after season and year after year, we needed that therapy bench. Her divorce and my cancer passed, and other problems came and went, but they always seemed better with a friend to listen. The kids outgrew the park, and our therapy bench became a poolside chair or a bonfire, but the setting didn't matter. The darkest days of my life came when my son was diagnosed with brain cancer. She shared my sorrow and then my joy when he became cancer-free a few years later.

We had more happy times than I could ever count. My husband shared many of those times with us, but he politely excused himself from our shopping trips or trips to the garden center. We shared in the joy of all our kids' accomplishments along the way.

Knocking on a stranger's door was one of the most life-enriching things I have ever done. I know her ex-husband said she needed a friend, but it turns out I needed one more. I love her like a sister, and I always will. I am still quiet and reserved, but I now understand we need to try new things to discover the beautiful possibilities the world can offer, like my friend Jenn.

~Michelle Bruce

25

Interfering

We cannot live only for ourselves. A thousand
fibers connect us with our fellow men.
~Herman Melville

lived in Southwick, Massachusetts, a little municipality with one church, one drugstore, and two traffic lights. After a while, I got to know most everybody since we all attended each other's garage sales, gathered at high school events, and got our cars fixed by the one and only mechanic.

Gossip ran rampant in our little town, but I tried to stay out of other people's affairs. Even if they needed help, I didn't feel right making the offer. I was afraid they would be insulted or angry, not receptive.

Then came the Frank dilemma. Frank was in his late sixties, a Vietnam veteran. His wife had died from cancer ten years earlier and they had no children. Frank's only true friend and companion was his dog, a German Shepherd named Morgan. Morgan wasn't a support dog per se, but he was this man's steady ally and his rock when bad nights haunted Frank. Everyone in town considered them a team and let Morgan come into their establishments. The two were often spotted together at the barber shop, bakery, or drugstore. More often than not, on a hot day, they could be seen swimming in the pond by Frank's cottage.

Then one day I realized I hadn't seen Frank in town for a while. Morgan had been an old dog, close to sixteen, so I began to make discreet inquiries at the grocery store and gas station. It had been a stroke, the clerk at the market told me. Morgan had to be put down. I wanted to knock on Frank's door and tell him I was sorry and ask if he was okay, but I was afraid to interfere.

Frank's loss was unmistakable. He looked terrible and he started shuffling as he walked. No one heard him laugh anymore. His shirts hung loose, and his pants bagged at his knees. My heart broke for him, but I didn't know what to do. So I did nothing.

My work as a court reporter took me fifteen miles away to the city of Springfield. One day, I found myself at the lunch table with Shari, one of the court clerks. She mentioned that she was looking for a good home for her dog Jax because she worked long hours and there wasn't a doggy daycare within thirty miles of her. Jax was almost a year old and full of energy, frisky and playful, and it bothered her that he spent the day alone. Even though she lived in a house with a doggy door to the back yard, sometimes Jax got himself into trouble from sheer boredom by chewing furniture and gnawing walls. As she talked, the proverbial lightbulb blinked on over my head.

Frank needed a purpose, a reason to get up and eat breakfast again. He needed a dog. I told her all about Frank, and she agreed to meet him. I went home happy and sure of my intentions, but unsure how to get the courage to meddle in Frank's life. Maybe he wouldn't want another dog. Maybe it would be too distressing for him. What if I opened up old wounds? I paced around my living room trying to come up with a solution. Whatever I did, it had to be handled gently on all levels.

Every day, Frank waited on his porch for the mail to arrive. Knowing that, I timed it so that my bike and I would be at Frank's property right before the mailman arrived. I waved to Frank on his porch, and then rode my bike up his driveway without invitation. I confided to him that I had a problem and needed some advice. I knew he'd fall for that. He was that kind of guy.

With a nervous hitch in my voice, I managed to blurt out my tale about Shari's dog and her inability to get him properly trained. I asked him if he'd be willing to help her out. He shuffled his feet and looked anywhere but at me. I could tell he wasn't thrilled with the idea, and my hopes dimmed. *This is exactly why I keep out of people's lives,* I reminded myself. But then he mumbled something about sleeping on it, and I rode away thinking, *I just planted a seed.*

A few days later, I accidentally-on-purpose ran into Frank at the coffee shop, and I pulled out my second direct hit: a photo of Jax. I lamented to Frank, as I placed the photo in his hand, that it was such a shame that this gorgeous dog had to be cooped up in a tiny apartment for sixteen hours a day. It was a lie and a terrible exaggeration, but I was committed to this scheme now. When Frank saw that Jax was a Shepherd, his eyes softened. He bit his lower lip in thought while I quietly picked up my coffee and left. I "forgot" to get the picture back.

Two days later, I made sure to ride my bike past the cottage. Sure enough, Frank called me over. He agreed to meet with Shari and the dog, but he didn't promise anything. On the day of the meet-up, Jax bounded out of the car and ran up and greeted Frank like he'd known him all his puppy life. Frank patted him and scratched the dog's ears and said things like, "Well, aren't you a handsome fella, huh?" We sat on the porch and talked "dog" and "military" for over an hour before Frank committed to training sessions three times a week for a month.

Well, the change in Frank was really something to behold, not to mention what it did for the dog. After a few weeks, I got reports of the two of them being spotted all over town with Frank patiently putting Jax through his paces. On the last agreed-to training day, Shari asked Frank if he would adopt Jax. He said "yes."

I'm happy to report that Frank's step became lighter, and he began to smile again. He and Jax went everywhere together: shopping, running chores, even ice fishing out on the lake. It made me laugh to see them seated next to each other on blankets, both staring intently at the dark hole in the ice, patiently waiting for a fish to bite.

A few months later, while riding my bike, I spotted them by the end of their driveway, and Frank beckoned me over. He peered down into my face and waggled a finger at me. "I always knew that dog never lived in no apartment," he said. "I just wanted you to know that." And with that, he gave Jax the command to fetch the newspaper. They walked side by side up the gravel path and in through the front door.

My first foray into meddling in someone else's life hadn't been a disaster, but nonetheless I promised myself I would never do it again. Until I do.

~Jody Lebel

26

The Oroville Dam Crisis

*Dare to reach out your hand into the darkness,
to pull another hand into the light.*
~Norman B. Rice

My dad's first engineering job was helping build the Oroville Dam back in the 1960s. So when the crisis hit, we took it seriously—filling our cars with gas, stocking up on food and water, and buying extra propane tanks. "When the water goes over the dam's emergency spillway, we all need to head for the hills," said Dad. "They should have concreted that dirt wall long ago. When the water hits that dirt, it's going to erode the hillside. That will compromise the dam. We're all in trouble now."

I left my dad's engineering office and went to buy another round of groceries that Friday, although I wasn't sure this would help. My dad didn't know if we were high enough to escape the flood where we lived at the base of the Sutter Buttes. If the Oroville Dam broke, it would be a disaster like none of us had ever seen. The Sutter Buttes, an ancient volcano in the center of the Sacramento Valley, would become an island like Hawaii, but without the beaches and hotels. Our plan was to hike into the Sutter Buttes if the flood waters overtook our home.

I didn't really believe the dam would break. None of us believed that. So on Sunday evening, with water running over the emergency spillway all weekend long, and the news broadcasting everything was fine anyway, we weren't prepared when officials suddenly called for a mass evacuation of our valley. Nearly 200,000 people were told to get to higher ground as fast as possible because the dam could fail within the hour, sending a thirty-foot wall of water downriver.

An hour earlier, our fourteen-year-old son John had injured his arm playing football in our yard with his cousins. My husband Scott had taken John to Urgent Care in Yuba City, a stone's throw away from the Feather River. It was the same Feather River that flows out of the Oroville Dam where the wall of water would come from.

I jumped on my iPhone trying to reach Scott. They were treating John's fractured wrist even as they closed the clinic, kicking out all the other patients with lesser needs. A homeless man in the Urgent Care parking lot began screaming, "God is testing us! He's testing us with this flood!" as people ran for their lives.

"Please get home as fast as you can," I said before hanging up with Scott as friends began calling, seeking refuge with us. "We don't know if we live on high enough ground," I told people. "You are welcome to come, but we might have to hike into the buttes if the flood gets here."

It took hours for Scott and John to make it home in gridlocked traffic. Several families said they were on their way to our house, but by midnight, nobody had arrived. All the cities along the Feather River were facing evacuation. The roads were a mess. I could hardly sleep that night. Miraculously, the dam was holding.

Early the next morning, our house was eerily quiet. The families headed to our home the night before had stayed in Yuba City because the roads were jammed.

"I'm going to drive up to Sutter and see what's going on there," Scott said as the sun rose over the buttes that morning. A half-hour later, Scott returned. "You're not going to believe this," he said. "Pass Road is filled with refugees. People slept in their cars last night. Babies in sleeper pajamas are toddling alongside Pass Road."

I quickly gathered food and told Scott to load a case of water into the back of the truck. "Let's go see how we can help," I said with a sinking heart. I felt so bad that our children had slept in warm beds, while families slept in cars just up the road from us.

A half-hour later, we returned to our home with a line of vehicles in our wake. We had handed out some food, and when we encountered some families with small children walking around on the road, we couldn't stand it. "Come home with us," I pleaded with these shell-shocked families. "We will take care of you. We will keep you safe."

Several families came. Only one mother among the refugees spoke English. Her name was Tillie. I've always regretted that the Spanish I learned in high school and college didn't stick. But I remembered, "*Mi casa es tu casa.*" Our home was their home during this evacuation.

We welcomed in these flood refugees like friends. The children played with our boys' toys. Everyone used the bathrooms and relaxed in our living room. The men, after quietly eating our leftover spaghetti from the night before, washed our dishes and swept our kitchen floor. I'd wanted to bring the women and children home, but the men frightened me. Now, I left the kitchen so those daddies didn't see my tears as they did my chores. These were good men doing their best to protect their wives and children. Tillie told me how her husband brought along their children's life vests and planned on putting their little ones in their vests before placing them in the tallest trees they could find when the water came. The older children hugged me and thanked me for bringing out more toys for them to play with. I found baby wipes in our bathroom so the mamas could change diapers.

By the time these families left our home, I had fallen in love with them. "If a levee on the river breaks, come back to us. We will take care of you," we told them as they packed up their children to go. "If the Oroville Dam breaks, get out of this valley as fast as you can. It will be a catastrophe."

"If the dam fails, I'm going back to Mexico," said one of the men. I didn't need Tillie to translate for me. Though he spoke Spanish, I understood. I stepped over and put my arms around the man. "If you need anything, anything at all, we are here for you." I know this man understood some of my English even if he didn't speak it very well.

My husband hugged the man after I did, and I could tell Scott felt it, too—a bond with this man we couldn't ignore or escape. In the midst of the Oroville Dam crisis, these people were no longer refugees and strangers among us. They became a part of our family and remain our friends today.

~Paula Scott Bicknell

27

Ten Past Three

*Each friend represents a world in us, a world possibly
not born until they arrive, and it is only by this
meeting that a new world is born.*
~Anaïs Nin

"He's a bit of a weirdo, if you ask me. No wonder his kids are so strange." I could hear the other mums tittering at the school gates. I stood alone, waiting for my daughter to come out, too shy to intervene. I checked my watch: ten past three, another five minutes to go.

I saw Paul blush and stare at the ground. Nobody ever talked to him. I thought it was cruel, but I told myself he didn't help himself. He was always so serious. Never smiled or said "hello." Every day, it was the same — ten past three, leaning on the steel school gate, staring at the notice board full of old memos about swimming club or parents' evening events that had long passed.

The other mums kept talking under their breath, occasionally laughing coldly out loud. I wondered whether they would turn on me as well. I never talked to anyone either. Did they think I was weird, too?

I should have introduced myself when Poppy had first started school, but that was months ago, and the moment had passed. The other parents had all formed little groups. It felt a bit like being back at school myself. So many times, I'd stood on the edge of the playground, always wishing I had the guts to go and join in. Nobody ever came to me, and I never went to them. Sometimes, I wondered what might have been if only I had the guts to take a chance. Things might have been different, happier.

Perhaps I looked just as strange as Paul did, standing there by myself, looking at my shoes, longing to see Poppy run out of the school gates so we could go home, shut the door and have tea together. I hoped Poppy wouldn't become as shy as I was.

Paul's twin boys were a year older than Poppy. That meant he'd been waiting at that gate every day for the past year. *Did he endure this awkwardness every day? He must dread it,* I thought. Still, perhaps there was a reason. *Was he just plain weird, as the other mums said?* One couldn't be too careful, especially when it came to children. That's what I told myself.

I faked a yawn and checked my watch again. Only two minutes gone. *This is excruciating,* I thought. That school bell couldn't come soon enough. The mums' kept looking over their shoulders at Paul. He kept blushing. I wondered whether his boys realised that their dad always stood alone. Then, with a pang of regret, I wondered whether Poppy realised that her mum stood by herself as well.

Suddenly, I felt my feet moving! An inner voice said, *What on earth are you doing?* I found myself walking toward Paul. As the other mums gazed accusingly at me, I could feel my cheeks get hot. *Was I making a terrible mistake? What if Paul really was a weirdo?* As he watched me walk toward him, he looked bewildered, scared even.

Well, you've got to say something now, I thought. *Otherwise, you're the one who looks like a weirdo!*

"Hello, you're Paul, the twins' dad, aren't you?" I stammered. Silence. What had I done? *You can't stop now,* I thought. *Those mums will eat you alive.*

I stuttered on. "I'm Sal, Poppy's mum. I just thought, well… I thought I'd come and say 'hello.'" *No stopping now!* "It seems so silly not saying 'hi' when we stand here every day, same time, you know…" My cheeks were burning. *Please, just say something, anything!* I thought.

More silence. My shyness was crippling me, and I was dying inside, knowing that my risk had not paid off. Just as I was about to turn on my heels, ashamed, and go back to my spot at the gates, Paul spoke. "Hello, Sal. Yes, I'm Paul." He held out his hand. I took his, and we shook. As we did, I glanced back at the other mums. They were staring with their mouths open.

"Please excuse me for not saying 'hello' before," he said. "I find social situations a bit difficult, you see." I did see, of course, because I did, too. "I really appreciate you coming over. It means a lot."

We started talking—not about much, the upcoming school concert and plans for the holidays. Before I knew it, the school bell had rung. Children came flying out of the gates, shirts hanging out of clothes, hair ruffled, cheeks rosy. As it got noisier, Paul and I realised we could no longer hear each other. And for the first time at those school gates, in front of the suspicious mums, we just laughed naturally. I think it was a big moment for both of us.

Poppy smiled when she saw me talking to Paul. She wasn't used to seeing me chatting with someone! Paul's twin boys buried their heads behind his legs, but smiled shyly. I think they knew that friendship might be around the corner, too.

From that day on, Paul and I would chat with each other at ten past three each day. As we talked more, I was lucky enough to find out more about him and his family, to know there was nothing weird about him. His shyness was due to a mild autism, which his boys had inherited. They could get by, but social situations for all of them were tricky. Paul confessed that he had started to dread the school pick-up as he was aware of the other mums being nasty. He didn't blame them, he said. He knew he might look a bit serious and weird. But that was just because he wanted the ground to swallow him up sometimes.

I shared about my shyness. We laughed to think that for several months we'd both been standing at those school gates, too timid to introduce ourselves to each other or anyone else. Poppy and the boys became firm friends. They see each other most weekends now and spend hours running around the garden playing. Their friendship, and ours, has enriched our lives so much.

I know now that finding the guts to say hello that day was a life-changer for us all. I'm so glad I could put the past behind me, ignore fears about anyone who is different, and do something positive.

And the other mums? It took a while for them to pick their jaws up from the ground, but after a while they stopped staring and sniggering. On the last day of term, Paul and I went over to say "hello" to them. They weren't so bad. One of them even confessed she laughed when she felt insecure. She had never thought how it might make others feel. We might not become best friends with them, but the awkwardness has stopped, and we often chat all together.

I never look at my watch with dread anymore. In fact, I look forward to ten past three. Soon, the new term starts. If I see any parent standing alone, I'll take that chance and say "hello."

~Sal Patel

28

Comedy and Courage

Trust the still, small voice that says, "this
might work and I'll try it."
~Diane Mariechild

was living in San Francisco and taking a lot of improv classes and going to open mic nights. At that time, Robin Williams lived in San Francisco, too. He owned a house in the Sea Cliff area of "The City." Sometimes, he would show up at open mics.

One of the improv classes I attended regularly was taught by Jim Cranna every Saturday afternoon at the Fort Mason Center. It was a refurbished military quarters used for various and sundry purposes such as theatre, dining, and all types of artsy classes. Sometimes, as many as twenty-five to sixty-plus folks showed up. Jim made sure to fit everyone in so they could improve their craft.

It was business as usual at the class one day. The usual cast of comic actors and some new ones were testing their comedy chops — playing improvisational comedy games.

The class lasted for three hours, and we would go to the nearest mini market located in the building and get a snack or coffee during breaks. One day three of us were standing outside the building, when lo and behold, Robin Williams walked by, enjoying the fresh bay air. My fellow comics were completely frozen. They saw him, but they couldn't summon up the courage to just say "hi" to Robin, who was with a friend. They kept whispering, "What do I say? What do I say? I just can't go up to him and say 'hi'!"

I froze for a moment, but then I composed myself. I thought, *It's now or never. Seize the moment!* I told them, "Hey, if you guys can't handle it, then I will ask him to come and join us for the second half of class." I could hear them mumble under their breath, "Yeah, sure, right. You're going to ask Robin Williams to come to our comedy class. Good luck with that one!"

So I calmly went up to Robin and his friend and I asked him to join us. "We're having an improv comedy class. We're on break now, but we would be most humbled and honored if you would join us for the second half of the class." Robin looked directly in my eyes and said with little hesitation, "Okay." It was like a grown-up child being asked to come and play. With that, he and his friend followed me up to the class.

When he saw Robin, Jim said, "Oh my, look who Micheline is bringing to class." Jim's eyes were all aglow in sheer astonishment and delight. "Why, it's Robin Williams!" Robin and his friend stayed the rest of the class and at the end of the class, Robin and Jim performed a skit. It was amazing to watch Robin psych up in order to get into character. We actually watched him shape-shift as he prepped physically and mentally for his made-up character. He gave it his all. We were mesmerized watching this master comedian perform. It was truly magical.

What a delight for all of us that Saturday afternoon! All I know is that if I hadn't mustered up the courage to ask Robin to join us, none of us would have had that experience. But something inside of me said, *Just approach him with dignity and respect and ask him to join us.* I was humbled by his grace and humility. Here he was — an internationally famous actor and comic — but he was so very, very nice. He was responsive, unpretentious and kind.

That is the Robin Williams I will always remember and the one I keep in my heart. I'm so thankful that I found the courage to ask, so that all of us could meet such a wonderful and talented human being.

~Micheline Birger

29

Jerry

*An effort made for the happiness of
others lifts us above ourselves.*
~Lydia M. Child

I live in a small, rural town in Connecticut. In our town, a man, probably in his late forties or early fifties, is often seen wandering about town, usually pushing an old shopping cart. Sometimes, he is just walking slowly and carrying a plastic bag. His gait is stiff and labored. His clothes are rumpled and appear old. He picks up trash and bottles and cans that he finds for recycling. At first glance, most people assume he is homeless and most likely an alcoholic or drug addict.

I had my first good look at him one day when he was in the grocery store turning in the tickets he had collected for the five-cent recycled bottles and cans deposit. I noticed how the customers around him at the courtesy counter looked at him in disgust.

The weather that day was really nasty with a cold, driving rain. This man was soaking wet and the water was literally dripping off him. I was walking out of the store, and he turned to leave at the same time. Our eyes met, and I impulsively asked him if he needed a ride somewhere. He smiled genuinely and accepted gladly. He had goodness in his soul; I could feel it.

I'd never done this before. I am a sixty-two-year-old woman, and time has taught me to be cautious. I've never picked up a hitchhiker or a stranger. If I see someone in distress, I will call the authorities for assistance. But something compelled me to speak to this man.

When we got to my car, I noticed that he did not smell at all and there was certainly not a hint of alcohol on him. As I drove, he talked a little bit. His sentences were almost childlike. He told me that his name was Jerry. He commented to me that he used to have a car and a job, and he drove everywhere. But then he had a bad accident, so he couldn't drive anymore because of a brain injury. He had to take a lot of medicine.

Jerry explained that he likes to be outside, so he walks a lot. He likes to pick up trash so the town will look nicer. And anything he can recycle gives him a little bit of extra money until his disability check comes in. He also told me that the grocery store doesn't want him to go inside anymore because they said it bothers the customers.

Jerry lives with his parents on a rural road just outside the center of town. I drove him to his residence in a modest mobile home. He thanked me and went inside.

Now, whenever I see Jerry, I honk my horn and wave to him. He waves back with a big smile on his face. I've asked him a few more times if he needs a ride, but he has always declined, saying he likes to be out in the fresh air.

I wonder how many people incorrectly judge this man? Jerry is just a man who had something terrible happen to him and is just trying to live his life peacefully now as a traumatic brain injury survivor. What happened to Jerry could happen to any of us. I don't read the Bible regularly, but I know bits of it. I'm reminded of Matthew 7:1 where Jesus said, "Do not judge, or you too will be judged."

Everyone has a story. Most of the time, we don't bother to listen to the stories. We go about our day with our minds stuck in our own little worlds. I advise everyone to take the time to observe and really listen to what people have to say. Take a chance and start a simple conversation with a stranger. You will be amazed by who you meet and what you can learn.

~Debi Smith Pouliot

When Shrinking Violets Bloom

The shell must break before the bird can fly.
~Alfred, Lord Tennyson

A s a child, I was very shy. I grew up in a strict environment where children should be seen and not heard. When I did open my mouth, I usually ended up putting the proverbial "foot" in it. Any attempt at repeating a joke would fall flat, or I'd blurt out something stupid and be teased or reprimanded. Eventually, I learned to stay silent unless spoken to first. I was okay with close friends or family, but new situations and unknown environments would render me mute. Public speaking would leave me with stage fright, paralyzing fear, or an embarrassing stutter.

The problem got worse as I got older. Though I enjoyed going out, it was always in a group. I relied on my friends to break the ice when meeting new people. In fact, I met my husband Don through a third party. Our relationship, subsequent marriage, and the huge network of people he knew or was related to led to constant social interactions, something that I was deplorably bad at.

I became overwhelmed. I was used to a quiet, aloof family that rarely had company. We had no relatives close by. My husband, however, had five sisters, a brother, and more relatives than I could count. Meeting them all and trying to keep track of their names, let alone trying to make conversation, was mind-numbing. My timidity prevented me from appearing friendly, and I know I didn't make a good first impression.

The same held true when we started going to different gatherings. If we were attending a party, I would become pathetically needy, stressing repeatedly before we even arrived that Don stay by my side throughout the entire function. If he so much as made a trip to the bathroom or went to refresh a drink, he wouldn't hear the end of it during the ride home.

My husband is very laidback, with the patience of a sloth setting out on a thousand-mile journey. At first, he was very understanding about my insecurity. In fact, he seemed to find it endearing. Eventually, though, he started declining invitations for get-togethers, assuring me he'd rather stay home and watch television. I realized he wasn't being truthful, and *my* behavior was the problem. I wanted to change it, but how?

I began to read self-help articles, looking for ways to overcome my debilitating shyness. Nothing I read seemed to apply to me. The conversation starters seemed completely out of my comfort zone. I knew nothing about politics, world events, or rocket science — and who on earth could possibly be interested in my robotic, boring packing job in a factory?

If anything, the more I read, the dumber and duller I felt. My confidence level plummeted farther south than even demons dare to venture. Trying to validate my self-worth in a mirror simply made me feel ridiculous — and in need of a diet if the mirror was full-length. Silly as I felt, I compromised and tried anyway, but after speaking to my reflection for only a few minutes, I snapped my compact shut in frustration. How could I possibly convince total strangers that I was an interesting, captivating conversationalist if I couldn't even convince myself?

I tossed the useless magazines aside and continued to agonize. I knew that I couldn't spend the rest of my life hiding at home in my prison of self-imposed terror. I had to change, and I vowed to do so at the next event we attended, which just happened to be my husband's company picnic the following week. I had no idea how I was going to break past my barrier of silence, but I swore I would not leave that party without trying to speak to at least one person.

When we arrived that Saturday morning, there were already more than eighty people there. After introductions were made to people whose names I mumbled and quickly forgot, I felt that familiar dryness fill my mouth. My deer-in-the-headlights expression was my husband's cue to drag me away.

"Why don't we go get ourselves a soda, honey," he invited for what was probably the hundredth time since we met. This time, his voice didn't have that understanding ring to it. His resigned tone gave me the resolve I needed to put the socially destructive monster inside me away once and for all. I took a deep breath.

"I'll get it," I replied. "You stay here with your friends."

Ignoring his shocked expression, I trotted away before I could change my mind, making my way to the refreshment table at the end of the field.

As I reached into a cooler filled with ice and soft drinks, I spotted a woman sitting by herself at a picnic table watching the crowds mingle.

I was instantly filled with empathy as I took in her rigidly defensive body language. Her knees were clamped together, her back ramrod straight. Lips drawn tightly caused a nervous tic to flutter on her cheek. White-knuckled fingers clutched the purse in her lap like a protective shield.

I surprised even myself when I didn't hesitate to grab an extra soda and walk over to sit next to her.

"Hi! I'm Marya," I stammered, pushing a cola toward her. "I couldn't help admiring your pretty blouse and wondering where you bought it."

I had no idea why I asked that since I hadn't even noticed her clothing, but I could see her shoulders visibly relax as she named a popular store. Then she told me her name was Violet.

"You look like I feel, Violet," I confessed, "as if you'd like to be anywhere but here. I never know what to say at these things."

"You, too?" she replied incredulously, and surprised me by instantly launching into a monologue of how she had no choice but to attend since she was the company director's private secretary. She explained how difficult it was for her to socialize and meet strangers. Before I knew it, we were deep in discussion. It was only when we heard a throat clear behind us and turned to see my husband that we stopped talking.

"About that soda, honey…" he grinned teasingly, but I could see the pride in his eyes that I was finally attending a function without being glued to his side. I pushed the now warm drink toward him and continued the conversation while he wandered off to mingle without me.

I don't know about Violet, but that was the last time I ever shied away from getting to know people. The discovery that a simple, interested question, compliment, or common interest will prompt most people to talk about themselves allowed me to break through my self-imposed tradition of shyness. I now eagerly embrace the opportunity to attend any event we're invited to.

I still tell jokes that fall flat, and I blurt out things that can cause an uncomfortable silence, but then, who doesn't? I'm only human — but now I'm a sociable one.

~Marya Morin

STEP OUTSIDE YOUR COMFORT ZONE

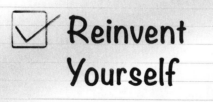

✓ Reinvent
Yourself

31

Following My Heart

I don't focus on what I'm up against. I focus
on my goals and I try to ignore the rest.
~Venus Williams

When I was seventeen years old, I dreamed of becoming a doctor, but my dream seemed unachievable. I am a first-generation American born to Jamaican immigrants, and the first college graduate in my immediate family. My parents instilled in my brother and me the belief that we could become anything we desired as long we worked hard, but I still didn't think that meant I could go all the way to becoming a physician. Perhaps it was because there were no black doctors around me to emulate, or perhaps it was because I didn't like science in school, especially physics, which was almost my undoing.

I decided to attend college in upstate New York and major in accounting. I enjoyed business, and accounting would give me a stable career. That decision led me to the world of investment banking and Wall Street. I had a very good friend with connections at Morgan Stanley and he managed to get me a temporary position on the trading floor when I graduated from college in 1991.

Talk about a different world! I had grown up in Amityvile, a small community on Long Island, and yes, the town featured in *The Amityville Horror*. It's the kind of community where everyone knows each other; I attended school with the same classmates from kindergarten through twelfth grade. We were very close-knit. My exposure to Manhattan, forty miles away, was intermittent; my mother used to take my brother and me school shopping there once a year. But each trip increased my love of the city. I just knew that once I graduated from college, I wanted nothing more than to work in exhilarating and sophisticated New York City. And that summer, I got my wish!

Working on the trading floor of Morgan Stanley was exciting but temporary, and my goal was to find a permanent accounting position. I interviewed throughout New York City, and I eventually landed my dream position just six floors above the trading floor in the accounting department.

My eight years at Morgan Stanley and subsequent six years at Citigroup were great. I loved crunching numbers. However, deep down, I knew there was more for me to do. I could not pinpoint why I felt the way I did, but I knew that I possessed the potential to do more. I thought maybe the next step was to become a college professor. During my investment banking career, I obtained an MBA, and I thought the next logical step would be to teach business on a collegiate level. Then my father died, in June 2000.

His death was a seminal event. As previously noted, my parents told me I could do anything I wanted, but it was my father who gave me confidence. He had such high aspirations for his children. He used to say, "Randi, first you will get your bachelor's, then a master's, and then you will get your doctorate." I never paid any attention to him at that time, but somehow he instilled something in me.

Once he was gone, I knew, perhaps on a subconscious level, it was time to do more. Then, 9/11 occurred, just five blocks away from my office. After watching the destruction unfold that day, I realized that I needed purpose. Working as an investment banking accountant could be grueling at times; there were many times we would work on holidays or late on weeknights. I decided that if my work was going to take important time away from being with my family, it should at least be for a good reason.

Within a year, I was enrolled in pre-med classes at a local college. Somehow, I managed to work full-time and take courses such as Biology, Organic Chemistry and, yes, Physics! I aced my courses.

Soon after, I took the Medical College Admission Test, the dreaded MCAT. My grades and MCAT scores were sufficient for admission to Stony Brook University School of Medicine.

I loved medical school, but it was challenging. When I enrolled in August 2005, I was thirty-five years old. There was only one student older than me. Medical school was a challenge, but I persevered and graduated on time. I went on to do my residency in pediatrics, which also was not a walk in the park.

When I decided to change careers, I knew I would be a pediatrician. I loved children and wanted my career to involve molding and guiding their health and wellbeing. I'm now a board-certified pediatrician serving the most vulnerable population of my community, back in Brooklyn where I was born. Yes, I made some major sacrifices, but I could not be happier.

If only my daddy could see me now.

~Randi Nelson

32

Chicken Soup for the Soul

Fifty

*Coming out of your comfort zone is tough in the
beginning, chaotic in the middle, and awesome
in the end… because in the end, it shows
you a whole new world.*
~Manoj Arora

The day I turned fifty, I swore I must have passed through some sort of time warp. *Surely,* I thought, *I cannot be at this destination this soon.* There was still so much to do. So many things I had put off until I had "more time." But, at fifty, I realized we don't get more time. We just keep getting less.

For half of those fifty years, I had the pleasure of working as a public schoolteacher and school administrator. Hundreds of students graced my life with their trials and triumphs. Many a lecture I offered on holding on to hope and following one's dreams. I poured encouragement into the youth sent to me. Several listened intently and came back years after graduation to share their stories of success. But at fifty, I realized that I had not heeded my own advice. I had certainly fulfilled my childhood dream of becoming a teacher. But there were still other dreams I had held onto for years and failed to bring to life.

As little kids, my sister Margie and I imagined ourselves the next Sonny and Cher or Donny and Marie. We stood for hours in my room with hairbrushes in our hands, singing along to albums on my record player. We tacked up sheets to the ceiling for stage curtains, and then invited our parents and five siblings to watch our performances. We both joined the school choir in elementary school. Later, as teenagers, we sat outside on summer evenings with George, a boy from down the street, and Cindy, my sister's best friend (who later became my wife!). George and I played our guitars as we all sang the latest Bee Gees songs or any other songs with simple chord progressions. We thought we were hot stuff.

I always dreamed of being a singer performing on stage before an adoring crowd. Despite the fact that my job as teacher and later as an administrator required me to speak before large groups, I never had the courage to make my singer's dream a reality. But the year I turned fifty, I was presented with an opportunity to do just that.

A teacher who worked at my school approached me one day before the end of the school year and told me that her husband, a high school theatre instructor and director of a community acting troupe, was planning a summer production of the musical, *Godspell*, a 1970s retelling of the Gospel of Matthew set in New York City. She pestered me each day that last month of school until I agreed to try out for a part.

On the Saturday of tryouts, I almost backed out, but my wife and daughter convinced me that I needed to take this chance. I went on stage and sang "Prepare Ye the Way of the Lord" and "All for the Best." Two days later, I received word that I had the lead part — as Jesus! I had four weeks to memorize forty-two pages of dialogue, my four songs, and the choruses for all of the other songs in the show! I practiced in the car, the shower, even in the little inflatable pool in the back yard with my daughter as my coach.

After two weeks of rehearsing, we were told to put our scripts away. "If you get stumped, just say 'Line!'" we were directed. I used that word multiple times that night. Embarrassed yet determined, I took my script with me to the office each day the next week. When my work as a school administrator was complete, I went into the cafeteria and emoted to the milk cartons! When the custodians, curious about all the commotion, checked in on me, I moved to the band room and performed for my imaginary audience there. By the end of the week, I had most of my dialogue and songs memorized.

The cast was an intergenerational and interracial group of talented individuals. The youngest was five years old. The oldest was fifty. The teenagers were some of the best singers I had ever heard. I worried about keeping up with them.

In Act II, Jesus chastises the nonbelievers via the rocker, "Alas for You." During most rehearsals, I played it safe and sang the song fairly blandly, almost as a ballad. But one night, during the last week of rehearsal, I decided that if the kids could sing so powerfully, then I could do the same. We were all on stage having little conversations as we awaited our turns to practice our individual songs with the voice coach. When it was my turn, I channeled my inner Alice Cooper and let the Pharisees have it! I remember opening my eyes to see that the others had stopped their conversations and were looking at me now with mouths opened wide. Their reaction was my reward and the reinforcement I needed to give it my all.

Performance night arrived sooner than my nerves could handle. I stood quavering backstage in my full costume: a Superman T-shirt, bell-bottomed jeans, rainbow suspenders, and red, white, and blue tennis shoes. The rest of the cast approached the stage from the audience, singing the opener, "Prepare Ye the Way of the Lord." I looked to my right and noticed that an exit door was only ten feet away. *Ten feet — ten seconds — I could escape this,* I mused. Then I thought of my family sitting out there. I entered stage left on cue and launched into my first number, "Save the People."

Once the first song was over, my nerves were fairly stabilized, and I was able to make it through the rest of the program. I messed up my lines once, but the others covered for me. Because the story is a free-flowing dialogue between Jesus and his followers, we had agreed that if I got lost somewhere in the forty-two pages of the script, someone would just prompt me with a line like, "Hey, Jesus, why don't you tell us the story about…" That worked great, and those kids made me look good!

The program ended with me crucified and carried out of the auditorium on the shoulders of my fellow cast members. They dropped me unceremoniously in the foyer as they rushed back to the stage for their curtain call and reprise of "Day by Day." I jumped up, brushed myself off and peeked in the back door awaiting my signal to join them on stage. I noticed an older woman in the back of the auditorium wiping tears from her eyes. I knew then that I had done the right thing in pursuing this dream. It was clear to me at that moment that our dreams and all we do to achieve them are inextricably connected to the lives of others.

Renewed, I ran down the side aisle to center stage and sang with more confidence than ever before.

~Tim Ramsey

33

No More White Walls

Our home tells a story about us, so we may as well
take the opportunity to make it a stylish one.
~Deborah Needleman, The Perfectly
Imperfect Home

A small bell chimed to announce my presence as I pushed open the shop door. There went my hope of entering unnoticed. A salesman hurried to meet me with a broad smile. "How can I help you today?"

I resisted the urge to make a hasty exit and forced myself to greet him instead. "I'd like to see some paint swatches."

Our home was more than ten years old and way overdue for a fresh coat of paint. The past ten years had been good to us, too, as we developed special friendships. It was because of those friends that I found myself in the paint store.

It started innocently enough with visits to each of their homes. Then I invited them to ours. Two friends, Jan and Linda, graciously admired our home, but were curious about one thing. I steeled myself for what I knew was coming. Jan was the first to ask. "Beautiful... but, um, can I ask why all the walls are white?"

It was a natural question. Their homes included color-coordinated rooms, accent walls, and color-themed bathrooms. Every room proclaimed their confident decorating abilities. On the other hand, every wall in our home was stark white. The label on the paint can may have had a fancy name such as "Pearl Onion" or "Ice Cube," but I had to face facts: It was still white.

How could I explain my reasons for all white walls? It's not because I don't enjoy color. I had admired their homes. I watched HGTV, and I'm a fan of home makeover shows. I read *Better Homes and Gardens*. I learned to differentiate between "warm" and "cool" colors. I even knew the difference between saturation and intensity. And still my walls were all… white. When it came to actually selecting colors, I became paralyzed with indecision.

I learned the colors of the rainbow in grade school by memorizing the acronym ROYGBIV. Red, orange, yellow, green, blue, indigo, violet — so pretty when they form a bow in the sky. Or adorn wildflower petals. Or when they paint the clouds in glorious sunsets. I've always enjoyed splashes of color… as long as they stayed outside.

When it comes to painting my walls, I panic. Too many choices. *What if it doesn't look good when I'm finished?* Of course, I know I can repaint, but I barely have enough time to paint it once, let alone redo it. So in looking back at more than thirty years of marriage and four different homes, every wall in every home has sported a boring shade of white.

Not anymore. I was ready for a change. I *needed* a change. So I smiled at the salesperson and followed him to the rack of paint chips.

"What colors did you have in mind?"

It was a simple enough question. With my friends' encouragement echoing in my thoughts, I said I was thinking about starting with blue for the dining room. And perhaps gold for an accent wall in the living room. He nodded approvingly and pointed to groups of cards. Perhaps this wouldn't be so hard after all.

"What shade of blue were you considering?"

It was then the colors betrayed me. The wall of paint chips induced a familiar feeling of panic. We had moved way beyond ROYGBIV. Later, I learned this one store offered 231 shades of green, 152 variations of red, 188 shades of blue, and 154 variations of yellow. Even my old friend, white, was disloyal — with 184 different shades. Honestly!

Blue? No such thing. Too easy. Instead I read names such as Adriatic Sea, Oceanside, and Poseidon. Next to them were Gulfstream, Côte d'Azur, and Amalfi. *Amalfi? Really?*

I didn't fare any better searching for the right shade of gold. Auric, Nugget, and Alchemy were nestled next to Overjoy, Midday, and Nankeen. *Seriously?*

Giving in to curiosity, I glanced through the reds. Habanero Chile, Fireworks, and Heartthrob joined Valentine and Heartfelt as options. The green family also sported its own creative labels, including Julep, Argyle, and Picnic. I shook my head when I noticed one paint chip labeled Gecko. I may live in Florida, but not in a million years would I put a lizard on my walls.

Still, I was determined to do this. So I grabbed a handful of blue and gold paint cards that seemed to be the right hues, thanked the salesperson, and left. Back home, we held the various chips against our walls, compared them to our furniture and window treatments, and tried to imagine how the rooms would appear. The graduated intensity of color on each card made it even more difficult to choose. On some cards, it was almost impossible to discern the difference between the shades.

We finally settled on two choices. I called them blue and gold, but their official names are Caspian Tide and Mushroom Bisque.

Once we chose the colors, the next step was the prep work. Covering the furniture, taping the edges of the walls, and laying a drop cloth took almost as much time as the actual painting. The job lasted four days from start to finish — one day to prep, one day to paint, and one day to remove miles of blue painter's tape from the walls and ceiling. The last day was reserved for scraping permanent paint flecks from our hair and skin. With every drop that had landed on me, I marveled at how the decorators on television makeover shows can finish an entire room in one afternoon and not get a speck of paint on themselves.

I do have to admit, the final product looked terrific. Color really does make a difference. It even made me feel different. And I was thrilled to invite those same friends back to see the result.

In fact, the dining room and living room look so good that I've been eyeing our bathrooms. There may be a place in our home for Habanero Chile after all.

~Ava Pennington

34

Climbing the Mountain

And the day came when the risk to remain tight in a
bud was more painful than the risk it took to blossom.
~Anaïs Nin

"That sounds so exciting. I do envy you." I kept my voice bright, but Sally had known me a long time and wasn't fooled. She stopped talking about her new job.

"I just wish I hadn't had to move," she said. "I miss our times together. I guess you do, too." I could hear the regret in her voice.

Instantly, I felt bad for letting her know that I wasn't dealing with her leaving as well as I hoped. We had been best friends since school, spending most of our spare time together, helping each other through good and bad times. A couple of years ago, she had been through a nasty divorce, but had picked herself up and re-trained as a teacher, something she had always wanted to do. I was thrilled for her. The only trouble was her new job was 200 miles away.

I had always been the quiet one. Sally had helped draw me out of myself, and now I felt lost. We chatted a little more about this and that.

It wasn't until later that evening that I thought about the fact that while Sally was brimming with stories about her new life, I hadn't had much to tell her in return. My life was fine, comfortable, but I had to admit, more than a little stale. And to get through the lonely evenings, I'd started to buy the odd treat — a donut here, a chocolate bar there — and the kilos were starting to pile on.

My friend at work, an older lady with a sharp tongue but a kind heart, had noticed that I seemed a bit lackluster, and I found myself telling her how I missed Sally. If I'd expected sympathy, that wasn't what I got.

"You know what you need?" she said, looking at me over the top of her glasses. "To get out of your comfort zone. Find a new hobby. Make some new friends." She dipped her head back into her work. It was clear the conversation was over.

At first, I was miffed. But while driving home that evening, I took a long, hard look at my life. *When was the last time I had done anything different, exciting even?* I had to admit it had been a trip I had taken with Sally, and it was a long time ago.

That night, I took out a pad and paper and wrote a list of ideas about how I could make my life more exciting. After all, it was up to me to make things different. By the time I finished, I'd made quite an extensive list.

The only problem was where to start; it seemed overwhelming. I was just about to head off to the fridge, but then I looked at it again. I noticed that most of these items came under two headings: meet new people and improve fitness. I would like to say I jumped out of the chair and joined the nearest gym, but I didn't. I pushed the list to the back of the paper rack to deal with my good intentions another day.

A few days later, I was reminded of my list. I'd been to the supermarket, and as I was loading my car, I saw a group of walkers returning home. They looked a muddy and bedraggled lot. It had been a drizzly day, and the sky, which had never been bright all day, was now turning dark.

As they got closer, I could hear glimpses of their conversations. "Looking forward to my tea." "I'm getting ready for a hot bath." They were unloading jackets and rucksacks into cars, and switching walking boots into day shoes. They looked cold and tired, but there was also a happiness and contentment about them. "See you next week" was the last comment I heard as they folded themselves into their cars with cheery waves.

That night when Sally called, I told her about my plan. "That's great!" she said. "Just make sure you get all the right gear and don't take on anything too strenuous too soon. We don't want to have to call out mountain rescue." I could hear her amusement. Feeling encouraged, I contacted a walking group. I didn't know if it was the one I had seen, but I hoped it was. They had seemed such a friendly bunch.

The following weekend saw me kitted up with full rucksack and waterproofs. Setting off to the meeting place, I felt excited like I hadn't in years. However, on the journey there, I began to worry. What if the group didn't like me or the walk was too strenuous? It had been a while since I had done real physical exercise. What if I got lost? The thoughts kept coming, and I almost turned back.

The meeting place was a small café at the foot of a very large mountain. My stomach did a flip as I studied the size of it. I could see the group getting ready across the car park. Boots were being tied, and maps were flapping in the wind. At that point, my nerves failed me, and I was just about to reverse out again when I saw a tall man with a wide smile making his way over to me. Somewhat reluctantly, I got out of the car.

"Are we going up there?" I asked. The mountain seemed even bigger as I looked up. He took in my new boots and jacket and smiled.

"No, that's for the experienced walkers. We're taking the lower route. It's about five miles. The weather's good, so it should be a breeze."

He led me over to the rest of the group, and I felt a little better when I recognized a couple from the other day. At least I was with the friendly group I'd seen.

We set off down a track between fields. As we walked, no one really spoke. I worried about this for a little while, but as we walked on, the breeze against my face, the warmth beneath my jacket, and the gentle uphill pull on my muscles did their trick. I became lost in the experience.

After a while, people started chatting to each other. Before I knew it, I was chatting with them. It was so easy. Any lulls in conversation were just more time to enjoy the view. When we stopped for lunch, I didn't even miss the cream cake I'd opted not to bring with me. I was too busy talking.

As we meandered back down the hill toward the warmth of the

café, I felt a lightness I had not felt for a long time. I had found new friends and a new way of keeping fit, as well as a new passion. After wishing my newfound friends a safe journey home, I took a moment to look at the top of the mountain. *One day, I'll be there,* I thought to myself.

~Michelle Emery

A Brand-New Day

As you begin to live according to your own guidance
and your own daring everything changes completely.
~Leonard Willoughby

reset my odometer to zero that morning as I pulled out of my driveway. Now, six hours later, it registered 350 miles, the sun was dropping out of sight, and I was lost. I had spent too long at Walmart figuring out what I wanted to buy in case I couldn't find a grocery store for a few days. Now I was at the mercy of dark street signs and the fact that my GPS sent me to the wrong address, just as the lady I was renting from had predicted. And, of course, I needed more than one bar on my cell phone to call her for more directions.

Even so, I was super excited, and my heart was light. I had just driven away from absolutely everything I had known for the last five decades. Why had I decided to leave it all — to pack my clothes, my laptop and my life, get in my car, and drive away? I could say that I was in a rut, that I needed a change, and that would be true. But to be more exact, my life had fallen into a deep pit. The dirt was falling in, and if I didn't do something, it was going to bury me.

When we realize that very little in our lives brings us satisfaction, we should reassess. And as I looked back at the past fifty years, I realized there was very little I was satisfied with. There was no change in sight for me, either. I would continue to work at a job I hated, and go home every evening to a marriage that wasn't working. My anxiety level was through the roof. Physically, I felt it daily. Panic attacks were a part of my breathing pattern, and heart palpitations kept me awake at night.

And then I asked myself some really hard questions. *What are you doing? Why are you here?* And then again, *Why are you really here?*

And there was my epiphany. The answer to the last question was a realization about myself that I didn't like.

For the past fifty years, every decision I had made was based entirely upon what I thought others wanted me to do. I wanted a different kind of life, but I was afraid of disappointing my family, so I stayed in a place that I longed to leave. Even when there really was no reason to stay, I didn't leave.

And then I realized that living the life I wanted might mean living the life others didn't want me to live. As I looked down the road to the future, I hated what I saw. As long as I stayed, nothing would change. Nothing at all!

So, three weeks ago, I sent an e-mail to a company looking to hire medical staff. Before the end of the day, they called me with a job 350 miles away. And I took it!

For the first time in my life, I did not search for approval from anyone else; I did not ask for opinions. I merely stated what I intended to do. And that could be what shocked everyone the most.

The reactions were mixed. From my husband's "What about me?" attitude followed by stony silence, to my brother's insistence that there was truly something wrong with me, I got exactly what I expected — and I was okay with that.

Three hundred and fifty miles is like a reset switch. Just like a computer, this trip was effectively clearing my memory and rebooting my brain. And as I exited I-95 and drove through the small southern city of Emporia, Virginia, I knew immediately that this was a place to begin again.

My cell phone finally connected, and I had Becky on the other end, talking me into the lakeside subdivision one turn at a time. A tiny lamp on the screened-in porch of the bungalow beamed a welcome to me, and the warmth of this December night wrapped itself around me. I already loved it!

That was a year and a half ago, and I have no regrets. My anxiety has evaporated; I haven't had a heart palpitation since I drove away. I have joined Habitat for Humanity, something I always wanted to do. I have a fulfilling job in a hospital, and I spend my weekend mornings writing on the screened-in porch of the bungalow, and my afternoons riding my bicycle on backcountry roads.

And I have peace. No more worries about tomorrow, and no more longing to live my life differently. It's a new start with a new purpose. With fresh dreams, I am re-discovering who I was before life and all its disappointments overwhelmed me. Happiness, contentment and the chance to start over awaited me after a very long drive south on I-95, and I wake every morning to a brand-new, fulfilling day.

~Patty Poet

36

From Plumbing to Prose

If you put yourself in a position where you have to
stretch outside your comfort zone, then you
are forced to expand your consciousness.
~Les Brown

For most of my adult life, I worked as a plumber. But by my mid-forties, after surgery on both shoulders and years of chronic back and knee pain, I realized it was time for a career change.

This was easier said than done. I was a middle-aged master plumber with no college degree and a lack of marketable skills. That's how it seemed to me anyway. My wife saw things differently.

"How about becoming a writer?" she asked one evening.

"A few short stories published in small literary magazines doesn't make me a writer," I replied. "Besides, I make more in an hour of plumbing than I have for all of my short stories combined."

Undeterred, she said, "There are other types of writing. I think you're talented enough to do it."

Well, that made one of us. But because my wife is usually right, I started searching online for writing jobs where I could utilize my knowledge of plumbing. I honestly had no idea these types of jobs were even out there, but I soon began writing home-improvement and plumbing articles for a couple of content mills. These companies were sort of the bottom of the barrel and the pay was low, but it was a start and gave me a few writing credits to put on my resumé.

From there I moved on to freelancing for a couple of online HVAC (heating, ventilation, and air conditioning) companies. The pay was better and the work steadier. I still wrote the occasional short story, and even self-published several novels and a series of Maine humor books.

About a year ago, I wrote an essay about my son's high school graduation and submitted it to a parenting blog. It was accepted for publication and led to my having more than twenty essays published on various parenting blogs in less than a year. This was yet another market that I had never paid attention to. I expect it to continue because my sons give me a lot of material to work with.

This is a direction I never saw my life taking. In three years, I've gone from working as a master plumber to writing parenting posts. When I tell people who haven't seen me in a while what I'm doing now, they look at me in disbelief. I don't blame them; sometimes I don't believe it myself. I'd like to say I took the leap of my own accord, but it was a combination of injury and my wife's belief that drew me into writing as a career. Looking back, it's a move I wish I'd made much earlier in life. If only we all had a crystal ball. It just proves that some of the best things in life are unexpected.

There have been many benefits to such a drastic career change. The pain in my back and shoulders is greatly reduced. I don't come home from work every day complaining about sore muscles and cuts and burns on my hands. I no longer wrap my arms around toilets more often than I wrap them around my wife. And, best of all, I now work from home and get to spend more time with my family.

Of course, it's not all peaches and cream. It's been a little difficult financially, and I still don't make nearly as much money from writing as I did plumbing. But overall the pros far outweigh the cons, and I can happily say I'm the only person I know who's gone from being a plumber to a writer.

~Gary Sprague

37

San Antonio Living

Life shrinks or expands in proportion to one's courage.
~Anaïs Nin

I hit it off with the bubbly host of *San Antonio Living*, Shelly Miles, when she interviewed me about a story I had published in *Chicken Soup for the Soul: From Lemons to Lemonade*. Shelly interviewed me three times over a four-year period, and then asked me if I would be interested in doing a monthly DIY (do it yourself) segment. *Wow!* I remember thinking. *Shelly Miles likes me! She wants me to be on her TV show!* I had a momentary surge of self-confidence that lasted just long enough to e-mail her back with an emphatic, "Yes!" Unfortunately, as soon as I pressed the send button, I began to cry, "No, no, no!"

What had I done? I was no television personality. I was almost forty-two, overweight, and had minimal experience appearing on television. Yet I had just signed on to make regular appearances on a lifestyle show on the NBC affiliate in the seventh largest market in the U.S. Every insecurity I'd ever had came rushing to the surface.

I spent the weeks leading up to my segment giving myself a lot of pep talks. I don't know whether they helped or not, but I did make it through that first show without passing out on live television.

When I watched the show later, I cringed. *Oh, my gosh! Does my voice really sound like that? Do I really look like that?* I decided if I was going to go back the following month, I was in major need of a makeover. In a desperate attempt to look fifty pounds lighter and twenty years younger, I decided to get a haircut and try out bangs.

I'd never had bangs. I immediately hated the way they looked, and it definitely didn't make me look thinner or younger. I was depressed for a week. Then my husband told me in the most loving way possible to snap out of it and start working on my next segment. I listened. The next segment went well, as did the one after that. I felt my confidence grow with each new show.

I had lunch with a friend who gushed about my television appearance earlier in the week. "Great tips!" she said. "And you seemed like you were having so much fun!" Actually, I was having fun. The realization came as somewhat of a surprise after all the fretting I had done.

As the months flew by, I found I was becoming less critical of myself. I began to feel more at ease in front of the camera, even with my awful haircut.

I've been doing the show for two years now. If I had it to do all over again, would I do it the same? The answer is no, absolutely not. I would *never* have gotten bangs! Thankfully, that is my only regret. I'm super happy I waded through all of my insecurity and followed my path. Just the other day, I was in Hobby Lobby when a woman approached me. "Aren't you that DIY lady from *San Antonio Living*?" she asked.

"Why, yes. Yes, I am," I answered. And I finally believed it.

~Melissa Wootan

38

The Makeover

We cannot become what we want to
be by remaining what we are.
~Max De Pree

The first half of my life had been devoted to my mother, husband, and four sons, shaping my days around what they needed from me. But now I was on my own. The children were grown. I was single. And my mother had moved 1,200 miles away to start her own new life.

It's time, I decided. I was turning fifty, after all. *The second half of my life will belong to me.*

First up was changing my look. When I saw women in long skirts, I thought they looked great, but I needed to muster up the courage to change my look so dramatically. I checked out the shoes, jewelry, and blouses that went with the skirts. Even the haircuts looked different.

My birthday arrived and one day I adopted my new look. I slipped into my new long skirt with appropriate shirt, added big drop earrings, bangles on my wrist, and sandals. I was embarrassed as I walked from my gift shop in a small, historical town to the bank and post office.

I went to the post office first. No one said a word. Wow.

On to the bank. No one said a word about my new look. This was much easier than I thought it would be. I went shopping that night and bought several colorful long skirts. Then I piled up all my old conservative clothing to give away.

Over the weekend, I had a second pair of holes put in my ears to accommodate the diamond studs my last husband, who recently passed away, gave to me. That made room for the dangly ones in the lower holes. A feeling of joy washed over me. This was fun!

My girlfriend Anne took me to her favorite hair salon.

"Time to wash away the grey," she said.

As I sat patiently in the chair, the hairdresser turned it one way and another, looking closely at my skin color.

"Hmm," she said.

When I left the salon, I had red hair! It was a bit startling when I passed a window and caught a glimpse of myself. It didn't look like me... until I got used to it. Then I couldn't remember what I looked like before!

Then I started traveling. I flew several times to Europe, spending the same amount of money that it would have cost me to travel sixty miles away to the Jersey shore. I traveled extensively in the United States.

The last major change I made was buying a different car. I turned in my dark four-door sedan and bought a red Camaro.

I couldn't believe the little box I used to live in. Now that my mind had been opened, it would never close again. My attitude was different. I was happy and filled with gratitude.

A friend asked if I was trying to be young again. I thought about it and realized, no, I could care less about being young again. I wouldn't want to go through that again.

That was over twenty years ago. That little change of clothing changed my whole life! I have since written a dozen books, and stood in front of groups of women, teaching them to tell their stories. I encourage them to take charge of their lives, open their minds, and go back to school regardless of their age. Life is good!

~Arlene S. Bice

39

Books to Barbells

*One of the greatest experiences in life is achieving
personal goals that others said would be "impossible
to attain." Be proud of your success and share
your story with others.*
~Robert Cheeke

One summer night in 2007, I stepped on a stage in a bodybuilder's posing suit, spray-tanned, dehydrated and exhausted. Most of my family and friends thought I was out of my mind, especially considering that just a few weeks before I had wrapped up my seventeenth year as an elementary school librarian.

I had turned forty-six that year and gone looking for a challenge. I found more than I bargained for when I saw a poster for a natural bodybuilding competition workshop at my local gym. I walked into that meeting only knowing that a natural competition meant that no performance-enhancing drugs were allowed. How hard could it be to work out for a few weeks, find a cute suit and prance across the stage the night of the contest?

As I found my seat in the room, I thought I knew how hard this journey was going to be. The training plan was challenging but not out of the question. I was comfortable in the gym, in shape even though I wasn't a professional athlete. The diet, though, was more rigid than I expected. There was plenty of protein, green vegetables and any beverage I wanted as long as it was water. My beloved peanut butter was nowhere to be found on the recommended foods list.

Just as I got my anxiety level over sugar withdrawal under control, we were shown acceptable examples of posing suits. Yes, they are called suits, but they are little more than scraps of fabric glued to the body. The last part of the workshop showed us the mandatory poses that we would be asked to execute as we were scored by the judges. We were also told that the judging would take place on the morning of the contest.

The real show would be that evening when we would be asked to pose to ninety seconds of the music of our choice. That information was shared as if we would all see the fun in choreographing our moves to music. Leaving my seat two hours later, I thought of every excuse not to take on this challenge. I knew, though, that not doing this was the easy choice. I wanted to know that I wasn't too old to challenge myself, that my body was still capable of responding to tough training, and that I had the self-confidence to step on that stage in little more than two triangles and a thong. The hard choice was the only one that would let me know the answers.

Over the next sixteen weeks, I adopted "Stick to the Plan" as my motto. Life narrowed down to the essentials of work, sleep, diet, and time in the gym. Of these four, the diet proved to be the toughest. Chicken, broccoli, egg whites, and sweet potatoes were on an endless rotation.

My husband, in a show of solidarity, followed the same meal plan and lost ten pounds. He also declared that he would never eat another sweet potato again. The lack of beverage choices became my personal challenge. I resorted to drinking water from pretty glasses in an effort to trick myself into believing it was something better. Glassware did not make the choice any easier, but it did give me a boost to hold onto a pretty piece of stemware.

What I didn't have to trick myself into believing were the changes I saw in the mirror. I didn't just have biceps; there were defining lines showing the results of my workouts. One of my youngest students asked if my arms looked that way from holding up the library books when I read aloud. Teachers and parents at school, along with total strangers, asked me how I looked so fit. Each week I saw changes in my body and my mindset. I had answered the question as to whether I could stick to the training plan, but the other question remained: Could I show off my body in front of an audience?

Peak week is the week leading up to a contest. This is the time to ask the body to give just a little more without giving it any extra fuel. The workouts slow down, the diet becomes more monotonous, and we stop thinking that posing in front of any available mirror is strange. I spent the week cutting out all sodium, carefully tapering down my water consumption, and bouncing from emotional highs to emotional lows. Spray tanning changed my normally fair skin to the same shade as my dining room table. The tanning also brought out lines and veins that I had never seen before. The morning of the show, I was sprayed once more, covered with oil, and lined up behind twelve other competitors.

The morning judging was a blur — literally. The stagelights made it impossible to see past the row of judges, but there was no mistaking the cheers and yells of my husband, friends, and family. We executed the bodybuilding poses that had felt so strange just a few months earlier. The hours of practicing the exaggerated poses finally felt like second nature.

My relief as we left the stage was quickly replaced with a new set of nerves for the night show. I substituted "pizza dinner" for my usual "Stick to the Plan" motto. Hearing my familiar posing music helped me to step onto the stage one more time. When everyone in my weight class had completed their routine, the judges asked us to return to the stage for the awards. I felt like I had already won, though. Not because I was better than everyone else, but because I hadn't given up. I stuck to the plan and pushed myself out of a stereotype of age and profession and into finishing a tough challenge. I did not need a trophy to tell me that I was a winner, but seeing the first place trophy set in front of me added a sweet validation to all of the sacrifice and discipline.

At the end of that night, I knew that my physical changes were temporary, but the mental changes could be mine forever. Drinking just one large glass of water robbed my body of some of those lines and cuts. Knowing that I had learned new things, that I hadn't let nerves get the best of me, and that I hadn't quit when it got too hard, showed me a mental toughness that I hadn't known was inside me.

I trained and competed successfully for eight more years after that first contest. Each time, I grew as a competitor and a person. I learned that we can all do hard things. Like bodybuilding, those hard things mold and define us. My posing suits still hang in my closet right at the front to remind me that I'm stronger than whatever challenges the day may bring.

~Mary Jane Michels

40

My Life 2.0

*We must be willing to get rid of the life we've planned,
so as to have the life that is waiting for us. The old
skin has to be shed before the new one can come.*
~Joseph Campbell

thought I was tough, capable and grounded, the one to whom others turned for help… and then the unfathomable happened. I was at work waiting for my husband to pick me up and take me to a doctor's appointment. He was late, quite out of character. I called, texted, e-mailed, no answer… weird. He *always* had his phone with him. He was a community activist, often credited (or criticized) for engaging in "ambitious" projects. His goals were always greater self-sustainability for the community and its members. He was a truly noble fellow. We met doing social reform activities, and I'd been his copyeditor, executive assistant, and passionate champion for more than thirty years.

At first, I was mad, then really worried. I walked to the bus stop to go home. We lived fifteen miles out of town, in rural Hawaii, and the bus line ended about twelve miles out. On that long, slow ride, calling again and again, I alternated between anger and worry. I got off the bus at the end of the line and stuck out my thumb. Who wouldn't pick up a sixty-three-year-old woman? A former young co-worker happened by, picked me up and took me all the way to my front door. I didn't want to concern her, but I knew something was wrong when I saw my husband's car in the carport.

I found him in the bathtub in cool water. He was conscious but babbling. I guessed he'd had a stroke. I called 911 and the paramedics had him airlifted to Honolulu.

My dear husband was given a thirty percent chance of survival. During the ensuing days in the ICU, I couldn't even cry, holding onto hope that he would beat the odds.

He didn't, and I went home to a house that held thirty years of marital memories but was now devoid of any warmth. I was in shock. I looked around, and all I could see was stuff — mostly *his* stuff. I was a minimalist at heart, and he was a collector. Whoever said opposites attract was right! I spent days trying to get started and would find myself with an armload of stuff, not sure where to put it, then seeing something else, and finally just stopping in the middle of a room and turning around and around, spinning, reeling.

I even started getting really angry. How could he leave me with all this stuff?

As the days went on, and friends drifted in to help, I realized that I needed to have a plan for *my* life. This was too much house for just me, and it was too far from work and other friends and activities as I tried to build my solo life. I made a decision: I would downsize and move. I set a target of eight months, gave notice to my landlord, and began the real work.

I had to make a plan. I made four categories for the stuff: keep, give to family or friends, sell, and donate or trash. I made spaces for each category: folding tables in the carport for stuff to sell or donate; shipping cartons for stuff to send to family on the mainland; shopping bags labeled for friends; and trash bags for obvious discards. What was left, I'd keep.

Did I say that I was a home-share host? (That's how I chose the eight-month target — that's when my last reservation ended.) This complicated matters a bit! I couldn't just put the place in turmoil. I needed the guests to keep up with the rent, so I had to be a responsible, cheery host. The first few guests after my husband passed were hard to welcome but turned out to be complete blessings! A counselor and mentor for young impoverished kids was the first. I informed her before her arrival of my loss, and she came with an open heart and big hugs. The next was a healing practitioner, a young man looking for a wife! He was funny and joyful and tolerated the parade of people who came to my assistance. He joined in our impromptu get-togethers.

Those two guests really helped me find the courage to do this. I had always been the stable one, the one to whom others turned when in turmoil. My guests helped me realize that I could reach out for help now myself—that strong people can still need help themselves! I needed those hugs and all those friends, people who would force me to take a break, take a walk, eat, go to bed... all those things that get left out in the chaos of change.

The traumatic experience began to take on the quality of a game. I would set a space target: that shelf, three feet by two feet, today! It kept me focused, and I learned to resist the temptation to start another space before one was finished. I learned how to delegate—to let others help.

Evenings were still hard, but I got through them with the help of a friend who was staying with me and also going through a big life change. We even discovered a totally silly TV series we could stream and binge watch when we needed a break. We made up hand gestures that signaled it was time to dive into that show. (I still go to that show for relief four years later!)

I held five yard sales, moved to a small place "in town" to try that out, and eventually moved to the mainland to be closer to family and other support systems. That move consisted of ten plastic tubs, two large suitcases and one carry-on. The whole process of downsizing was amazingly cathartic. I place so much value on the *quality* of life now, not the stuff. I find I have all joyful memories in my heart, and the grief has melted away. It was a lot of work launching My Life 2.0, but it was eminently doable, with time, and planning, and a lot of help from my friends.

~Jean Bevanmarquez

41

Running Away with the Circus

Life is a circus ring, with some moments
more spectacular than others.
~Janusz Korczak

A few days before my fiftieth birthday, I experienced a traumatic brain injury. At the time, I was a long-distance runner, and sports had always helped me keep my life-long depression at bay. But depression after a brain injury is much more finicky and severe, and I needed something new in my life.

So at age fifty — menopausal, depressed and brain-injured — I did what any woman would do: I joined the circus!

I was athletic as an adult but not as a kid, and I had never taken dance lessons or ballet or gymnastics. I was strong, but neither very flexible nor graceful in the least.

Since the onset of my post-concussion depression and anxiety, I had been isolated. I took time away from work, my social circle dwindled, and I felt very alone. I was often afraid to leave the house. Even booking my first circus class was a huge leap of faith for me.

When I walked into my first aerial acrobatics class, I wasn't surprised to find that I was the oldest student; in fact, even my teachers were young enough to be my daughters! But I was determined to stretch beyond my comfort zone, and the "kids" welcomed me. One of my classmates said to me, "Wow, *my* mom would *never* do this! I have to bring her here to see you!"

After a group stretch and warm-up, my coach Katelyn asked which apparatus I'd like to learn. There were silks, trapeze, and hoop. I eyed the aerial hoop, also known as a lyra. Oh, how I wanted to sit up in the hoop and learn to fly like a bird!

Alas, I didn't have the arm strength to lift myself up onto the hoop. I was deflated. My excitement was replaced with self-doubt and disappointment. When I expressed my frustration to my coach, she told me to just keep trying, and that many people can't lift their body weight. At that point, I realized, *Hey, I'm trying to lift my body weight! How cool is that?*

So I kept trying. And trying. For three weeks, I tried, and I got better and stronger. Then it happened. My hands gripped the bottom of the hoop, and I lifted my feet to touch the hoop. I hung, upside down, by my knees! And then I pulled myself up so that I was sitting in the hoop. The entire class applauded!

Every week, I practiced and listened to my coach. I took home the strangest bruises I'd ever had. I also took home the confidence I needed to start talking about my injury and its impact on my life. I had a new group of friends, people who hadn't known me before my accident, and they accepted and supported me.

Still, in the darkest throes of depression, I would drive to class feeling so depressed that I flirted with self-harm. It was difficult to get motivated, because the rest of my life seemed to be collapsing under the weight of my post-concussion syndrome.

But when I walked into the gym, my mood would immediately lighten. I was amongst some of the most caring, compassionate and fun people I had ever met. I started learning new tricks. I developed flexibility, even at age fifty. I started to love hanging upside down in the air, and I wasn't afraid of falling.

Several months later, a sign-up sheet appeared. It was for an upcoming student showcase. Students were invited to perform a three-minute routine, illustrating what they'd learned in class.

Rather hesitantly, I asked my coach, "Do you think I could do something? Do I know enough? Am I good enough?"

"Absolutely!" she said. "Let's work together to create some choreography."

Choreography! Wow, things were about to get serious! Within a week, I'd chosen my music and started playing out some tricks and transitions. My coach agreed to spend one-on-one time with me, intense times when I would work non-stop for an hour, running routines over and over until I got them right. Now, I was going home with blisters and calluses on my hands, but with a spirit that soared beyond anything I'd ever imagined.

Then came the big event: the showcase. Several of us were performing on silks, trapeze, and hoop. I was scheduled to go on stage about halfway through the show. My heart was beating at a ridiculous rate. I was nervous and excited as I watched my classmates perform their routines, the ones I'd observed and applauded at practice week after week.

When my name was called, I stood up. As I waited for the first notes of my musical accompaniment, I surveyed the room. My beautiful and patient coach... my classmates... my brother, cousins and husband... this was where I needed to be.

I soared through my performance. Everything I'd practiced, the blisters, and the bruises — they were all worth it!

A cloud lifted that day. I was now a fifty-one-year-old, menopausal, brain-injured *circus performer*! Since that initial show, I've done several student performances. My recovery has not been easy, but when I'm grieving the loss of my "old self" or when I'm depressed, I remind myself that I am a survivor. When things became unbearable, I didn't run away; instead, I ran toward the circus.

~Cat Kenwell

Chapter 5

STEP OUTSIDE YOUR COMFORT ZONE

☑ Face Your Fears

42

A Tough Journey to a Magical Destination

The size of your dreams must always exceed your
current capacity to achieve them. If your dreams
do not scare you, they are not big enough.
~Ellen Johnson Sirleaf

will never forget that phone call. "Good afternoon, Ms. Thompson. I am calling from the University of Liverpool to tell you that you have been awarded the Master's of Business Administration with distinction."

I thanked the caller without realising that tears of joy were running down my face. I had overcome self-doubt and fear to pursue this MBA. It was a moment of triumph that would change my life, and build my critical-thinking skills, self-confidence and opportunities. It would help me to reengineer and redefine myself personally and professionally.

Now let me share the torturous journey that led to that phone call. Throughout school, I had found myself failing exams. Teachers called me bright, but somehow I never excelled academically in the way that was expected of me. To this day, I'm not sure why. I would perform well in class, and grasp and articulate the issues, but give me an exam, and I would either underperform or fail outright. This happened at every stage of my life — in junior and high school, and at university and postgraduate level. Getting my law degree and passing the bar was an exercise in perseverance, a cycle of failing and fearing exam results.

Finally, I entered law practice and did relatively well. I got involved in social causes. I ran for national political office and was elected to Parliament in Barbados. The Prime Minister appointed me to Cabinet as a Minister of government. Life was good, but my academic history gnawed at me and filled me with self-doubt. I wanted to prove myself academically. So I opted to do an online MBA with the University of Liverpool.

When I shared my plan with my work colleague John he said, "You are really busy, have ministerial responsibilities, the largest constituency in the island, and you plan to earn a master's degree? Do you know how demanding a master's program is? How will you find the time? I do not think you can get this done."

I explained that the online option would give me more flexibility. "That is part of my point," he argued. "You have two secretaries and a personal assistant who do everything for you. How are you going to do an online degree? You are not even computer-literate."

Sounding more confident than I felt, I responded, "I will learn."

He looked directly at me, shook his head and laughed. "I think you should be prepared to fail."

Given my past, John's comment filled me with dread. At home later, I kept replaying John's cautions. I had a comfortable life and career. Was this dream of further academic qualifications really worth it? Was I just being stubborn and vain? The years of academic failures had been painful and embarrassing. I had been told I was second-rate, not good enough.

I decided to ignore my fears.

The university made it clear that their online degree and pass mark were exactly the same as offered in their brick-and-mortar classrooms. The degree comprised eight modules and a dissertation. Each module lasted eight weeks. Students were required to write four well-supported, academic essays every week. We completed a training module in the software the university used, and then the academic modules started. Within two weeks, the class size dropped by a quarter as students found the program too rigorous.

I would work all day, and attend constituency activities, Parliament and required functions, including those at night. I would then go home, spend two hours with my husband, work through the night, sleep for three or four hours, then get up and go to work and repeat the cycle the next day. I enjoyed the work and the enrichment gained from studying with people from all over the world, but it was very demanding. Plus, the Prime Minister had made it clear that my first obligation was to the country, and I would be given no time off for my studies.

At the end of the first module, I got a B. I breathed a sigh of relief and decided to start the next module immediately. After passing the second module, I got to Finance, the third module. I did not know the program Excel existed, so I did my Finance assignments in Word. This, added to my poor computer skills and slow pace, the requirements for the module and my dislike of mathematics put me under enormous pressure. I told my study partner Kumar and my husband Mac that I was going to drop out. I could not carry on any longer. Mac encouraged me to hang in there, not to doubt myself.

Kumar promised to support me through the program, and he did. We hooked up with another student, and the three of us worked as a team. They did the math and the formatting. I did the analysis and projections. This was wonderful at one level, but it also created more pressure for me as I was now worried about letting them down. Some nights, when I approached my computer, I would become totally overwhelmed by the thought of being up all night wrestling with another Finance assignment. I stayed in the course only because of my promise to my husband and my sense of responsibility to the team.

When the Finance module came to an end, another friend persuaded me to start the fourth module while I waited for the Finance results. Initially, I resisted, but then I agreed and was enjoying that module when the results for Finance came back. I had received an A and a near perfect score. I was shocked. I now had four modules and the dissertation left to complete the program. I started to believe that passing was not beyond me. I got ambitious. I ended up with six As and two Bs. To get the distinction, or first-class honours, I also had to score an A on the dissertation.

I was late submitting my dissertation. My tutor called to say that if I did not get the dissertation uploaded within half an hour, I would be marked as having failed to submit. I had not slept in nearly two days, trying to perfect the paper and format it to meet the university's requirements. My heart was racing. I felt that my dissertation was good, but not good enough for an A, so I would not get the distinction. Despite trouble with the technology, I managed to get the dissertation uploaded with only seconds to spare. Then I started the long wait on the results. My wait was rewarded with that congratulatory phone call.

I would later do a second master's and then become Assistant Secretary General of the United Nations, but it all began with finding the strength to step out of my comfort zone.

~Liz Thompson

43

Taking Action

Nothing diminishes anxiety faster than action.
~Walter Anderson

was on the Taconic State Parkway in New York heading for Vermont. I was just a few miles away from my favorite rest stop, a diner just off the parkway on Route 295 in Chatham. I made this trip often and always stopped at the diner for a cup of coffee. But on this particular day, just before the exit, I passed out. As I slumped forward, my chest hit the steering wheel, and I came to with a start. I couldn't have been out for more than a few seconds because I was still driving in my lane and still doing fifty-five miles per hour. I pulled off at the next exit and into the diner's parking lot. I sat in my car for over an hour having a full-blown panic attack.

My weekend getaway was done, but that was okay. I just wanted to go home and stop feeling so awful inside. I trembled for the entire two-hour drive home.

Just a few months before, I had ended a three-year, abusive relationship. It wasn't easy walking out the door — my confidence and self-esteem had eroded away to nothing. But when the death threats started, I knew it was time to go. Because I worked for the man I had just left, I was out of a job, home, and money as soon as the door closed behind me. Going back to my parents' house was my only option.

Within a few short months, I was feeling much stronger, healthier mentally and physically, and determined to put all the abuse behind me and move on. But after the mishap on the highway, something happened that I didn't expect—driving now terrified me. That ill-fated trip would be the last time I drove anywhere for the next year and a half. I stayed home and eventually became too afraid to leave. My world got smaller and smaller.

But then, the best possible thing happened: I became ill. Becoming ill meant I had to see a doctor. To see a doctor, I had to leave the house. My illness wasn't easy to diagnose. Over the course of several months, I went to see many doctors and was sent to different hospitals. Leaving the house became easier each time, and soon it was no longer an issue. But I still couldn't drive. My father drove me everywhere. Eventually, he realized he was only enabling me, and he knew he had to stop. One day, he said, "You need to get in your car and go for a drive. I can't drive you everywhere anymore."

Just the thought of driving the car caused me to have a panic attack. I said to my father, "I can't. I'm not ready."

"I don't know how to help you get over this," he said. "You need to find someone who can help you. The only thing I can do to help is to stop being your chauffeur."

I would do anything to please my father, so after I sulked for a while, I began looking through the Yellow Pages for help. This was during the early days of the Internet, so doing a Google search on phobia clinics wasn't possible. It took weeks to contact all the doctors, hospitals and clinics in the area that specialized in the treatment of anxiety and phobias, and to receive and read all the information they sent. I chose the White Plains Hospital because it was the closest, and their treatment program was the most comprehensive. My treatment started with a phone consultation. At the end of it, the doctor said, "We have a self-help group that meets once a week. I think you should start coming to that and then…"

"Whoa!" I said abruptly. "The only way I can get to those meetings is to drive there. I can't do that. If I could drive to White Plains, I wouldn't need your help." I thanked the doctor for his time and hung up.

When I told my father what happened, he stood up, reached into his pocket, and pulled out his keys. "Here," he said. "Go for a drive."

"I can't."

"You can. Just go up and down the driveway. And when you can do that, drive to High Street and back." High Street was only two houses away. I could read the street sign from the living room window. "When you can do that," he continued, "drive to the end of the road and back. Then drive around the block. After that, go to the library, the corner store, or the post office." Each location was no more than a three-minute drive from home. But then his plan got a lot scarier. "Each day, drive a little bit farther. When you can get to the grocery store, you can get on the highway. It's only a five-minute drive to the first exit. Get off there and come home. Then try for the second exit. Keep working at it until you can drive to White Plains."

With my mouth agape, I looked at my father in horror. I was certain he had gone stark raving mad. But within a few days, to please my father, I was driving up and down the driveway, to High Street and back, and to the end of the road. That was easy, but the rest took time. I drove a little bit farther every day, and it was scary. Four months later, I walked into the self-help group at The Anxiety & Phobia Treatment Center at White Plains Hospital. My anxiety level was at a ten — the highest level possible — and it would remain there for many months. But I learned how to cope with the anxiety, and the panic attacks eventually dissipated. As I began to overcome my fear of driving, my world became much bigger, and I was much happier.

One day, I awoke early and decided to go for a drive. Three hours later, I called my father and said, "Guess where I am, Pop? I'm in Vermont!" It was a triumphant moment, but in no way did it mean I was cured.

Driving long distances to places I've never been before still causes me anxiety. I still use the coping mechanisms I learned so many years ago. They still work — and I can drive in spite of the anxiety.

From my father, I learned one of the greatest lessons of life: If you think you can't, you can't. But when you tell yourself you can, you can do anything you set your mind to.

~L.M. Lush

44

The Conqueror

Do the thing you fear, and continue to do so. This is the
quickest and surest way of all victory over fear.
~Dale Carnegie

have always been terrified of heights. When my brothers and the other neighborhood kids climbed trees, I would watch them and cheer them on, but seldom tried it myself. When I was shamed into climbing a tree, I would only manage the first two or three branches before I would invent some excuse for climbing down.

As an adult, I didn't do any better. I was awed by the view when we visited the Grand Canyon, only to have it spoiled when my husband went too close to the edge, driving me wild with anxiety. Though he laughed at my alarm, he eventually realized that I was genuinely afraid for him and agreed to stay on the trail.

I spent many years teaching high school, and the stories my students told about their adventures stirred something inside me. I felt like I was missing out. At the annual school retreat, I watched dozens of screaming teens plummet from the cliff overlooking the lake and speed along a cable connected only by a harness. They tried to cajole me into giving the zip line a try, but I laughingly declined. There was no way I was jumping off a cliff.

When my husband was awarded an all-expenses-paid vacation to Maui by his company, I was thrilled. He came home with a list of activities that we could enjoy and among them was ziplining through the forest. He had done it in Guatemala, and our son and his wife had tried it in Costa Rica. I remembered how much my students had enjoyed it, too. I said yes, I would do it!

On the day of our ziplining adventure in Maui, it turned out that our group was too large. Four people had to stay back. Another woman dropped out, and my husband's boss and his wife gave up their spots. I volunteered to be the fourth person, but my husband dropped out instead, insisting that I needed to try ziplining. He told me that I shouldn't let my fears limit me.

My adrenaline began rising the moment we signed the release forms, and it continued to elevate when we were fitted with our helmets and harnesses. By the time we headed single file across the suspended footbridge toward the first tower, my legs were shaking. I tried to listen to the instructions, but I was too focused on simply breathing.

We went in pairs. I ended up with the man whose wife had dropped out first. He was excited; I was terrified.

I followed my companion up the rope ladder and across the platform. By the time a crew member hooked me onto the line, I was practically hyperventilating. When they told us to push off, I was certain that before we reached the next platform, my heart would stop and I would ruin the trip for everyone. Of course, I wasn't being rational. I was freaking out!

As I hit the next platform, I nearly knocked over the crew member assigned to catch us. He testily told me I mixed up my positions. That's what comes of not listening to the instructions. Instead of sitting up and slowing myself down at the end, I had leaned back with my legs straight in front, rewarding his efforts to stop me with a bruised rib or two. I apologized profusely as he unhooked me, and then I staggered to the ground. The others came flying in two by two, and everyone was laughing and grinning like they were having the time of their lives. I determined that I would not spoil this for my partner and would pretend I was enjoying myself.

We moved to the next platform and repeated the process of hooking the safety harnesses. This segment was longer, and it spanned a large, forested ravine. The view was spectacular, but so was the drop! Surprisingly, as we sped across the chasm, I was so amazed by the beauty of the tropical forest that I forgot to be afraid. I did notice, however, that my partner had made a race of getting to the end. I took that as a challenge.

There were five segments in all. Though I got close, I just couldn't outpace my zipline buddy. He laughed at my attempts, and I found that I was laughing, too. I was truly having a blast. The rush of adrenaline I was experiencing was no longer caused by fear or dread, but by exhilaration and sheer fun. By the time we pushed off on our last section, I was disappointed. The adventure was coming to an end.

As we all marched single file across that swaying footbridge that had marked the beginning of my journey, I felt stronger, taller somehow. My smiling husband was waiting for me at the other end. As I drew closer to him, he put his arms around me and said, "My conquering hero. I am so proud of you. You did it."

Yup. I did it, and I am proud of myself, too. Perhaps I'll try skydiving next — or not. I'm not completely crazy.

~Marcia Wells

45

The Elevator

Fight your fears and you'll be in battle forever. Face
your fears and you'll be free forever.
~Lucas Jonkman

Today was the day. I was tired of the jokes and ridicule. I wouldn't back down as I had so many times before. Today, I would ride the elevator.

I had hyped myself up the entire eleven-minute drive to work, and now it was game time. I stepped out of the car and as I turned to shut the door, I saw my reflection in the driver's side window. "Eye of the Tiger" played briefly in my head. Smiling at myself in the window, I shadow-boxed for a moment and turned to face the music.

Pride comes before the fall.

The sixty-eight steps to the front door were rather enjoyable. The weather was perfect. I bounced along, happy and determined. But when I reached the front door, my hands were already sweaty.

"You're okay," I said to myself as I brushed the hair out of my face. It stuck to my sweaty palm.

I have a real issue with the elevator in our office building. I have recurring nightmares of getting trapped, or the elevator plummeting to the ground, tossing my body about. My husband and I even passed on our number-one wedding venue because someone told me the elevator regularly broke down there.

In my defense, our office elevator breaks down regularly, too. And I only have to take the stairs up three floors.

But not today. Today I would take the elevator.

Reaching for the button, I noticed my hand was shaking. I almost walked away, but the door opened so I stepped in. For some reason, our elevators compensate when people get on. The elevator will rise up a couple inches with the doors still open. This was always the part that had me running for the stairs. Today I pressed the "3," and the doors slowly started to close. And then I was alone. Trapped in what was arguably the city's worst elevator.

What if it broke down? I would just press the call button, and someone would come get me. But how long would it take? Did I have food or at least a bottle of water in my purse? What if I had to go to the bathroom? I would never live that down. I would actually have to quit my job. And what if the help button didn't work? That had happened before. What if it was broken, and my cell phone didn't get reception? How loud could I scream?

I was crying as the elevator swayed back and forth. I inched closer to the emergency phone, glancing at the inspection certificate to make sure it was up to date.

The elevator stopped moving, and there was a long pause. I was certain the elevator was stuck. Just when I was sure I would faint, the doors opened, as if in slow motion. Cool air wafted in. I was on the third floor.

I did it. I rode the elevator the entire thirteen seconds.

I wish I could say I strutted off, head held high, but that was not the case. I cowered in my cubicle like an injured animal, grabbed my mirror and tried to clean up the mess my tears had made of my mascara.

There were no witnesses to my triumph over the elevator. That was okay. I had learned that I was bigger than my fears.

~Jamie Leigh Miller

46

No Regrets

To change one's life: Start immediately.
Do it flamboyantly. No exceptions.
~William James

have acrophobia, simply known as a fear of heights. I have always tried to power through it anyway. I have ridden roller coasters while plastering myself to the seat and closing my eyes, I've crossed long bridges holding my breath, and I can fly in planes as long as I don't sit by the window.

But I've also missed out on many adventures to avoid facing my fear.

One year, our friends from church were vacationing at the beach the same week as us. On the second day of vacation, they called and asked if we would like to join them on a parasailing adventure. They had paid for the excursion in advance, and someone had backed out. My adventurous husband said he would love to fill in for the cancellation, so I agreed we would go.

Now mind you, my understanding was that there was *one* cancellation, so only *one* person would be going out on the boat with them. One of us would stay behind. We didn't have to take a vote as to who that would be!

We arrived at the destination. After greetings and hugs, the group started heading toward the boat. I turned to head back toward a waiting area. "No," my friend Patti exclaimed, "you're going, too!"

I pointed at my chest and exclaimed, "Me?"

"Yes, you. We have *two* spaces available."

I expressed my fear and my refusal to do anything that involved heights, especially one that would put me in a harness high in the air over the ocean.

She was insistent that I come and assured me I could enjoy the boat ride. Not long after boarding the boat, everyone was handed a harness and told to put it on. I tried to refuse one, but again my friend and shipmate insisted I put it on — "just in case."

Everyone started pairing off and Patti looked at me and said, "You're going with me. We'll go last so you can watch how much fun it is." I did watch, and I stated unequivocally that I wasn't going to do it.

Then my husband went up and I decided I would watch his reaction when he came down. That would be the deciding factor.

When he came back down, he didn't look happy at all. He had no expression on his face — nothing. He is an adventurous person, so that concerned me greatly.

One other person went before it would be our turn. "I can't do this, Patti," I whispered. She ignored me. I started backing up, but before I could take another step, one of the crew members had attached me to the parachute harness. I exclaimed, "No, no, no!"

He said, "Ma'am, don't worry. If you want to come down, move your arms like this and I will bring you down. Just try it!"

There would be no backing out now. I closed my eyes as we ascended. After we reached the top, I kept my eyes closed, intending to do so until my feet hit the deck of the boat again. Patti kept describing everything she was viewing. I wanted her to just chat with me, but she wouldn't.

Finally, I peeked from one eye until I had the nerve to open both. I decided to just look straight ahead — that way, I would not be afraid of how high we were. After a while, I convinced myself that if I was going to make this worth the effort, I might as well enjoy the whole adventure. After all, I would never allow myself to be pushed into doing this again.

I looked slowly below me, and then up into the beautiful colors of the parachute. I was so excited and proud of myself at the same time. I couldn't believe it, but I was enjoying this experience.

As we were descending toward the boat, I was so thankful that I didn't let my fear rob me of this fun and exciting adventure. I was grinning from ear to ear over my accomplishment.

As my feet hit the deck, applause broke out. After listening to my whining, everyone on that boat knew they had witnessed a miracle.

Am I willing to try it again? Yes! Will I be fearful again? Of course, but I will be more committed to facing my fear.

Next up: asking for a window seat on the plane.

~Rhonda C. Hensley

47

The Phobia

*The quickest way to acquire self-confidence is
to do exactly what you're afraid to do.*
~Author Unknown

As long as I can remember, I have had a deeply rooted phobia about sharks. I'm not sure where it came from, but it has put a damper on my activities for years. Growing up in Southern California was quite a challenge. I would go to parties on the beach and spend the entire time fearing that a tidal wave would toss me into the ocean with the sharks. I woke up countless nights from nightmares where I was lost at sea and the shadows were lurking just below the surface, or a huge wave was coming and I was trying and failing to outrun it.

My fear was so crippling that I would completely stop breathing if I saw even a cartoon shark flash across the television screen. There was no way I could tolerate a commercial for *Shark Week*. I even had an accident in the hallway at my grandmother's house because I could not bring myself to go into her bathroom, where she had a copy of *National Geographic* on the counter featuring an article about great whites.

I spent many years of my life fluctuating between trying to avoid the ocean altogether and trying to convince myself that I was over the fear and it was a silly thing from my childhood. Counseling didn't work. Berating myself with countless verses from the Bible about not being afraid didn't work. Finally, I just decided it was something I was going to have to live with forever.

Then I met my mentors. I started listening to story after story about growth only happening in my discomfort zone. I heard over and over that the only limitations I had in my life were those I was putting on myself, and that if I didn't face my fear I would always be smaller than it. I couldn't let that happen. Something had to change, even if it meant getting very uncomfortable.

I started small. When I saw a picture of a shark on a billboard or a magazine cover, I made myself count to ten before looking away. Eventually, I was able to breathe while counting, so it was time to move on. Next I watched videos about sharks — not the dramatized Hollywood versions where sharks were attacking people, but actual videos of sharks existing in the wild and not bothering anyone. I started searching out articles about people surviving shark encounters and going back in the water even after being bitten. I went to Sea World and petted the nurse sharks. It was not exactly a great white or bull shark encounter, but it was still a big step for me.

The biggest step, though, came in September last year. My husband and I took a vacation in Nuevo Vallarta in Mexico. We booked a catamaran excursion that included snorkeling in the open ocean. It seemed like it took me forever to jump off the boat into the water… but I did it! And once I was in the water, I actually enjoyed myself. The fish were beautiful. We didn't end up seeing any sharks, but knowing we could have and jumping in anyway was such an empowering feeling! What's more, it has changed my life in other areas. Every time I face a challenge now, be it in business, family life, or anything else, I just think, *If I can snorkel in the open ocean, I can do anything!*

~Connie Brown

48

Mother Courage

*Birth takes a woman's deepest fears about herself and
shows her that she is stronger than them.*
~Author Unknown

"I have exciting news, Mom," Ann announced. "I'm moving to
Los Angeles." Visions of palm trees and movie stars flashed
through my head. I was beyond excited. For my entire life, I
dreamed of going to L.A. I loved Hollywood movies and the
tales of those who had made it big, and my daughter was going to be
living in that amazing place.

Then she actually moved there, to the opposite coast, thousands
of miles away.

"Mom, it's too expensive for me to fly home all the time. You're
going to have to fly out here." *Fly?* I broke out in a sweat just thinking
about it.

I'd spent many years avoiding airplanes. I once had my husband
drive an entire day to avoid taking a quick charter flight to a play my
daughter was in. The tickets were paid for, and the entire cast was flying
there, but I begged the stage manager to let us drive and meet them
at the hotel. When my husband won plane tickets to San Francisco,
I sent my son with him on the vacation instead. A few years later, I
took a two-day automobile trip with my daughters to Disney World.
I'd do *anything* to avoid flying.

It wasn't always like that. When I was a preteen, my mom accepted
a job as a reservations agent for an airline. Soon, my parents were

vacationing in Las Vegas and Aruba, waiting on standby for their seats on the plane. When I was thirteen, my sister Lisa and I flew for the first time to Disney World. Mom took a photo of Lisa and me posing in front of the airplane. Most of our flights were fine, but one time an engine failed before we took off, and we were forced to switch planes.

One horrible day, a plane from Mom's airline crashed, killing more than a hundred people. After comforting distraught family members on the phone all day, she came home from work in tears. From my bedroom, I could hear her crying all night. That's when my fear of flying began.

I began praying on flights. Mom believed if anything went wrong, it would happen during or just after takeoff. I'd count for a few minutes until I was certain we were safely up in the air. On a stormy flight to the Bahamas, we hit a huge air pocket, and the plane literally dropped. My stomach lurched, and I became hysterical. Beside me, Lisa laughed. She thought it was fun, like a roller coaster.

Then came the fateful flight. My parents and I were taking my Grandma Angelina to Italy. She hadn't seen her birthplace since she was seventeen years old. We took off from the airport in New York and were heading out over the ocean when the oxygen masks fell down. By this time, I'd been on enough flights to know that this was not a good sign.

People panicked. Dad helped me put on my mask, but there wasn't oxygen coming out of it! I trembled in fear and stared helplessly at the people around me. The pilot announced that the pressurization system had failed, and we were flying back to the airport. I gazed out the window as we came in for a landing, fearful of the ambulances waiting on the ground. By some miracle, we landed safely. We waited at the airport for another plane. Food and refreshments were served to keep us happy, but I wasn't buying it.

"I'm not getting back on a plane," I said to Dad.

"Don't worry, we'll be fine."

"I don't want to go to Italy anymore," I insisted.

"Of course you want to go," said Mom. "It's the trip of a lifetime. You'll regret it if you don't."

Soon, buckled in an airplane seat, I gripped Dad's wrist. And we had a beautiful trip to Italy. We visited Rome, Sorrento, Pompeii and the Vatican, where I gazed in awe at artwork on the ceiling of the Sistine Chapel. The highlight was seeing Sicily and the house Grandma was born in!

But here I was, years later, facing this dilemma again. My daughter could not afford to fly home constantly just because I was a fearful mess. If I didn't go, I would hardly ever see her. I booked the flight.

For weeks, I tossed and turned in my bed. I contemplated canceling the trip.

Ann called me. "I'm looking forward to your visit. It will be nice not to be alone on my birthday."

Alone on her birthday, far away without loved ones. What kind of mother would not get on that flight?

Soon, I was back on an airplane, alert and medicine-free. I wanted to be awake if anything awful happened.

Some athletic men sat near the emergency exits. *Oh, good,* I thought, *they'll save me.*

We taxied to the runway. The engines squealed. I clutched my armrest so hard my knuckles turned white. The woman next to me smiled. "Is this your first flight?"

"No, it's around my twentieth."

She burst out laughing.

"The engines," I whispered. "Do they sound right to you?"

"They sound fine," she reassured me. "You know you're much safer up here than on the ground."

I counted the minutes until we were safely cruising in the air. Nearby, a woman watched a movie on her laptop. Some cute children asked for snacks.

God wouldn't let a plane go down with all these adorable children on it, I thought.

The flight attendant seemed cheerful. *She's not afraid,* I thought.

A man read a magazine, and another was snoring. We hit some turbulence. It felt like riding in a bumpy car. No one looked worried. Soon, we were cruising smoothly again.

I forced myself to read but couldn't concentrate. The only thing that calmed me was talking to some patient people. It must have worked because time flew by, and the seatbelt light came on for landing.

Reality hit me. Soon, I would see Ann and a place I dreamed of my entire life!

When we touched down at LAX, the weather was sunny and in the 70s. Ann picked me up in her car bearing a hand-painted sign that said, "Welcome to Los Angeles."

"Where do you want to go?" she asked.

"I want to see everything," I said. For a week, we explored L.A. I touched Judy Garland's prints in the sidewalk and Elton John's star on Hollywood Boulevard. I browsed elegant shops on Rodeo Drive, tried on Harry Potter's sorting hat at Warner Brothers, strolled the Santa Monica Pier, and visited Griffith Observatory and La Brea Tar Pits (Ann's idea). We hiked to the Hollywood sign, admired the gates of the homes of many famous people around Bel Air, and met a rock star who posed with me for a photo.

Most importantly, I smiled as Ann blew out the candles on my homemade birthday cake in her new apartment. It was my dream vacation — all because I faced my fear of flying.

~L.A. Strucke

In Over My Head

The water is your friend... you don't have to fight
with water, just share the same spirit as the
water, and it will help you move.
~Aleksandr Vladimirovich Popov

There were no swimming lessons in my childhood, but I managed to teach myself the basics. I learned that I would be fine as long as my head stayed above water and I could put my feet on the bottom.

In my late teens, I had a job at the Algonquin Resort in St. Andrews By-the-Sea in New Brunswick. I used to swim at Katy's Cove with my co-workers, taking comfort in the fact that there was a lifeguard on the beach. I always kept my head above water; that was the key for me. Then, one day, my head went under. I don't remember if I was tired or if another swimmer caused a wave; I just remember the panic. I couldn't call for help, and the lifeguard didn't see that I was in trouble. A friend held me up until I regained control, but I never had the courage to go in deep water again.

They say that opposites attract, so of course I married a man who had grown up swimming every summer day at a lake. He was even a scuba diver. He tried to teach me to swim, or at least to float, but it didn't work, so I took beginner swimming lessons at the YMCA. I learned to float, and I did learn to swim well enough to join my husband in a pool, but I still wouldn't go in a lake where the water was dark and I couldn't see the bottom.

In spite of encouraging words from my husband's scuba buddies, I stayed within arm's reach of the edge of the pool and I continued to keep my face out of the water. When my confidence soared sufficiently for me to swim in the middle of the pool, my husband bought me a mask, snorkel, and fins. I was then able to put my face in the water and even learned how to do a duck dive — in the safety of a pool, with its reassuring blue bottom and nearby sides.

In the early 1980s, we went to Cuba on vacation. It was lovely, and the warm, calm shallow water off the sandy beach was perfect for snorkeling. The fish were beautiful, and I could see the bottom. I could put down my feet and stand up when water seeped into my mask or I got water in my snorkel.

The resort offered an introductory scuba session in the pool. Scuba diving was the reason my husband had agreed to a Cuban vacation, and I knew he would be pleased if I signed up.

Vladimir, the instructor, was handsome, but he knew little English other than a reassuring "no problem." The translator told me how good and safe the equipment was, and then instructed me to swim the length of the pool and back with my mask and snorkel. That was easy. Then came the scuba gear. The translator told me to swim with Vladimir to the far end of the pool, staying near the bottom. When I got there, he said I was to fill my mask with water and clear it underwater. My heart sank. I did know how to clear my mask underwater, and I had done it before, but I hated having water in my mask. When the time came, I let my mask fill with water, but I couldn't do it. I put my head above water, tipped out the bottom and let the water drain out. Then I put my head back underwater with a clear mask, and Vladimir and I swam back.

If a part of me had wanted to fail the course, it didn't work. Vladimir gave me a thumbs-up and said, "No problem. You dive tomorrow?" I took a deep breath and looked from Vladimir to my husband. Then I nodded.

The next morning, I pulled on a short dive suit and waded out to the boat while the men loaded the gear. The anxiety fluttering in my stomach increased as the boat kept going farther and farther, and

I could no longer see land. As Vladimir helped me put on the gear, my husband asked for my weight belt, but there wasn't one — not even a single weight that could be put in a vest pocket. *That's okay*, I thought, but Vladimir dashed my hope for a reprieve with his cheerful "no problem" as he turned on the air and helped me sit on the railing of the boat that was rising and falling with the waves. I hesitated, with one hand holding my face mask and mouthpiece in place, and my other hand over the strap at the back of my head.

Then I took a deep breath and rolled backwards into the water. I went completely under, but I popped up like a cork. My mask was still in place, and I could breathe through the regulator. That wasn't so bad. My husband descended with the other divers and was gone. Vladimir signaled for me to descend as well, but the buoyancy of the dive suit made it impossible with no weights. Not easily defeated, Vladimir went down and returned with a round piece of brain coral that he tucked into the curve of my left arm. He made the all-clear sign, a circle made with his thumb and index finger.

I returned the all-clear. He took my hand in his, and we descended into a different world. I saw fish swimming along with us and sea fans swaying in the current. I could look up and see the boat or look down and see the bottom. Soon, I noticed that my heart wasn't racing, the butterflies had left my stomach, and I had loosened the grip on Vladimir's hand. At that moment, I realized I wasn't afraid of water — I was afraid of not being able to breathe. With the scuba gear, I could breathe underwater.

When I rolled into the ocean that day, wonder replaced my fear, and determination was born. In December 1986, a few months after my thirty-ninth birthday, I became a certified open water diver in the cold water of the Bay of Fundy. I have enjoyed the beauty of the Great Barrier Reef, dived on wrecks, and marveled at the depth of the Great Blue Hole in Belize. There's a wondrous world below water, and it's all there for me now.

~Rose Burke

I Choose the Roller Coaster

*Your power to choose your direction of your life allows
you to reinvent yourself, to change your future, and
to powerfully influence the rest of creation.*
~Stephen Covey

t always starts with a feeling. Something isn't right, and I can't figure out what. I'm so anxious I can barely sit still. It keeps me up at night, pacing and pondering. Days pass, but the feeling does not. And then, all of a sudden, the answer will come to me.

The situation is always different, but the conclusion I reach is always the same: I need to make a change. A big one.

Some call it intuition. I've followed it many times in my life, and it has never led me astray.

If there's one thing I've learned about myself, it's that sometimes I need to make radical changes in order to be truly happy. I have no choice.

It can be really scary to leave a marriage or a highly successful career, but every time I've followed that feeling, my life has transformed for the better.

That feeling has come back. It's tugging at my insides even as I type this.

When I launched a new blog called the Positive People Army, it ignited a fire in me. I'd always known that I wanted to make a difference and spread positivity, and this blog became the way I would do that — or at least a great start.

I labeled it my Passion Project.

As the weeks passed, more and more people started reading, sharing, and following. Some folks even decided to join in and submit their own articles.

The blog was flourishing.

I should have felt pure joy. But the more popular the blog became, the more angst I started to feel. Why did I feel this way?

Writing and sharing positive energy was exactly why I created the Positive People Army, and I was getting exactly what I wanted.

So what was I missing?

It reminded me of a time when my eldest son was about to turn eighteen. As his birthday approached, a strange uneasiness began to come over me. I just couldn't put my finger on why. Then, one day, the answer came to me — or, rather, it was thrust into my face.

During an argument, my son actually yelled, "You're not the boss of me anymore!"

My heart sank, and I suddenly understood what had been making me so uncomfortable. It was the thought of his impending transition into adulthood. He was going from someone who needed his mother to someone who didn't.

Throughout Michael's life, I've tried my best to readjust and grow as a parent, but this particular circumstance was very different.

Since the time he was born, I had made every decision in his life. I picked the food he ate and the clothes he wore. I decided which school he went to and what extracurricular activities he would enjoy.

In essence, I was the manager of his life. It truly was the best job I could ever have asked for, but he no longer needed or wanted a supervisor.

I couldn't get his words out of my head. *You're not the boss of me anymore.* They echoed through my mind for days.

After many sleepless nights, I finally admitted my discomfort to my husband. I told him how saddened I was to be losing Michael.

He looked at me sympathetically, held my hand and said, "Sweetheart, you will never lose Michael. He loves you so much. You just need to readjust your role and give yourself a new title. The two of you will be just fine."

His words hit me like a sack of bricks. He was right!

Why had I thought I would ever lose my son? All I had to do was modify how I was parenting and give myself a new label.

With that thought, I decided to retire as "Manager of Michael's Childhood." I then gave myself a fancy new title: "Consultant to His Adulthood." It had a nice ring to it! And it was a simple change that worked.

Michael is now twenty years old, and both of us have settled into our new roles quite well.

Remembering this moment helped me realize that maybe I needed help finding the answers, like my husband had helped me regarding Michael.

A number of days later, I ran into a wonderful friend I hadn't seen in a while.

The moment she saw me, she started gushing about the blog. She shared her favourite stories and congratulated me on releasing such a positive force into the world.

I blushed and thanked her for her kind words. Then I sighed and confessed that I was feeling some unease about it, but had no idea why.

We talked about how I felt writing the posts and how much it meant to me to receive other people's stories. She asked me what my hopes and dreams were for the blog.

Then the most amazing thing happened: I got the answer.

While I was speaking to her, I unintentionally changed the mental label I had given the blog from my Passion Project to My Life's Project.

The moment I said it, I stopped myself. My entire body shuddered, and I could feel goose bumps rising on my skin.

"Oh my god," I said to her. "I think I just discovered why I've felt so funny. I want the blog to be more than just a hobby. I hadn't even realized this until I said it!"

My girlfriend laughed and said, "I guess you need to start figuring out what that means and get to work on making it a reality."

It's terrifying to admit something like this out loud, and even more so to actually write it down. But I knew deep down that if I didn't, it wouldn't happen. Without people knowing what I want, the opportunities will never be offered to me.

I struggled to write the post for almost a week, afraid to put it out there in the universe, but I just had to do it.

And within twenty-four hours of writing the first draft, I was e-mailed and asked to do my first radio interview about the blog. The universe had answered me in record time. It was an amazing sign and an incredible start to this journey I have ahead of me!

Once again, making a mental change had made all the difference in the world.

I realize this won't happen overnight, and I could either be incredibly successful or fail miserably.

The way I look at it, I need to decide what kind of life I want. Do I want my life to be a carousel, going round and round in a predictable pattern? Or do I want my life to be an unpredictable roller coaster ride — joyous, scary, and beautiful?

In my heart, I know there's only one real choice. I choose the roller coaster, and I'm going to ride it with my hands up.

~Heidi Allen

51

Swimming through My TEDx Talk

*When we share our stories, what it does is, it opens
up our hearts for other people to share their
stories. And it gives us the sense that we
are not alone on this journey.*
~Janine Shepherd

was always terrified of public speaking and even changed colleges to avoid a public speaking requirement. So one afternoon when my daughter Hannah called and said I should do a TED talk I thought, *No way,* even though I had no clue who "Ted" was or why he'd want me to speak.

Fast-forward to last summer when I read this headline: "Who Is TED and Why Is He Coming to Newport?" By now, most everyone knows about TED talks. TED stands for Technology, Entertainment, Design, and their tagline — ideas worth spreading — speaks for itself.

I learned that our island's inaugural TEDx theme was "Tides of Change," which was perfect for me. I've spent much of my life in the intertidal zone and was already kicking off my shoes and digging my toes into the damp sand.

My memoir was published in 2014, forcing me to talk to people. I'd spent three years saying "yes" to new challenges, feeling the fear but doing it anyway. I was ready to cross TED off my list. I applied and was chosen from more than sixty submissions.

I watched so many TED talks that the intro music infused my dreams. One of my favorites is one in which Tim Urban talks about procrastination. While he was supposed to be writing his talk, he admits to finding the Google Earth map of India and zooming in to about 200 feet above the ground, then spending two-and-a-half hours scrolling around "to get a better feel for India." I nodded as he recalled thinking, "Yes, it's always been a dream of mine to have done a TED talk *in my past!*" Tim's dream had come true; I still had work to do.

I took seven pages of notes about preparing a TED talk, and then wrote eight drafts of "Just Keep Swimming"—all twice the allotted length. I sent it to Hannah and some others for review. All agreed—start over. Staring at a blank Word document, I agonized over this: *What is my idea worth sharing?*

Three weeks before the event, I began writing "Why We Should Share Our Stories," and it all came together. After reading my memoir, my daughter Bella's dance teacher asked me to write my story as a dance. For the past year, thirty-six girls, including Bella, have been performing *Epilogue* in competitions. This would be the last of three reasons we should share our stories that I'd present, culminating with the live performance.

I began practicing. TED talks have to be delivered without notes. I divided mine into sections to memorize, highlighting key words, and imagining how I would move between three locations on the round red rug that's the hallmark of all TED talks. I practiced everywhere—in every room of my house, in parking lots waiting for my kids, and the best place of all—while swimming daily in the ocean.

One Saturday, I swam under an ominous sky. "Let's pretend we're at a cocktail party," I said to myself as I stroked along the shoreline. I liked the idea of walking onstage with a glass of wine, in case I needed it. Every day in the ocean is different, and the visibility was so poor I could barely see my hand. I was reciting the darkest part of my speech—about the deaths of my sons, Noah and Jonah—when all of a sudden the water turned inky. Looking up, I realized black clouds covered the sky and it began raining, matching the mood of my story at that moment. I swam on.

The next day, I finally swam through my whole speech without forgetting any lines. My fingers and feet were numb, but the water was a clear, pale green. I rarely see anything more than seaweed, so swimming over two quahogs feeding was a first. Likewise for three skates I swam over — their silky silhouettes camouflaged by the sandy bottom — just as I was reciting how, like sea glass, the sharp edges of our pain are worn smooth. These magical moments helped me memorize my speech, which I was definitely afraid I was going to forget as soon as I stepped on stage.

I'd begun dividing my life between BT — before TED, and AT — after TED. Finally, the last BT day dawned. During my final rehearsal swim, I was reciting the news of my son Isaiah's birth when a school of ephemeral fish darted past — a perfect wrap. I was as ready as I'd ever be, although I truly wished I could swim my speech instead of standing on stage reciting it. Swimming was something I knew I could do. But, as most bereaved parents know, we've already done the hardest thing — burying our children. After that, everything in life should be easy. *Be brave and do hard things,* I reminded myself.

It was tough swallowing my nerves all day, waiting almost eight hours to step onstage in the red cowboy boots I'd chosen because they screamed, "I am not afraid!" Wearing red boots means you must, as my son Micah says, "Be a warrior, not a worrier." And the minute I pointed my toes forward with a glass of icy Chardonnay in hand, everything fell into place. "Let's pretend we're at a cocktail party," I said, swimming right on through my speech with the black clouds, quahogs, skates, and fish all awaiting their cues.

I finished my talk, forgetting only one passage. Nobody noticed; it made no difference. Safe to say, one of the happiest moments of my life was delivering my final line, the introduction of the dance, then hurrying offstage to join Hannah in the audience. I settled in as the dancers took their places, sipping my wine with relief. I wished time would stand still as Bella and my beautiful back-up dancers shared the gift of *Epilogue.* I listened to the words I'd written and recorded, fulfilled with every movement of the final example of why we should swallow our fears and share our stories: It might just lead you to someplace that's simply amazing! And I was simply amazed.

Now, at last, it is AT. I was scared, but I did it! And like Tim Urban, I am so happy that I have a TEDx talk in my past.

~Kelly Kittel

Chapter 6

STEP OUTSIDE YOUR COMFORT ZONE

☑ Be Spontaneous

52

Not Just Another Thursday

If you're offered a seat on a rocket ship,
don't ask which seat. Just get on!
~Sheryl Sandberg

I groaned as the alarm on my iPhone sounded. Knowing my children would be waking up soon, I picked it up and quickly scrolled through my favorite apps — a morning ritual. Something caught my eye on Facebook. It was a post from a local television casting company, asking for last-minute applications for people to play marketing executives on *Empire*. I had always wanted to be on television, but the practical side of me ruled out pursuing such an impractical dream. Still, I decided to e-mail them my photo and information. I chuckled to myself as I did so, actually feeling embarrassed. After all, I'm a suburban mother, not an actress or a hip, young marketing executive. Right as I hit Send on the e-mail, I heard my son wake up. I hopped out of bed and forgot all about it.

An hour later, I buckled my son into his carseat, and we headed to preschool. We were a few minutes early and it was raining, so we waited in the car before going inside. While he sang along to the radio, I grabbed my phone again and scrolled through e-mails. There was a response from the casting agency: "When can you be to the set?" My heart started pounding. I hadn't actually expected to get a response of any type, much less one asking me to come to the set!

I put my phone in my purse and rushed my son into his classroom.

After kissing him goodbye, I wrote back saying that I could be there at 10:15. Within minutes, I had another e-mail waiting for me. This one contained a parking pass, directions to the set, and an employment form. I texted my husband, "CALL ME ASAP!" He called immediately and asked what was wrong. I filled him in after first swearing him to secrecy and asked him what he thought I should do. His reply: "Are you kidding me? Go for it!"

My mind racing, I thought through the logistics. I could use a vacation day from my job as a sales representative, and my babysitter was already planning to pick up my son from school. There was no reason I couldn't go. Before I could change my mind, I called the casting director to tell him I was on my way. There was no backing out now.

After making the forty-five-minute drive into the city, I pulled into the parking lot where I was told a shuttle would be waiting. Climbing into the van, I smiled nervously and hoped I didn't look as clueless as I felt. After being dropped off at the set, I was guided upstairs into what looked like an old warehouse. After filling out my paperwork and showing my identification to the security guards, I was led into what they called a "holding area" on the set. Now I had to clench my jaw to keep it from dropping open. I was awestruck. Having never been on a television set, it was incredible to see all the different set designs.

While waiting for my turn, I met a few other extras who all had done this type of work before. They said that typically they weren't able to see themselves on the shows they filmed because they were either shown too briefly or edited out. They also said they rarely met the actual stars of the show. They were surprised that this was my first time doing this. I explained I had responded to an ad I saw on Facebook on a complete whim.

After waiting a short time, a production assistant came and told me it was time to come with him. I followed him and once again had to pick up my jaw from the floor. This had officially become the craziest day of my life. The scene that I was asked to participate in involved me standing right next to Terrence Howard—an actual movie star whom I had seen in too many movies to count! On top of that, my job in the scene was to pretend I was judging some dancers while they performed the most incredible routine that I had ever seen. I pinched myself. I had to be dreaming! I spent the next several hours in awe. Being on a real TV set was just as incredible as I had imagined it would be. I really could not believe my luck.

After my scene finished filming, I was given a ride back to my car. I called my husband and filled him in on all the details. My children were dying to hear what had happened as well, and wanted to know if Mommy was going to be on TV. I told them that while I did get to see a TV show being filmed, it was unlikely I would actually be shown myself. They asked a few more questions before forgetting all about it and returning to their toys.

A few months later, I was at the gym on an elliptical machine suffering through a workout. I had recorded all the episodes of *Empire* since my day on the set, but never saw myself or even the scene I had participated in. I figured something had happened where they had to cut it out for editing purposes. Suddenly, a TV screen about thirty feet away from me caught my eye. The show playing was *Empire*, and I thought I saw myself. Then I thought I saw myself again! I texted my husband, who was home with the kids, to make sure it was recording just in case. A few minutes went by, and then he texted me a picture of myself on the TV screen!

At that point, I was done with my workout. I raced home and walked into my house to find all four of my kids jumping up and down screaming. Not only had the scene not been edited out of the show, but I was shown several times. I went from being an ordinary mom to the coolest mom ever in their eyes. It was so exciting!

Looking back on the experience, I think about how taking one simple chance completely changed not only my day, but my life. It only took me a minute or so to send in that e-mail submission, but it required that I make myself vulnerable and face the fear of rejection. In the past, I wouldn't have done it. This experience has given me a renewed excitement for my life along with a fresh new belief that dreams can come true at any age for those who are brave enough to step outside their comfort zones. It just goes to show that extraordinary days really can come from ordinary mornings.

~Lindsey A. Knuth

53

A Humbling Experience

*Judge tenderly, if you must. There is usually a side you
have not heard, a story you know nothing about, and a
battle waged that you are not having to fight.*
~Traci Lea LaRussa

t was my very first impression of Salt Lake City, Utah. My best
friend had dropped me off in front of The Cathedral of the
Madeleine, near Temple Square, before heading to the university.
Thinking I'd start my tour with this building, I climbed the stone
steps and pulled open the outer wooden door. I found myself inside
a small entrance, facing a second, locked door. As I turned to leave,
I noticed a man, a vagabond, asleep in a corner, his head resting on
a small backpack. Suddenly feeling like I was intruding, I exited the
cathedral as discretely as possible.

Outside, I paused on the sidewalk and inhaled the cold winter
air. My encounter with the vagabond brought to mind an article I had
read on the plane. It was an interview with a pastor who had spent
a day walking around downtown Toronto, handing out change to
everyone who asked. At the end of the day, he counted how much
money he had shared with the needy, and it was less than ten dollars.
The lesson he wanted to impart with his story was that we shouldn't
show so much restraint about giving to those in need, because none
of us will go broke if we part with a couple of dollars now and then.

I could see the wisdom and truth of his words, but I still mistakenly
believed that most homeless people were either drug addicts or drunks,

and that giving them money would only serve to fuel their vice. When confronted with a similar question, the pastor pointed out that the Bible tells us we must strive to offer charity in whatever manner we can to whomever is in need. It is up to God, not us, to see that our gifts are righteously used. That last message was now causing me to re-examine my beliefs regarding homeless people.

"Miss?"

I turned to see the vagabond walking toward me. "Yes?"

"You wouldn't happen to have a bit of money to spare, would you? Enough to buy breakfast?" he asked.

"No, sorry," I answered. "All I have is Canadian money. I don't think that would be of much use to you."

"No, it wouldn't. Thanks."

I hesitated a few seconds before offering, "I have a McDonald's gift card. I could buy you something for breakfast."

"Thank you," he replied.

I followed him down the street to the nearest McDonald's. He looked to be about fifty years old and was dressed in layers of what I figured must be every garment he possessed.

After ordering breakfast and a coffee for himself, he asked me what I was having. I told him I'd already eaten and that I was anxious to start my visit of Temple Square.

"You have time for a coffee, Miss," he said. "The buildings don't open for another hour."

I couldn't figure out if he wanted company for breakfast or if he felt awkward after realizing that I had detoured by the McDonald's solely for his sake. His comment caught me off guard, and I was unable to come up with a polite reason to excuse myself, so I ordered a tea and resolved to sit with him for a while.

When we left, he thanked me again for the breakfast and asked if I was heading directly to Temple Square. I told him I was.

"I know this town well. I'll show you around," he offered. "To thank you for your generosity."

"It's not necessary."

"I insist."

What to do? I must admit that it was kind of him to offer to be my tour guide in exchange for breakfast. I didn't want to spend the entire day with him, but I didn't want to be impolite either. So, I reluctantly accepted his offer.

We started by the Temple gardens, followed by the Joseph Smith Memorial Building, the South Visitors' Center, the North Visitors' Center, and finally the Conference Center and the Tabernacle. We spent six hours together!

Initially, his presence bothered me. It troubled me to be accompanied by a vagabond. I worried about what others would think and how I would be seen.

At first, I tried every excuse I could think of to part ways with him: I need to rest a bit; I'd like to take some pictures; I need to call my friend; I need to use the bathroom... Nothing worked! He always waited for me patiently.

Eventually, I gave up and accepted my fate. That's when I began to see things differently. I realized he was a fantastic tour guide. He knew absolutely everything about everything: the details of the Temple's construction, the names of the plants in the Temple gardens, the history of Hotel Utah and of the renovations that transformed it into the Joseph Smith Memorial Building... everything!

Little by little, I got to know him and started appreciating the way he would tell me about his life while we walked. Over the course of our time together, the vagabond disappeared, and James appeared. James was an educated man and had once been a tradesman in Tennessee. He had resorted to sleeping on church steps following an injury and a series of unfortunate events that had left him without a job, house and money. He wasn't an alcoholic or a drug addict.

We parted ways in front of the Conference Center.

"I have to go meet my friend," I said. "Thanks for the guided tour. I had a nice time." I was sincere.

"Happy I could be of some use."

I pulled the McDonald's gift card from my pocket.

"Here. It's not much, but it should buy you dinner," I said, handing him the card.

"I can't accept… You've done so much already."

"I insist. I don't need it."

"Thank you."

"Goodbye and good luck," I said, holding out my hand. Instead of shaking it, he removed a necklace from around his neck and placed it in my palm. It was a large metal cross studded with plastic "diamonds."

"Keep it close to your heart. It'll protect you," he said.

It's not the type of necklace I would typically wear. I thought of protesting, but the sincerity with which he gave it made me think it would be futile to do so. He shook my hand, thanked me once again for my generosity and left me with a "God Bless."

Almost ten years have passed since that day. His necklace has become a permanent addition to my purse, constantly reminding me to never judge a book by its cover… or a man by his appearance.

~Kim Tendland-Frenette

54

I Am a Karate Mom

Our spontaneous action is always the best. You cannot,
with your best deliberation and heed, come so
close to any question as your spontaneous
glance shall bring you.
~Ralph Waldo Emerson

Every week, I sat on a hard plastic chair in a cold, tiled waiting area with at least a dozen other parents. The fluorescent lights flickered a rhythm off the mirrored wall, and the smell of sweaty feet and small children hung in the air. Sound bounced off the cinder-block walls just like our energetic children bounced around on the training-floor mat.

It was my husband's idea to sign up our youngest son, Silas, for karate lessons. He was an impulsive, distracted, and extremely hyperactive seven-year-old. My husband, who'd had a brief experience with martial arts in college, thought karate training would help Silas burn off excess energy while learning focus and self-control. So, waivers were signed and tuition paid, and I carted him to class every Wednesday and Friday night.

For one hour twice a week, I sat patiently in uncomfortable seating and watched my son as he slowly developed a sense of accomplishment by learning to throw a solid punch and maintain his balance as he made a difficult kick. Every week, he bowed out of respect as he entered the training room, and bowed again as he left. He was quiet and attentive during class, soaking up every word his sensei said. I often wondered if this was the same child who had trouble sitting still at the dinner table; the one who threw hour-long temper tantrums when his sister ate the last cookie; the one who couldn't remember to put the milk back in the refrigerator.

While it didn't happen overnight, and I can't exactly explain how, karate did exactly what my husband had hoped. We started to see the positive effects at home as our son became calmer and more patient.

Martial arts transformed my son. What I didn't know was that it would transform me, too.

I am a karate mom, but maybe not the typical sort. Since Silas first stepped onto the dojo floor, I've made sure that he, and then each of my other three children, made it to class on time. I've washed karate uniforms and packed sparring gear. I've driven them hours away to tournaments and cheered from sidelines. I've taken pictures of proud moments and bragged about them on social media. My bookshelves are lined with trophies and my walls with promotion certificates. That is all typical, but what's not typical is that not all of those trophies, promotion certificates and proud-moment pictures belong to my children.

One evening, my husband and I sat watching Silas's class learn their first kata, a choreographed combat pattern. The children were quiet and focused, working hard to match the movements of their sensei, Tim Cunningham. Sensei, a Japanese word that can be loosely translated as "teacher," is a quiet man in his sixties, and yet he moved through teaching kata to ten small children with power, grace and presence. He commanded a room full of children without ever raising his voice. In that moment, karate seemed like such a beautiful art. I leaned over to my husband, Keith, and whispered, "I think I might want to do this."

Keith turned to me with a look of complete surprise on his face. "Okay," he answered.

Two weeks later, I stepped hesitantly into the martial-arts world at the age of thirty-six. Silas had helped me tie on my shiny, new white belt and showed me how to bow before I entered the training floor. Then I took one small step onto the mat. It was a single small step, but it was a step far outside of my comfort zone. I was not particularly athletic, coordinated, or confident. I had played T-ball rather poorly as a child, barely managing to hit the large ball from its stationary position atop a waist-high tee. The most physically active I had been in recent years was wrestling squirmy and reluctant children into their pajamas before bedtime.

I was only an awkward mom, with a case of mild social anxiety and a wildly perfectionistic streak. I was almost paralyzed with the fear of making a mistake or looking like a fool. I knew absolutely nothing about martial arts beyond what I had witnessed watching my son's class from the waiting area. I was in completely uncharted territory.

The first class was the hardest. I wanted so desperately to be "good" at karate. I longed for that confidence, presence, and grace that I had observed in Sensei Cunningham and saw developing in my young son, but I was not a natural. I struggled through that first class feeling awkward, clumsy, and silly. I left feeling embarrassed and incompetent, as if gaining any semblance of competence in karate was far outside my reach. I was fairly certain that I would never go back again, in spite of having already paid the first month's tuition.

Silas wouldn't let me quit that easily. So, I went back to the very next class, not because I wanted to, but because I wanted to be a good example for my children. I am so glad I did. In the years since those first awkward, hesitant steps onto the training mat, I've learned a lot of important lessons. I've learned physical balance and body mechanics. I am a small-framed woman who stands 5'4" when I'm really trying, yet I can hip-toss grown men, and force them to "tap out" from a quickly implemented arm bar or chokehold. I can land punches and kicks with speed and technique. I know how to unbalance an opponent, both physically and mentally.

But there are lessons I've learned along the way that I didn't really expect. I learned that I don't have to be perfect in everything; that even though something doesn't come easily, it doesn't mean it isn't worth learning; and that having patience with myself is far more important, and far more difficult, than having patience with others.

I am not the typical karate mom because I don't just watch my children from the sidelines. Two months before my fortieth birthday,

I went through a grueling physical and mental test and came out on the other side with a black belt. In fact, all six members of my family now hold that rank. And we are all better people for having done it.

Last night, after tying on my black belt, I stepped out onto the training floor surrounded by my own class of small, active children. They bounced around me, begging for attention, eager to get started. I walked them through how to land a solid punch and keep their balance as they throw a difficult kick. Many of those kids are there in my karate class because their parents want to help them burn excess energy, and learn focus and self-control.

"Those chairs are pretty uncomfortable," I tell the parents. "You should think about joining us out here on the mat."

~Alice Jones Webb

55

Life Is Better Upside-Down

*We should consider every day lost on which
we have not danced at least once.*
~Friedrich Nietzsche

My first exposure to pole dancing was on Halloween in my last year as an undergrad. One of my girlfriends, Beth, invited me to a show downtown. She had a spare ticket, and one of our friends was performing. Initially, I resisted. After all, what would my family think?

"There'll be food," she assured me. Food is a godsend for students. "I'll show you a couple of spins, too."

Admittedly, I was intrigued. Pole dancing was exotic, taboo. Besides, we hadn't had a girls' night in ages. "Why not?" I said. "Could be fun."

Once there, I nibbled on the promised finger food, eyeing the dancers as they played on the poles between routines. I felt overdressed. Some of them wore six-inch platform heels; others were in neon leg-warmers. Most wore nothing more than very short "booty" shorts and cutoff shirts. Beth showed me a spin called "ballerina" and laughed when I got stuck on how to hook my leg on the pole.

The show entranced me. The dancers glided as if their heels were an extension of themselves, their movements slow and sensual. One routine featured two girls on the same pole; another involved a chair. I admired their strength and fluidity. I could barely spin around the darned thing.

Afterward, Beth pointed to a flyer. "Let's sign up for classes. Just think, we could dance like them!"

We approached the manager and stated our intention to buy a membership. Glancing over my shoulder at the poles, I inserted my credit card and held my breath as the machine beeped. *Payment accepted.*

We pledged to begin our memberships in mid-January, a New Year's resolution. The day of my first class, as I was getting off the bus, my phone buzzed. It was Beth: "Can't make it — sorry! Got an exam tmrw. ☹"

I'd signed up. There was no backing out now. I braced myself and entered.

The studio had transformed in the daylight. Sunlight shone through the windows onto wood floors, bathing the room in warmth. Girls were already stretching on blue yoga mats, wearing crop tops and tanks, booty shorts and leggings. Some of them wore heels. Heels!

Then there was me, in baggy blue shorts and a faded shirt I got from a box of Sugar Crisp, feeling like I was back in high school gym class. Prior to pole fitness, I had never worked out. I was the chubby, asthmatic kid nobody ever wanted on their team. Gym was the only course where I couldn't study my way to an A.

I took off my shoes and inched into the room, hoping nobody would notice me. The instructor spotted me immediately.

"Hi, I'm Meghan!" she said. "Is this your first class?"

I nodded.

"Don't be shy. Grab a mat and find a pole."

I set up shop at the back. We began by doing hip circles to upbeat pop music, which made me feel like a hula dancer. Then we did some variation of push-ups on our hands and knees that Meghan called "cat spirals" and described as "scooping out a tub of ice cream with your chest." Then there were plows and hip extensions. Soon, I ached everywhere, and that was just the warm-up!

After what felt like forever (fifteen minutes), Meghan said, "Mats away. Time to get on the pole."

She then demonstrated a body wave. After a few minutes of trying to coordinate my hip, butt, and chest in a way that looked sexy and not robotic, we switched to practising the "fireman," in which we spun in a cross-legged position on the pole. Those were fun, if dizzying.

Finally, we did strength-building. Meghan showed us a pole hold, grasping the pole with both hands and lifting her legs behind her. When I tried it, I felt weak and let go. My arms quivered, and my abs burned.

"You did great today," Meghan said.

My shoulders sagged. "I'm so bad at this."

"It's your first day! We all start somewhere." She smiled sideways at me. "You ever done something like this before?"

I shook my head.

"Then why do you expect to be perfect on try number one? Building strength takes time, and flow comes with practice. You'll get there — trust me."

She said it with such certainty that I believed her.

My trial month ended in the middle of February. It had been a fun four weeks. On the day of my last class, Meghan asked, "You going to sign up for more?"

"I don't know," I said. The price of a three-month membership was intimidating for someone on a student budget. "I might move to another city when I start grad school. It depends where I get in."

"I understand," she said. "Best of luck."

After a few weeks, however, I found myself missing the class. During the day, my mind swam with memories of my time at the studio, the rush of doing spins, and the pleasant ache in my muscles after a class.

And so, in June, I caved and renewed my membership.

"Nice to have you back," Meghan said. "It's been a few months, hasn't it?"

"I'm addicted," I confessed, and she laughed.

I wanted to invert like I'd seen at the Halloween show, and I said as much. Meghan told me that I needed enough strength in the preparatory strength-building moves like the pole hold. They didn't teach inverts at the beginner level.

I set a deadline: By the end of summer, I'd be strong enough to move into the next level of classes. Every day during open practice, I came to the studio and practised the strength-building moves. I even began a pole diary ("fitness journal"), complete with stick-figure sketches in the margins and happy faces on days when I nailed a new move. Eventually, I could hold the strength moves for more than five seconds, and I'd nailed every move on my checklist.

One day in late August, Meghan approached me at the end of class and smiled. "We're moving you up. You're ready."

Kathi was my new instructor, a slender woman with short, magenta hair and a wide smile. The previous week, I'd bought myself booty shorts and a studio-brand crop top as a treat to myself — kind of how a superhero dons a uniform once she's embraced her superpowers. That was me, Spider Woman. The baggy blue shorts were banished.

"Hot damn!" said Kathi. "I remember you. Where were you hiding that body, girl?"

I blushed, but smiled. We warmed up like we usually did, and after giving the others a move to work on, she said, "Time for your first invert. I'll spot you." She explained it, and then demonstrated for me.

I gripped the pole, sucked in my breath, and lifted with all my strength.

"Shoot your legs! Shoot your legs!" Kathi said. "Breathe!"

I wrapped my legs around the pole and squeezed. From behind me, I heard applause. My heart pounded. I inhaled deeply and smiled so wide my cheeks hurt. There I was, only months before struggling to do a body wave, now inverting for the first time.

Life was definitely better upside-down.

~Laura Johnson

56

A Greyhound Encounter

In helping others, we shall help ourselves, for
whatever good we give out completes the
circle and comes back to us.
~Flora Edwards

When I tell people I'm shy, they tend not to believe me. I don't come across as a quiet, introverted person, but there is more to shyness than that. I do love to meet new people, make new friends and help a stranger here or there, but I am usually hindered by my anxiety, which prevents me from going over and making an effort.

That was why a seemingly innocuous encounter on the Greyhound bus meant so much to me. It showed me that I could indeed get past myself and reach out.

It was an overnight trip from Ohio to New York, and I was taking it with a few friends of mine from the boarding school I was attending. I was headed home to surprise my family for the holidays and was pretty excited about it.

We settled into our seats for the long ride ahead, well-stocked with candy and an optimistic pillow or two. The passengers formed quite the motley assortment, a microcosm of our great, diverse nation. The bus slowly settled down for the night, as each of us tried to make ourselves as comfortable as possible. A majority of us tried finding comfortable sleeping positions as a peaceful silence descended upon the lumbering bus.

And then, the silence was pierced by a decidedly unhappy wail. It was an infant, and he was crying. Loudly. His father attempted desperately to shush him, but to no avail. He seemed unsure of what to do, how to handle this precious bundle in his arms. And he was all alone.

I wondered what would cause a man so young to be traveling alone with an infant. My heart went out to him; he looked ready to cry himself. And that baby just broke my heart.

So I turned to my friends, and with a conviction so unlike me, I said, "I am going to that baby!"

They looked at me like I was crazy and then proceeded to tell me that I was. I believed them, truthfully. This was so beyond my comfort zone that I couldn't even see my comfort zone with binoculars.

But there was a baby. And he was crying. And that was all that mattered.

So I took a step out of my comfortable seat and a running leap outside my comfort zone and I approached that hapless dad.

"Here, let me try," I said.

His look echoed my friends', but his had the extra element of sheer desperation. He looked around the bus, almost as if to ensure that it was okay to entrust his baby to a stranger, and saw that there was nowhere for me to go anyway. He shrugged and wordlessly handed the baby to me.

I took the distraught boy back to my seat and slowly began rocking him in my arms. I sang the lullaby I had grown up with in his ears.

We made quite the sight — me, an Orthodox young woman singing the age-old Jewish bedtime song to an African-American infant. People looked up, gaped, and then either smiled at the prospect of peace and quiet, or shrugged nonchalantly at just another night on Greyhound.

After a few moments, the baby relaxed in my arms and let his eyelids flutter to the rhythm of my lullaby. And then, miraculously, he was asleep.

I handed him back to the relieved father, who placed him carefully in his infant seat.

"Thank you," he whispered.

"No, thank *you*," I responded.

~Devora Adams

57

The Blue Dress

Everybody else needs mirrors to remind themselves
who they are. You're no different.
~Jonathan Nolan

pulled it out at random, one of the pile of thirteen evening gowns I'd selected to try on for my brother-in-law's wedding. This dress was a long shot, one I'd never wear, and yet something about the iridescent hints of the perfect blue seduced me. It glided on, pulling ever so slightly at the hips because it was close-fitting. As the zipper went up my back, corseting me tighter and tighter, the heat in the dressing room rose considerably. I managed to raise the zipper to a point at which the strapless dress stayed in place, and I felt respectable enough to leave the dressing room to ask for help.

"I think it's too tight on you," the saleslady said as she zipped up the bit I couldn't manage on my own. "You won't be able to sit down in it."

"You think?" I said, pretending to care.

But she wasn't there anymore; she was already on her way back to her usual command post, where she decided who could go in and how many garments they were allowed to try on. "Make sure you put it back on the hanger," she demanded, her back facing me.

It might, perhaps, have been the sensible thing to do, but instead I walked back into the dressing room and closed the door behind me. With the anticipation of a teenage girl about to read her first love note, I turned toward the seat directly across from the door and sat down defiantly. Realizing that I could, in fact, manage quite successfully, I glanced at the smile shining back at me from the mirror and confirmed something was up.

Maybe it's the lighting, I thought, for the woman I saw in the mirror wasn't quite me at all. I stood and watched her as she smiled at me and straightened her back. When I moved, she moved with me; when I spun round, she did the same. And as the moments turned into minutes, I realized the smile we shared had turned into uncontrollable joy.

I opened the door, searching for an audience, and headed to the mirror found at the end of most dressing room corridors. The dress ruffled audibly with each step, as if announcing royalty. I waited, and then, when a middle-aged mother and her twenty-something daughter emerged to discuss what the young woman was trying on, I asked, "Excuse me, I need another opinion. The saleslady thinks this is too tight on me. What do you think?"

The mother and daughter regarded me for a moment and practically bowed in approval. "No," the mother said. "It's perfect. It looks stunning on you." I would have blushed, but I was that other woman, the confident one. She didn't blush. Instead, I walked back into my dressing room and stared some more.

Could I pull this off? Could I wear this beautiful gown? Here was the thing: The dress was positively seductive, in a way I'm not. I chop garlic and onions routinely for my family's evening meals, and at the end of the day the balls of my fingers often smell like food. But the woman in the mirror could smell of nothing but perfume. I work as a third grade teacher and often hear myself say things like "Line up quietly, please!" and "Please don't pick your nose." But the lady in the mirror, well, she would never say those things.

I slipped off the dress and held it in my hands, all the while thinking how beautiful it was and how sorry I'd be if my children and my husband never got to see me in it. I began to imagine what it would be like walking into that wedding ceremony wearing the dress. I'd walk into the same church where I had married years ago, a young woman still finding herself. Wouldn't it be wonderful to walk down the same aisle as the person I had become: a wife, but also a mother and a teacher, and the latest version of me: the woman in the mirror?

Dressed and ready to go, but still unsure, I handed the pile of unwanted dresses to the saleslady and realized I was tightly holding on to that blue dress. I said, "I'm taking this one." And just like that, I became the woman in the mirror; everything I am and a little more of what I might be.

~Adriana Añon

58

Splash of Fame

Don't think, just do.
~Horace

n 1968, Andy Warhol said, "In the future, everyone will be world famous for fifteen minutes." In a short time, the phrase "fifteen minutes of fame" became a standard promise. Like most people, I never really expected to have even a few seconds of this assured and grand limelight. And then it happened.

We were aboard the *National Geographic Explorer* on a cruise to Antarctica. The ship carried 148 passengers and 100 crewmembers. Excitement filled the air as we witnessed sculptured ice formations twenty stories high, snow-covered mountain peaks and glaciers.

Motor-driven boats called Zodiacs ferried us across the frozen sea so we could climb snowy mountain ranges and mingle with penguins waddling around like little old men. Enormous seals dotted the shoreline. Heavy snowflakes covered our parkas, and frosty air bit into our skin.

Like all the other passengers, we relaxed in the tranquility of the excursion and relished the serenity of the White Continent. Then one morning we saw a sign announcing an open invitation to all passengers: Polar Plunge at 12:30.

My husband and I gaped at the sign. His face brightened, hinting he wanted to give this reckless feat a fling, but I had a churn of panic in my stomach. Hundreds of reasons for not doing such a ridiculous act clicked through my mind. "No way," I declared.

"For starters," I protested, "we are much too old. The water is freezing cold. Heights terrify me. I'm not much of a swimmer. In simple language, I'm a wimpy coward."

I could tell by my husband's expression my rebuttal didn't dent his building enthusiasm. "Not only that," I moaned, "but it means I'd have to wear a swimsuit in public with a boatload of people gawking at my fat, wrinkly body."

He gave me a quick hug along with his endearing smile. "We'll never have another chance," he insisted.

My resolve gradually weakened. My hearty "No way" gave way to a weak "Maybe." Finally, I heaved a big breath, mustered my courage and forced myself to say with fake enthusiasm, "Okay. Let's go for it."

Dressed in our swimsuits and shaking with trepidation, we gathered with the other participants in the lower part of the ship called the mud room. I eyed the group. A daring, testosterone-driven teen clamored to be first in line. A twenty-something woman in a bikini barely covering her slender body also stepped forward. Her partner wore Speedo trunks and swim goggles, indicating his aquatic expertise. The remaining few ranged in age from exuberant young people to middle-aged adults joking and laughing. We two eighty-year-olds were visibly the ancient, senior citizens of the group.

Our turn came all too soon. Shivering in the arctic air and trying to forget the perils of freezing water, we moved through the doorway and onto the Zodiac that would serve as the jump-off point. We stepped up to the edge of the bobbing Zodiac, and for a split-second gazed at the churning, glacial water below. My legs felt like wilted lettuce, but it was too late to turn back. We clutched our hands together, took a deep gulp of air, and took the polar plunge into the frigid ocean.

After what seemed an eternity, we bobbed to the surface and splashed our way to the safety platform. Wiping saltwater from our eyes, we staggered to the mud room. Thankfully, towels and bathrobes awaited our quivering Popsicle bodies. Through chattering teeth and hysterical laughter, I proclaimed triumphantly, "I can't believe I did that!"

On the deck above, passengers gathered to witness the episode and click photos of the crazy polar plungers. That afternoon, I claimed my fifteen minutes of fame from our cruise companions. We became the celebrities of the day. I must admit I reveled in their admiring comments: "You were the couple who held hands and jumped together? How romantic. Was it cold? Were you scared? Awesome! What will your kids say? Bravo… and at your age, incredible." Most notable of all, I heard, "You are so brave."

In my memory bank, I've stored my fifteen minutes of fame, and it will last the rest of my life. However, I have no inclination to skydive or bungee jump to experience distinction again. I still cling to my natural tendency toward self-preservation. My one-time, totally wild stunt is enough. Ah, but my splash of fame felt glorious.

~Barbara Brady

How Hard Could It Be?

It is a shame for a man to grow old without seeing the
beauty and strength of which his body is capable.
~Socrates

My friend Preston jogged beside me on the track. "You want a good workout? Then you should try a spin class at the gym."

I laughed at the idea. "Ooh, let's sit on a bike and pedal for an hour going nowhere. How hard can that be?"

He gave me a knowing smile and invited me to join him the next day.

"Nah, man, I've got better things to do. If I'm going to work out, I'm doing something that gets results."

Preston nodded as if he agreed with my logic, but added, "Come try it, just once."

Fifteen years ago, the Air Force pushed to improve its members' physical fitness, which was never my strong suit. Preston and I both lived on the heavy side, always bordering on or exceeding the body-fat standards. We both sought ways to improve our condition and get off the squadron's "bad-boy radar."

Preston could run faster than anyone I knew at his size. Whatever he was doing, it worked. I managed to trundle along, but my joints had already started deteriorating, causing stiffness and intense pain after high-stress activities like running, basketball, and racquetball. With no impact, indoor cycling should have been a natural choice for me.

I can't say for sure why I resisted. The thought of a heavyset guy flopping all over a bike didn't look good in my mind. Self-conscious about my total lack of physical coordination, I've never been a big fan of group activities where other eyes might be on me. I also didn't believe I'd get the level of exercise I needed to lose weight and improve my fitness. I used to bicycle everywhere in high school, and if ever the cliché applied, I assumed spin class would be "just like riding a bike" — both familiar and easy.

But I agreed to give it a shot, and knew I would enjoy proving Preston wrong. One day after work, I walked into the indoor cycling room and took a bike in the back corner, as far removed from the group as possible.

The instructor — a short, rail-thin guy made of wiry muscle in a Spandex riding suit straight out of the Tour de France — approached me and shook my hand. "Hi, I'm Shawn. You got water and a towel? You're going to need them."

"I'm fine," I said, confident I might not even break a sweat. "Thanks, though."

He guided me through adjusting the bike for comfort, probably because everything about me screamed, "I have no idea what I'm doing." Then he took the lead bike and turned up the music — some R&B with a heavy beat for pedaling cadence. "Spin is all about you and the bike," he reminded the group. "Doesn't matter what anyone else is doing. You pedal with the beat and adjust your resistance. On a fast song, you're pedaling quick, so resistance is light. Slower songs, you've got to turn it up to maintain that high intensity. But you control the resistance; no one's going to turn that dial for you."

Shawn kicked off the workout by telling us when to turn it up and when to increase our speed. Within minutes, my heart pounded like it wanted to escape my chest, and sweat dripped from my arms and face. About halfway through, I stopped caring when he told us to increase resistance. I barely kept up the pace, sucking in desperate breaths that never felt like enough.

"You are strong," Shawn growled as he tore up the "hill" of heavy resistance. "Your mind gives up long before your muscles will. Keep going."

Even though everything in me cried for a break, I knew he was right. My legs could still push against the resistance and keep the bike's wheel turning even though my will felt crushed.

I finished the class shaking, soaked, stripped of my utterly wrong notions, and absolutely in love with the experience. Though it hurt my pride to eat crow and tell Preston about it, I also committed to more spin classes and started convincing other co-workers to try it out.

A month later, the gym staff announced an upcoming workshop to train new certified instructors. "In a military environment like this," Shawn said, "where people move or work on changing shifts, we can always use more."

After class, I spoke with Shawn. "You mean I could get paid to do this? I could arrange my own workouts and pick my own music?"

"Yeah, man. It's pretty great."

I completed the certification, signed up with the gym staff, and arranged my schedule to fit in leading a couple of sessions each week. Where once I mocked the idea of spin class, I found myself on the bike in front of everyone, pushing my way up a hill, looking out over the panting, sweating bodies, and echoing Shawn's words: "Your mind will quit long before your muscles do."

I know because I almost quit before I started. Instead, I spent the next two years running classes, earning a couple of hundred dollars a month for something I would have done for free.

~David M. Williamson

Use the Rope

I don't think anything is unrealistic if
you believe you can do it.
~Richard L. Evans

My little five-year-old seemed all the smaller standing at the base of the huge rock-climbing wall as the teenage employee double-checked her harness. It was our second time at the park, and the place was somewhat crowded. On our first visit, Ruthie had begged me to let her try the climbing wall, but I had denied her, afraid that she was undersized. But life had dramatically changed since then. I had been diagnosed with stage 4 cancer, and suddenly life seemed too short not to let her try.

I stood outside the gated area watching the employee attach Ruthie's harness to a hydraulic-resistance safety rope. He gave her a thumbs-up sign, and she was off! She scampered up the wall with joyful abandon. At times when the next handhold was a long stretch, she paused a moment, and then jumped courageously to reach it. This tiny girl made it to the tippy-top, while kids twice her size chickened out about halfway up.

I marveled at how she did that so easily and joyfully. If cancer was the rock wall, I wanted to be Ruthie.

When she touched ground again, I leaned over the low fence. "How do you do that?" I asked.

"I just do it," she said with a shrug, and started on her second pass. Apparently, if I was going to learn the secret, I had to climb the wall myself.

I hadn't climbed a rock wall since I was sixteen. With added weight and reduced muscle tone, I doubted if I could even do it. I sure didn't see any other moms trying to scale the wall. Several months earlier, embarrassment would've stopped me before starting. But cancer does funny things to the brain. It makes us realize that we are braver than we think.

With determination, I entered the arena. I stepped into a harness, and the same teenage employee attached my safety rope and gave me the thumbs-up. As I began my climb, I was elated by my own bravery for trying something so bold. Then, only ten feet up, my fingers and toes started to tire, and there was absolutely no place to rest. My excitement shattered with the apprehension that I was going to slip and fall.

The climb was a lot like battling cancer — a mixture of exhilaration and fear. Exhilaration… as I dared new avenues of both physical and emotional health. Fear… that I might make a bad decision or that cancer might win. But any athlete can tell us that to be at our best, we can't be afraid. Fear will lock up our muscles and minds. To perform, we have to stay loose. I just didn't know how.

I marveled as I watched my daughter reach the top for the second time. She let go of the wall, clung to the rope, and began her descent. It was a very slow descent because she barely outweighed the resistance of the rope. Here was a clue to her fearlessness. With that rope, she couldn't possibly fall. She might slip, but she wouldn't fall. She was so light she could feel the rope supporting her when she climbed.

If I was going to make it, I would have to trust the rope, too. So I let go. Immediately, I felt the security of the rope; its upward lift felt much stronger than when I'd had both feet on the ground. Although I descended much faster than Ruthie, it was still very gradual. I realized that even though slipping might give me a momentary shock, I would be perfectly safe. With newfound trust in the rope, I gripped the wall and started climbing again.

Ten feet up. Twenty. Twenty-five. Now the holds were getting trickier. I hung on the wall, uncertain of my next move. I felt like I was treading water, trying to catch my breath and keep my head above the frigid emotion swelling around my chest and throat. I knew that feeling all too well lately. It was the exact same feeling I had every time I noticed a new ache and worried if the cancer had spread, or when I faced another round of scans. Arresting, panic-laced fear. At that point, I wanted to be done rather than swim in that terrible dread.

As I clung there, Ruthie caught up to me on her third climb. Her grips were getting trickier, too. She'd reached one of those spots where the next grip was beyond her reach. I watched as she concentrated, stuck out her tongue, wiggled her toes to just the right position, and then pushed off, momentarily attached to the wall with only one hand. The leap affected the hydraulics of the rope, and for that brief moment, the rope actually lifted her upward. She found the hold, got her footing, and continued moving.

Use the rope, I reminded myself, stretching out bravely. One hold. Two. Three. I was at the top. I did it!

That day on the rock wall instructed me for the long cancer battle ahead. As I've continued the fight, my rope has caught me many times. When my hands and feet were blistered from chemo, my sister made meals, did dishes and put kids to bed. When I was wiped out from an experimental treatment, my dad did laundry and directed the children's homework. My rope has lifted me, too. Friends have cheered me up, my husband has spent hours in long conversations with me, my children have showered me with affection, and God has provided vital spiritual reassurance.

When scans or medication changes or scary cancer stories start to envelop me in icy anxiety, I continue moving by whispering to myself the secret of doing something hard and scary: *Use the rope.*

~Heidi Johnson

Just Ask

*Stop trying to be less of who you are. Let this time
in your life cut you open and drain all of the
things that are holding you back.*
~Jennifer Elisabeth

Just *ask him,* I thought as the man at my lunch table got up to leave. I was eating there with my friends, the Davises from Davis Graveyard, who were friends with the man. The man turned out to be Scott Morrow, host of the *The Fearless Ghosthunter* radio show, and one of the speakers I'd specifically come to HAuNTcon to see.

He'd make a fascinating interview for my blog. All I had to do was ask, but I was afraid to. Interviewing wasn't my strength. I'd never done a face-to-face one. I'd certainly never requested an interview in person. I didn't know how to naturally work it into the conversation. What if he said no?

But I also knew I'd kick myself if I let this opportunity pass me by. I started to panic. It might be the only chance I got.

Do it! The voice in my head shouted.

"Could I interview you sometime?" I blurted out awkwardly.

Oh, boy. That was bad.

He cocked his head to the side and regarded me... how? Thoughtfully? Curiously? Cautiously? It was hard to tell. It made me even more nervous.

"I mean, I'm sure you're busy with the conference and all, but maybe I could e-mail you questions or something?"

Oh, boy. I am making it worse. Now I sound like a nervous idiot.
Which I was.

Shut up! Shut up! I told myself.

"Sure. I'll be around all weekend. We'll catch up and make it happen."

Wait. What? Really?

"Great. Thanks!" I said, trying to play it cool, in case it wasn't too late for that.

A couple of hours later, I found myself in his seminar. There wasn't time to talk afterward. Plus, it had been a long day. It was time to go home and get ready for the evening festivities, which included a costume ball.

The HAuNTcon conference was for the Halloween industry. People from haunted attractions all across the country had come to Nashville for it. And the costume ball was among the highlights — a great chance to network.

I'd been insanely excited about the ball when I first learned the conference would be in my back yard — not for the networking aspect, but because I lived for dressing up at Halloween.

But it wasn't Halloween. It was a cold January night. I was tired. And I didn't really know anyone at the conference other than the Davises. The couple of people I'd chatted with in seminars weren't going to the ball.

Then I started doubting my costume. It wasn't scary like I knew many of the costumes would be. It was sort of spooky. Its official name was Corpse Countess. It was a big, beautiful, silvery satin dress with a hoop skirt and a tattered hem that billowed out ethereally when I walked. White make-up gave me a ghostly glow, and my big white Marie Antoinette-style wig completed the royal spectral look.

It was one of the most lavish costumes I'd ever worn, but would people at the ball laugh? These were hardcore haunters. They liked blood, guts and gore. I was just a ghost.

And then there was my husband. He'd agreed to go with me, but begrudgingly. Halloween was not his thing. It was Friday and he'd had a grueling week. Work had called him out of town. He'd land at six, drive straight home and change, and then we'd leave. I knew he was going to be exhausted. Maybe it'd be better if we stayed home instead.

"Don't be nervous to go," my husband said. "So what if we have the worst costumes? Maybe they'll have a prize for that. And if it's that bad and we're not having fun, we can leave. You worry too much."

Yep. He knew me so well.

So we went. And to my astonishment, I was swarmed when we entered the ballroom. Everyone wanted a photograph. Of me. With me. I'd never experienced anything like it.

I got compliments galore on my big, ghostly dress. And then we hit the dance floor. The dress made it awkward to dance the way I normally would, but people loved that I was out there.

The ball ended up being a blast. I talked with so many people — including, at one point, Scott Morrow and his girlfriend, Sue. They both got a kick out of my costume.

But most amazing was what happened the next day. Scott found me sitting at a table after lunch between seminars.

"How 'bout we have a chat now?" he asked as he took a seat. "Great costume last night, by the way."

My nervousness from the day before was gone. Scott turned out to be incredibly down-to-earth and easy to talk to. We spent the next two-and-a-half hours chatting away.

Before we parted for the next seminars, he said, "Now that you've had a chance to interview me, I think it'd only be fair for you to be a guest on my show sometime."

I was stunned. *Really? How cool!* But I didn't say that.

Instead I said, "I'd love that! Thank you!"

We scheduled it to happen a few weeks later. In a pre-interview conversation a couple of days before his show, Scott said, "You know, our network is looking to fill more slots. You should apply for your own show. You've got the personality and an interesting niche. I think you'd be great."

I was flattered. In fact, I'd seen the notice on ParaMania Radio's site saying they were looking for new shows. I briefly considered it, but... What did I know about hosting a radio show? Nothing. However, I wasn't a stranger to radio. Several years earlier, I'd had a ten-minute segment at the end of a friend's show for a few months. I had even toyed with the idea of getting my own show. But I'd never pursued it — partly because I was lazy, partly because I was filled with self-doubt.

But here was someone telling me he saw something in me. *Maybe I should apply. What was the worst that could happen?* So before I lost my nerve, I filled out the application. To my surprise, it was accepted a week later.

I'm not sure this exciting new phase in my life would've transpired if I'd let my nerves win. I'm pretty sure it wouldn't have.

But you know what? I'm glad I'll never know the answer to that "What if?" question. It's more fun living this reality.

~Courtney Lynn Mroch

- ☑ Try avocados
- ☑ Go ziplining
- ☐ Sign up for art class
- ☐ Make a new friend
- ☐ Run a 5K
- ☐ Buy a bathing suit

Chapter
7

STEP OUTSIDE YOUR COMFORT ZONE

☑ Go Far Away

62

Off My Rocker in France

Retire from work, but not from life.
~M.K. Soni

At my retirement party, my co-workers gave me a lovely gift: a pillow and blanket woven with the image of the campus building where I spent the last decade of my thirty-year university career. As the celebratory cake was served, my friend got a dreamy look in her eyes. "I just picture you curled up in your rocking chair under that blanket with a cup of tea and a good book," she said. I knew she shared my love of both tea and reading, and I could hear in her voice that this was her dream of the ideal retirement. So I smiled and nodded, all the while thinking to myself, *I've got a lot more adventuring to do before that rocking chair!*

Less than six months after we both retired, my husband and I boarded a plane for the biggest adventure of our lives: a winter-long sojourn in the Languedoc-Roussillon region of France. Leaving the frigid, snowy landscape of the Upstate New York town we had called home for the past forty years was scary, but we were determined to spend three months to find out whether an expat retirement was for us.

We took a while exploring our options. We knew a lot of "snowbirds" — people who escaped our harsh winters with second homes in Florida or other southern destinations. But with our family roots in Europe — my husband's in Ireland and mine in Poland — and our love of history, art and architecture, we started to think about warmer regions in Europe. While we're not beach people, we wanted to be close to the sea, and we love exploring nature almost as much as tromping around museums and castles. So we landed on a little corner in the south of France, just over the border from Spain. It was the off-season, so we were able to cheaply rent a vacation home in a seaside village, with the Mediterranean and the foothills of the Pyrenees mountains both within walking distance. We were surprised that, other than the plane ticket, our three-month stay would be less expensive than a winter in Florida.

Our ground rules were simple: We would live like locals, not tourists. No fancy hotels, frequent dinners out or guided tours. We would walk everywhere or take a bus or train, the better to explore our new world. We'd avoid big supermarkets and malls, opting instead for local farmers' markets and artisans' shops. We'd drink the village wine, sample regional cheeses, and get our bread and meat from the baker and the butcher down the street.

I have to admit it was not without culture shock. While we'd both had a year or two of French in college, that was forty years ago. All I could remember was: *À quelle heure est le petit déjeuner?* Asking what time breakfast is served is a useful phrase, but it's only good once a day. We brushed up with tapes and workbooks, but learned most of our French just by living it. We watched French TV, tried to read the French newspapers (with dictionary in hand), and learned to ask for wine, bread and cheese in halting but passable French. We made plenty of mistakes along the way, but our French neighbors were so welcoming and kind that we were encouraged to keep trying.

Living in Europe gave us a lot more than language practice, though. I've got arthritis in both knees, and at home I had avoided stairs or climbing hills whenever I could. By the time our three-month trial period was over, I'd hiked in the foothills of the Pyrenees, took 200 stone steps up one of the highest church bell towers in our region, and jumped on and off more trains than I'd even seen in my first sixty-two years of life. I'm a bit of a scaredy-cat, but my husband and I climbed to the top of the summer castle of the kings and queens of Mallorca and stood on the roof looking out to sea. We walked out on a narrow break wall with the waves of the Mediterranean crashing left and right and only a rusty pipe as a railing, and scaled a rocky promontory to explore an ancient chapel with nothing between us and Africa but the blue waters of the sea.

I'm not always the most adventurous eater, but that first winter I tried cheeses that looked — and smelled — like something rotten, ate snails and octopus, and drank the strongest coffee I'd ever tasted in a cup the size of a big thimble. I cooked recipes written in a language I could barely understand on a stove with the temperatures in Celsius and measurements in liters and grams. We bought wine for the equivalent of $1.50 a bottle, out of a barrel, where the winemaker poured it from a spigot into a "cubi," which is like a plastic milk jug for wine refills. And it all tasted wonderful!

Our first three-month sojourn was so magical, in fact, that we returned for two more winters before buying our own tiny stone house well within our modest budget, high on a hill in a wine-making village surrounded by vineyards as far as the eye can see.

We live there half of every year, expanding our French abilities and visiting churches and museums some days, hiking in the vineyards on others. But mostly we do what we initially planned to do — we live like locals. We've made friends with our village neighbors, who have shared their homemade wine and gifted us with everything from bread and sausages to the tiny shoots of early spring asparagus picked in the countryside. We get "bisous," the cheek kisses French people use to greet friends, from people on our street and shopkeepers we visit frequently. And the bus driver, who is the same age as our son, has taken to calling us his "American parents."

We've changed it up stateside as well. This year, we downsized from our antique-filled rural home to move into a tiny loft apartment — the perfect "lock and leave" base to allow us to pursue more European adventures.

And on a recliner in that loft is draped my retirement gift blanket, just waiting for me to return and curl up with a good book and a cup of tea.

~Michele Bazan Reed

63

To Galway, with Love

We travel not to escape life, but for
life not to escape us.
~Author Unknown

t's no surprise that when Mom died, I was left in a state of limbo. She and I had been as close as a mother and daughter could be. I called her my best friend, and I meant it in every sense of the term. She and I loved one another unconditionally and learned a great deal from each other. She was my "partner-in-crime." When she wanted to go to Tommy's for some chili cheeseburgers at 3:00 in the morning, I eagerly joined her. When she sold her self-published Algebra II exercise book at a local math convention, I jumped at the chance to spend the weekend in Palm Springs with her peddling her creation. Our relationship wasn't perfect, but it was ours, and it was sowed in love.

After she died, I not only lost my best friend, but I was also left with an overwhelming sense of abandonment. One moment, Mom was here, and the next she was gone. Prior to losing her, all I had ever known was my small, tight-knit family and home in Los Angeles. But now, everywhere I turned, it was glaringly obvious that a large portion of that equation was missing and would be forever. The small blessing was that I had stayed home while attending university and got those extra years to connect with Mom. We had done a little traveling around our home state of California for her various business endeavors. I experienced more adult things with her during those years than ever before. We took a girls' cruise to Mexico, attended my sorority events, worked at the same school together, and gallivanted around Palm Springs several times.

As an Israeli immigrant who arrived in America in the late 1950s, Mom spent the next few years traveling across the country with her family in search of permanent residence. It was this perpetual movement that she had experienced as a child that made Mom avoid traveling very far, and specifically flying. This is why we never made it farther than our cruise down the coast to Ensenada or Gilroy, California, the proud Garlic Capital of the World (coincidentally, also Mom's favorite food). We took these small trips, bonded over our shared experiences, and made the most of our little adventures. And then, just like that, I was left with her house, her affairs to get in order, bills, a funeral to plan and a cloying feeling of loneliness.

Even so, a few months after her death, things began to settle slightly. With the funeral over and her finances put in order, my immediate responsibilities were dwindling. I noticed that having a to-do list helped divert my attention, even amidst my grief. But what was I supposed to do once I had checked everything off and was left only with my brand-new diploma and a heart so heavy it felt made of lead? I tried to fill my newly empty schedule with familiarity in order to find some semblance of normalcy. I cooked some of Mom's favorite dishes, but none of them ever tasted the way they did when she made them. I watched our favorite movies, but my solo laughter bounced off the walls of our now much emptier house, and my chuckles often turned into tears. I was stuck in a rut, to say the least.

It was at this low, and on a particularly dreary suburban morning, that I remember realizing I had to make a change. I had been watching some talk show to pass the night hours because sleep had not been coming easily. In this particular moment, I was becoming far too emotionally invested in a woman's quest to find the paternity of her son when a commercial came on. It was advertising travel within the state of California. I smiled as the camera panned over a familiar backdrop of either Arrowhead or Mammoth, where Mom and I had spent time playing in the snow together. A warm, silly smile spread across my face. But, as quickly as the ad had started, it began to close, and the warmth of my memories rapidly cooled. Then the whiteness of the snow on the screen faded altogether, and a black veil closed around a simple phrase that appeared and read: *Go find yourself.*

It was in that very moment, in that simple phrase, in those three little words, that I felt a spark. It ignited in me a little glimmer of hope. I found myself repeating the sentence in my head. *Go find yourself.* In that painful, debilitating time, these words sounded like a message of permission or release. I found myself reflecting, *Mom wouldn't want me to be moping. She wouldn't want me to keep trying to find her by reliving her life. She would want me to find myself and my own path.* So, what does any self-respecting, newly graduated college student do when she feels lost and needs to do some soul searching? She goes to Europe, of course.

Only a few hours later, I had booked a trip to Ireland so I could spend St. Patrick's Day in the rowdy streets of Dublin. I had stumbled upon an affordable tour for college students offered by a company both Mom and I had formerly worked for. I would be spending two and a half days in Galway and four days in Dublin. This would only be the second flight of my life, and I tried not to be nervous. There was nothing I could or wanted to do about my excitement, though.

A few weeks later, I found myself in the most beautiful place on earth. The rolling, vividly green hills welcomed me warmly from the window of the airplane. The moment I stepped off the massive vehicle, a brisk air hit me. It was cooling and calming and had just the right amount of wind to be exhilarating. I could tell almost instantly that this trip, and any travel I would take here on out, would be defining. I knew I had made the right decision to come.

Over the next several days, we would traipse our way through the countryside, seeing flashes of quaint towns through the windows of our tour bus. We stopped at many, tossing a pint back at quintessential Irish pubs, and shopping for authentic Irish products at the small markets. It was liberating to be wandering around in a new place, and also very eye-opening. I learned a great deal about myself in this foreign environment.

In Ireland, I learned that I had enough gall to do karaoke in a bar full of strangers, even with minimal alcohol in my system. I saw that when I was not being flustered by L.A. traffic, my latent sense of direction could navigate unfamiliar streets quite easily. I witnessed the heights of my own bravery when I got a tattoo the day after St. Patty's Day in a second-story Dublin tattoo shop. By stepping more than 5,000 miles out of my comfort zone, I discovered an intense passion for travel that I had never acknowledged before. However, it was while I stood on the edge of one of the Cliffs of Moher that I truly saw the big picture. Mother Nature has a way of doing that: putting things in perspective.

Water lapped hungrily at the massive rock formations, and we stood as close to the cliff edge as the high winds would allow. There were tourists all around drinking in the landscape as I was, but I hardly noticed them. I could focus only on the rhythmic waves, powerful winds, gorgeous greenery of the cliffs behind me, and the deep blue of the ocean in front of me. The meditative sounds and stunning scenery captivated me, and then reminded me that there was a much larger system at work than I could ever conceive of. All we can do is remain open to the adventures that life offers and take leaps of faith in our ability to navigate through them, for it is in those unfamiliar situations that we often learn the most about ourselves.

When I arrived home, it became clear that my adventures had revealed to me a very clear proverbial fork in the road. I had been given two options: 1) stagnate and dwell on the unfairness of life, or 2) use my trials and tribulations as a learning experience. But by propelling myself down the cobblestone streets of Ireland rather than the familiar streets of my neighborhood, I now knew in my heart that my direction, self-image, and life had changed forever.

~A.B. Chesler

64

The Gift of Getting Uncomfortable

I am not the same, having seen the moon
shine on the other side of the world.
~Mary Anne Radmacher

sat on top of the single, scratchy sheet covering my cardboard bed and looked around. I could see light pouring in from the straw ceiling, illuminating the sand and dirt that made up the floor. Outside my window, I could see the outhouse, which was really more of a euphemism for a covered area with holes in the ground that functioned as toilets. In the distance, I could see a camel dipping its neck up and down as it made its way across the sand dunes. As I took in the scene around me, I almost laughed as I thought to myself, *How did I get here?*

"Here" was a campsite deep in the desert of Oman, one of the many exotic and remote places my husband and I visited as part of the six-month, round-the-world journey we decided to take last year. While we were both happy living comfortable lives in New York City, we yearned to share an adventure and shed the predictability of our lives by traveling from country to country with no set itinerary.

Prior to this trip, I really wasn't the type of person who said "yes" to whims or was particularly spontaneous. In fact, I valued routines and stability and often avoided situations that would make me feel uncomfortable or were different from what I was accustomed to. Saying "yes" to this six-month journey was one of the first major whims I've ever indulged in my life, and while it was certainly out of character, something inside of me kept whispering "go."

So go I did. I had traveled a lot prior to this trip, but to developed countries where I could stay in Western-style hotels with all the comforts of home. Visiting places in the Middle East, Africa, and Asia sent me into a tailspin of culture shock. Suddenly, I was staying in places with limited electricity (if at all), toilets that I had to squat over, and showers with no hot water. Food options were often limited to local dishes, and the idea of taxis in many places was a ride in the bed of a pickup truck. Even when the temperatures climbed past 100 degrees in some places, air conditioning remained a distant luxury.

I also witnessed a staggering level of dire poverty and squalid living conditions that I wouldn't wish on my worst enemy. From walking over piles of cockroach-infested trash on the streets of an Egyptian village, to coming face to face with little children in an Ethiopian market dressed in filthy clothes with flies all over their faces, this trip opened my eyes to the truly devastating state that so many people in this world are forced to live in. I saw living conditions I couldn't even imagine if I hadn't witnessed them with my own eyes.

Being in these places and seeing what I saw were unsettling experiences. But had I not pushed through my feelings of discomfort, I would have missed out on some incredible experiences on this trip that taught me lessons I will never forget. In an Egyptian village, I saw groups of women caring for children who were not their own, and often not even part of their families. In this village — and in many parts of the non-Western world — the spirit of community is vibrant, and village members look out for one another and pitch in to help other families when needed, without expecting something in return. I was touched by the responsibility neighbors felt to one another, and could feel the love of the community radiating through that village.

In many of the places we visited, people speak little English, which made asking for directions or help very difficult. Many times,

I felt frustrated and sometimes scared that we were lost or very far from our destination. Feeling so uncertain in a foreign country is a very uncomfortable experience, and it was in those moments that I really missed having an Internet connection at my fingertips so that Google Maps could guide my way. But it was often in these moments of desperate confusion that total strangers went above and beyond to help us, sometimes to extraordinary lengths.

In Namibia, for example, we got a flat tire (and had no spare) in the middle of a remote area hundreds of miles from civilization. We were lucky to come across two fishermen who didn't speak much English, but could tell we needed help once they saw our deflated tire. These two men spent more than two hours in the blazing heat trying to plug the hole that was letting out air. When that didn't work, one of them gave us their spare and drove with us four hours to the nearest town where we were able to purchase a new tire. He then had to hitchhike back to where we started from, all the while carrying the spare tire he let us borrow. This man's kindness — to complete strangers with whom he did not even share a language — touched me in the deepest place of my heart, where I now hold the truth that humanity is bursting with goodness, beauty, and love.

And it was in the Omani desert where I sat under the stars that we could see so clearly, sipping tea with other travelers and our Omani hosts, when I realized how much human beings have in common. Here we were, a group of twelve people from all over the world, sharing our experiences and finding all the ways we could relate to one another. I talked at length with a woman from China about our fears related to becoming parents, while my husband spoke about the grief of losing his parents with a man from Italy whose father had died from cancer just a few months earlier. I learned that night that there is so much more in the world that unites than divides us.

So, to come back to the original question I posed to myself while sitting in my desert hut, *How did I get here?* I got here by saying "yes," not only to the trip, but to all of the new experiences and insights I gained from traveling. I got here by pushing myself to experience the world and humanity in ways I never could have if I hadn't consented to feeling uncomfortable. Permitting ourselves the freedom to push past our own boundaries is one of the greatest gifts we can give to our souls.

~Brittany L. Stalsburg

65

Granny Drives a Hummer

*Regret of neglected opportunity is the worst
hell that a living soul can inhabit.*
~Rafael Sabatini

My boss's eyes were wide and questioning. "You're quitting to move to Argentina?"

"I have this novel I've been writing, and I just can't seem to find the time to finish it here in New York. I've been trying for a few years now." It was seven, to be exact.

I knew that I sounded like a lunatic — which is why I was even more surprised when he responded, "That's great, Rach. I'm excited for you."

Afterward, as I walked to the subway from the Urgent Care Center where I worked as a Physician Assistant, I wondered if I had made the right decision. People normally did this kind of thing after a bad breakup, or a near-death experience, or maybe after they lost their jobs. But to walk away from a six-figure salary at the age of thirty-one to "write a novel" seemed crazy, even to me. That being said, I'd been saving up money and could afford at least a three-month sabbatical.

In college, I had majored in Spanish Literature and hoped that one day I would write stories like the ones we read in class. But I'd always loved working directly with people, too. So after years of volunteering in my local ER and Health Department, I decided to apply to Physician Assistant school. I took everything from Organic Chemistry to the GRE, got accepted into my state college's Masters of

Physician Assistant Studies program, and from there moved to New York to work at a top hospital.

I had also started writing. I was more than a hundred pages into my novel when I stopped. Doubts filled my head, and I told myself that no one would want to read my work. So the unfinished story had sat on my computer, untouched, for more than two years. But I had also written a couple of short stories that managed to make their way into publications, giving me a glimmer of hope — faint, barely visible, but present. I knew that if I didn't take a few months off to focus on finishing my novel, it wasn't going to happen. I also asked myself, *Even if it never got published, would my time in Argentina still be worth it?*

I wondered what my family would say when I told them about my plan to move, especially my grandmother. She was a nurse and had played a huge part in my decision to go into healthcare. Magee, as my siblings and I called her, had worked hard her whole life to provide for her family, and hadn't been able to travel outside the United States until she was in her seventies.

I thought back to 2007, the year I'd spent living with my family right after college, paying off student loans. I stayed with my parents, but my grandparents' house was in the neighborhood, and so I'd passed many an evening at their home.

Magee was turning seventy-four that November. "Please don't buy me anything for my birthday this year," she'd requested of us. She was a minimalist and preferred to keep her house clutter-free.

This worked out for me as I was making $8.10 an hour as a nurse tech at our local hospital. I decided to give her an experience gift instead, but struggled with what we should do.

As her birthday drew near, I got more and more anxious about it. I thought about dance classes (my granny loved her Zumba), a trip to a nearby city for lunch, or seeing a play together. Nothing seemed unique, though.

Then one day, as we were watching TV, waiting for supper to finish on the stove, a Hummer commercial came on.

Almost as if to herself, she said, "I've always thought it'd be fun to drive one of those things."

I looked over at her and smiled. Finally, I had my answer.

When her birthday arrived a week later, I told her I was taking her out for lunch, but secretly I had a pit stop to make first.

When I pulled up at a car dealership, she looked around, confused. "Are we here?"

I smiled and pointed over to the far corner of the lot where the Hummers were.

She gasped. "No. I couldn't!"

But I knew she could. She'd always been the active type who didn't let life's speed bumps slow her down. Besides, she was a terrific driver. As we ambled over to the Hummers, though, I could tell she was afraid. Even I had to admit they were much bigger in person than on TV.

Magee waited by one as I went inside the building to talk to the car salesman. I explained that it was my grandmother's birthday, and would he be so kind as to let her test drive one of the Hummers on the lot?

A spark lit in his eye, and he grinned. "C'mon!"

He helped my grandma in and sat in the passenger seat as I climbed in the back.

Before starting up the car, I could see my granny hesitate. She took a deep breath, winked at me in the rearview mirror, and turned on the ignition.

For the next fifteen minutes, we drove around some of Tallahassee's most beautiful back roads. The sun streamed through the branches of the overhanging canopy trees and threw mosaic-like shadows across the road. I cracked open the window and felt the cool breeze blow my hair back away from my face. Magee beamed, moving the steering wheel with ease as the car salesman told her about the Hummer's finest features.

When we got back to the lot, she handed over the keys, giggling like a schoolgirl. "That's the most fun I've had in a long time!"

The salesman passed Magee his business card and told her to call if she had any further questions, but I sensed that he knew this was a one-time thing. He wished her a happy birthday and even obliged us by taking a photo of Granny and me in front of the Hummer.

"What did ya think, Magee?" I said as we walked back over to my little beat-up Camry.

"To be honest, I was scared half to death! But I knew if I didn't do it, I'd regret it."

I nodded and hugged her.

All these years later, those words have stuck with me. Sometimes, life gives us opportunities that will never happen again. And, sometimes, we have to create them.

As I took a seat inside the subway car and we pulled away from the platform, I knew I was making the right decision. Whether or not my novel ever got published, the time spent in Argentina experiencing new things would still be worth it. Like Granny, I needed to grab onto the steering wheel and risk the ride of a lifetime.

~Rachel Elizabeth Printy

66

After the Jungle

The real voyage of discovery consists not in seeking
new landscapes, but in having new eyes.
~Marcel Proust

walked off the grid and into the Borneo jungle wearing a backpack weighing almost thirty pounds. I was with two British guys, Ben and Pete, a Dutchman named Steef, two Indonesian guides, Edo and Oddie, and four men from the Dayak tribe.

The Cross Borneo Trek, traditionally known as one of the most difficult and challenging jungle treks in the world, follows the historical 1894 route of Dutch botanist Dr. Anton W. Nieuwenhuis.

Uting, one of the men from the Dayak tribe, peered over the muddy edge of the cliff ahead of us. He adjusted his straw, feathered cap with one hand and reached out with the other toward me.

"No good," he said, "no good."

I sighed and grabbed his hand. He pulled me up the last four feet of the incline to rest for a few seconds on a narrow root plateau. I looked down at the trail ahead. It descended at a steep angle and ended on the rocky banks of the river below. We went down sideways, Uting first, supporting me as I followed. My left hand was sore from being held so tightly in his. I gripped both trekking poles with my right hand and jabbed the earth as we slid slowly downward. When we finally reached the river below, we both stepped into it. Uting's feet never wavered across the rocky bottom. He held me up again as we crossed and braced ourselves against the fast current. If either of us let go, I would assuredly lose my balance and find myself carried off by the great Kapuas River, the longest in Indonesia.

Every night, we made camp on high ground near the river. First, the men cleared trees and bush with machetes. Next, they put down a blue plastic tarp to serve as the tent floor for the night. Around the tarp, they built a frame from small trees, expertly whittling the ends to sharp points so they could drive them into the earth. Over the frame, they draped another blue plastic tarp, stretching it across the high middle branch to tie off at the edges and form a peaked roof. They built a fire in one corner under the tarp, with another frame above it for drying branches and clothes. Every night we did this, sleeping on the bumpy jungle ground with no walls surrounding us while rain pelted the tarp.

One morning, after a particularly strong rainstorm, Pete and I brushed our teeth on the banks of the river, balancing on large rocks as we leaned over the rushing water.

"You know," Pete said. "I don't know about you, but I find that as I lie awake listening to the sounds of the jungle, I systematically question every life choice I've ever made."

I had a mouth full of toothpaste, but I nodded. I knew exactly what he meant.

We called the youngest of the four men who led us through the jungle "Eagle." This was a westernization of his actual name, which none of us could pronounce. He was our lookout and advance scout. I don't think there was any part of his body that wasn't muscle. He was a part of the jungle in a way that made it seem like he had sprung directly from its floor, emerging whole and spectacular from the mud and roots wielding a machete in one hand and grasping the arm of a helpless tourist in the other.

Whenever we came upon a particularly dangerous part of the trail, Eagle would be waiting for Uting and me. These parts of the path were treacherous enough that the men knew I would need two of them to help me navigate. A few of these were river crossings where the current was exceptionally strong. Uting took one of my hands, Eagle the other, and we walked slowly across, bracing ourselves against the powerful water as it rushed to the sea. Another instance was a sheer twelve-foot drop-off to the rocky riverbank, with very few roots to grab hold of. Uting tied a rope from a tree above, and Eagle went before me, his hands on my back as I slowly descended.

One night, after making camp and cooking dinner, the Dayak men disappeared into the darkness wielding spears made from tree branches. An hour later, they showed up carrying an enormous wild boar they had killed with a single spear shot through the neck. They cut him open right away, and we ate seared wild boar by the light of the fire — the best pork I have ever had.

Another evening, while playing cards, Pete and Ben played some music from their phone into a small speaker.

"Bob Seeegar, do you know Bob Seeegar? He is rocking!" Oddie said.

"Bob Seeegar?" I asked. Then I recognized "Trying to Live My Life Without You" coming from the speaker.

"Oh, Bob Seger. Yes, I know his music. I grew up with his music."

And there we were — two Brits, a Dutchman, an American, two Indonesians, and four men of the Dayak tribe — rocking out to "Bob Seeegar" deep in the heart of the Borneo jungle.

Walking out of the jungle is vastly different from walking into it. I walked out a different person from the one who walked in. We never really know how deep our strength and resolve go until we've spent weeks scaling slippery rocks and steep cliffs, traversing rivers with intense currents, climbing root and mud stairs, and slogging through muddy bogs that come up to the ankles, all while wearing the same wet, dirty, smelly clothes day after day, and spending the nights trying to sleep on a tarp on the hard, uneven earth.

These are not things found in the everyday world of a westerner from a first-world country. These are the night terrors they talk about in *Game of Thrones*. These are the pictures in *National Geographic* magazine that cause us to wonder whether they are staged. These are the places travel magazines don't write about. This is the jungle where people have died, their stories told by the boatmen and villagers we met along the way.

We walked out of the jungle together into the village of Tiong Ohang, which has a couple of paved roads, WiFi at the hospital, and a colorful, clean local house with rooms for rent. Our rooms were on the second floor off a large, common, open-air living space with a balcony on one end. After dinner, we bought all the beer we could find in the village, to the point where the shopkeepers just started giving it to us for free because we'd spent so much money already. We sat on the balcony, laughing and talking in a crazy mixture of Indonesian and English. Eagle left at one point to procure more alcohol. He came back with a clear liquor in a plastic bag that could burn the hair from one's nostrils. We drank it from small glasses, toasting each other over and over.

I'm not sure yet about this new person who walked out of the jungle. I am still reconciling the jungle with my reality of subways and traffic, clean socks, and endless drinkable water from the tap. And I'm still trying to figure out all the ways that I've changed.

I don't know how to tell people about all the times I almost died. I no longer am even sure why it's important. Danger isn't confined to only a specific geography. Life is always just on the edge of death, no matter where we are or what kind of jungle we are walking through.

What I do know is that, despite its myriad dangers, the world is still a wondrous place filled with kind, honest people. I know we can't compare pain or journeys or trials. But I also know that walking the same streets day after day is no way to live — at least not for me.

~V.A. Nirode

Electing Risk

*The whole secret of a successful life is to find out
what is one's destiny to do, and then do it.*
~Henry Ford

On a bright San Francisco morning in the spring of 1996, I received a call from my friend Ellen. We had served together in the Peace Corps in Guatemala in the early 1990s. After we exchanged greetings, she asked cheerily if I would like to go to Bosnia. I was startled; a war had only recently ended in Bosnia.

Ellen went on to tell me that a mutual Peace Corps friend had told her that the U.S. State Department was recruiting former Peace Corps volunteers who had domestic election experience. Those chosen would be UN Volunteers (UNVs) and work as election supervisors for the first post-war elections in Bosnia. Ellen went on to explain the timelines and expected deployment date for the project. If I was interested, I had to respond in twenty-four hours. I told Ellen I would think it over.

For the rest of the day, I was torn by conflicting thoughts. *Bosnia may be dangerous; do I really want to put myself in that kind of situation? I am over sixty years old. I am too old to go off on a new and risky path. What will my kids think?*

Then different kinds of thoughts, more positive, began tiptoeing into my mind. *I wonder what Bosnia would be like. This could be a challenging new experience; I do like challenges. If I turn it down, I may never get another chance.* In the end, the positive thoughts won.

A few weeks later, I was on a plane to Vienna to be briefed. I was assigned to an area near Tuzla in the northeastern part of Bosnia and Herzegovina. My partner was from Connecticut and had been a Peace Corps volunteer in Poland. We lived with a young family with two young children. When we chatted, they told us of the many horrors of living through a war. The resilience and courage with which they faced the present and the future were striking. The Bosnians in the greater community, with whom we worked and interacted, were as strong and welcoming as our host family.

Election Day in our area went without incident. Long lines of citizens were eager to exercise their right to vote.

I spent three interesting and captivating weeks in Bosnia. A month or so after I returned home, I was asked if I would like to return and participate in a run-off election. I said "yes" immediately.

It has been more than twenty years since I made the decision to let my positive thoughts override my negative ones. I have gone on to work on many elections in Eastern Europe, Asia and Africa. I have managed camps for internally displaced persons (IDPs) in Herat, Afghanistan, and I've done development work in Kandahar, Afghanistan. When I accepted my first Bosnia assignment, I had traveled to three foreign countries. My count is now fifty-eight. I continue to volunteer internationally.

Had I listened back in 1996 to the voice inside telling me not to take a risk, I wouldn't be telling this story. Fortunately, I followed the voice that said, "Do it" and I found a new life after sixty!

~John Dwyer

68

Broke and Traveling the World

You don't have to be rich to travel well.
~Eugene Fodor

How in the world did we end up living in London for two months? After living in Oslo, Norway for five weeks? With many more adventures to come!

Our world seemed very bleak a year ago—no job, no home, and what felt like no future. We were very fortunate to be living with our older son, so we were not homeless yet. But we didn't want to continue to impose on a relative, even if it was our son.

My husband and I were so excited two years earlier when we sold our home and moved from San Diego to Manhattan. We have another son who lives in Brooklyn, we had a job waiting for us, and we love New York City. Little did we know what a disaster it would be financially and mentally. The job did not work out, and the apartment we rented was way too expensive for us. So a year and a half later, we returned to California with no money, no job and very depressed.

After several months of looking for a job and not finding one, I decided I would need to find a less traditional job as a freelancer or on contract. With that thought, it seemed like an ideal time to ask myself, *What do I really want to do if I could do anything?* Travel is my passion, so the first thing that came to mind was to be a travel writer. But could I compete with all the established travel writers in the industry? In addition, to be a travel writer, I was going to have to pick up the phone and make calls. I have what I call a phone phobia. To make this work, I would need to get over it.

I started my new career as a travel writer close to home. The first article I sold to a magazine was about the Gold Rush towns in California near where I was living. Things started to look up after that.

We wanted to travel, and we could swing the plane tickets, but we didn't have enough money to pay for hotels as well. We started looking at alternative living opportunities, like caretaker positions. That's when we discovered the world of housesitting.

Our first housesit, for almost a month, was in a tiny town called Coloma in California. This was where the California Gold Rush started at Sutter's Mill. We were very fortunate because the homeowner was looking for someone close by who had experience with Border Collies, which we did. And what did I have to do to get this first assignment? Talk to the homeowner on the phone. When my phone rang, I forced myself to answer. Sara was wonderful, and at the end of the call she said she would be thrilled to have us come sit for her dog, Tessa.

After several housesitting stints, from San Diego, California to Portland, Oregon, we started looking at housesits in other countries. We were so excited when we got our first international sit in Oslo, Norway for five weeks watching over four beautiful cats.

As I write this, we have been in London for a month with about a month to go. After this, we are going to several other towns in England and one in Scotland. The couple we housesat for in Oslo has invited us back for two weeks in July—not to housesit, but just as friends. After that, we have a housesit in Rome, and we round out this adventure with one more sit in Copenhagen for August. By the time we go home, we will have been in Europe for nine months, visited ten countries, completed twelve housesitting assignments, and taken care of two goldfish, twelve cats, and fourteen dogs.

Housesitting has changed our lives forever. We have met dozens of wonderful people in several countries (many of them are now friends) and have stayed in some amazing places. The memories, encouragement, successes and experiences in the last year are irreplaceable. I would like to say "thank you" to all the homeowners who have trusted us with their homes and, more importantly, their pets. They have made a difference in our lives and helped us take a big step toward a brighter future.

With our travels, I have been able to write and sell travel articles to several magazines, websites and newspapers. A year ago, I would never have believed I would become an international travel writer and live all over the world. And our journey does not end here; we have many more places to go.

~Cynthia Graham

69

The Oddity

On this shrunken globe, men can
no longer live as strangers.
~Adlai E. Stevenson

Majoring in Portuguese was a great way to turn big, impersonal Harvard University into a small college. I was the only student in the major so I had the two professors of Portuguese doting on me. The only problem was that there weren't enough "Portuguese and Brazilian Studies" courses available to fulfill the requirements!

The obvious solution was a semester abroad, which would get me a bunch of Portuguese credits. But, back in the 1970s, good old Harvard believed that no experience could match staying on campus. I had to petition some august assemblage of deans in those ivy-covered buildings for permission to study abroad during my junior year. It took months for the verdict to come down, and I felt like I was waiting for a Papal Edict or something of that magnitude.

I got the okay, and became perhaps the first Harvard student to get academic credit for studying abroad. At age twenty, I was on a plane to Rio de Janeiro for the greatest adventure of my life. I started with a six-week language immersion course and some Outward Bound–esque training that involved dropping us off twenty miles away with no money — to see if we could use our language skills to get fed and cared for by kind strangers.

Then I was off to the poverty-stricken northeast of Brazil to do research for my thesis for a couple of months. Somehow, I had heard about an esoteric type of Brazilian literature called *literatura de cordel*, meaning "literature on strings." These were crudely printed little booklets — *folhetos* — that were displayed hanging from strings in the marketplaces. These *folhetos* were the way that lower-income Brazilians shared folklore, fairy tales, and stories about miracles and religious figures and local heroes. In addition, there were famous improvisational singers — *cantadores* — who would engage in singing battles against each other, surrounded by hundreds of their fans. Their songs and exploits would become fodder for new *folhetos*.

When I look back on it, it was pretty crazy. I traveled all over the interior of Brazil by bus via the Amazon Highway, speaking only Portuguese. I had a gold ring on every finger, there were no cell phones, and no one knew where I was. It's remarkable that nothing bad happened to me, but I expected the best and that's what I got. (I also told everyone that my gold rings were fake. This was in a place where even wedding rings were just some kind of worthless beaten metal, so everyone believed me.)

People were so kind and helpful. When I needed to meet someone for my research, the connection would be made. I was known throughout the *literatura de cordel* community in the vast Northeast of Brazil as *a pesquisadora americana* (the American researcher). Wherever I went, there were newspaper interviews and sit-down lunches with the local bigwigs of the community. I went to the singing battles and they would sing about me, the *pesquisadora*, and I'd sit up there with the *cantadores* in front of the crowds.

I went into communities that had never before seen someone as pale as I was. In one town, deep in the interior, I found myself surrounded by about fifty women and children of *Indios* descent. They stood around me in a circle, staring, and occasionally one of them would be brave enough to run over, touch my waist-length blond hair or look into my blue eyes, and then run back to the circle, giggling. I was an oddity — a freak. I took a couple of steps in one direction to see what would happen and the whole circle moved with me. I took two steps back and the circle moved back with me.

I was traveling among the poor and I was living like them too. I stayed in the most disgusting, ramshackle $5-a-night hotels you can imagine, filled with the sick and downtrodden who were on religious pilgrimages to the places I was visiting, which were hotbeds of local saints, religious heroes, and legends of miraculous healing. I still vividly recall one tiny hotel bathroom where I was eye to eye with the largest cockroach I'd ever seen, several inches long and no more than two inches from my face as I raced through the fastest shower of my life.

I spent those months interviewing poets, *folheto* vendors, the people who printed them, the *cantadores*, local scholars, and everyone else I could find who had anything to do with the popular literature community. And boy did I collect stories. That's what my thesis ended up being — one story after another about the lives of all the colorful characters I encountered.

Of course it was the best semester I ever spent "at Harvard" and what I got from that time in Brazil was invaluable. It set me up for everything that was to come in my adult life, giving me faith in the kindness of strangers, teaching me inner strength and resilience, training me to connect with people I didn't know and elicit their stories, and preparing me for the hard, lonely trips that were to come in my business career. Those months in the northeast of Brazil, which were scary, surreal *and* magical, created reserves of strength and trust inside me that I still draw on, four decades later.

~Amy Newmark

70

The Experiment

It is mutual trust, even more than mutual interest,
that holds human associations together.
~H. L. Mencken

Fall 1992. I have just arrived in the United Arab Emirates to teach English at the university in Al Ain. The English Department chair calls me into his office.

"How would you like to participate in an historic experiment?" he says.

"Historic experiment?"

"Yes. We would like to integrate our teaching staff on the women's campus with men. I am offering this opportunity to four carefully selected teachers."

"When do you have to know my decision?"

"Now. Classes start in one week."

"Yes. I am honored," I say. "Thank you."

As a new instructor, I want to start off on the right foot with my new boss, even though I know that, in a Muslim country, interacting with female students is a high-risk activity. If the experiment fails, I could be sent home the next day with my wife and children.

I report to the women's campus for teacher orientation. During a break, I explore the classroom building to locate my assigned room. I walk briskly down the hallway, turn a corner, and collide full-force with someone coming the other way. The impact rocks both of us back a step. As I apologize profusely, I discover that I have run into a student. She is wearing a traditional abaya, a black garment covering her from head to foot but leaving her face bare. She stares back at me in wide-eyed horror. Then her expression changes to pure disgust. She yanks her abaya across her face, stumbles around me, and races down the hall, out of the building. I remain in the hallway stunned and embarrassed, but with a better understanding of the challenge that lies ahead. I have second thoughts about my hasty decision to volunteer.

During orientation, I seek support from the other men in the experiment: two British nationals, Kevin and Nigel, and an Egyptian, Hedi. They are also nervous and uncertain. We agree that the key to our success is to respect our students' need for physical distance from us, to establish trust, and to demonstrate the highest standards of professionalism. Hedi tells us that his challenge is not as daunting as ours since he is an Arab and a Muslim, while we are neither.

"I don't envy you," Hedi says. "But I am sure you will succeed, *inshallah* (God willing)."

The first day of class arrives. I still do not feel ready. At five minutes to nine, I take my class roster and head to the classroom building. At the entrance, I meet Kevin.

"Well, then," he says, "it's into the breach! 'Ours is not to reason why...'" I am glad he doesn't finish the quotation. We wish each other luck and enter the building.

I navigate my way through hallways filled with perfume and the black shapes of young women in abayas scurrying about trying to find their classrooms. I wonder how they can see through their face coverings. I make wide turns around each corner until I reach my classroom. The door is open. I take a deep breath and enter.

Sixteen students cloaked in black sit silently in the last two of four rows of chairs spread across the room. They stiffen as I enter. All have covered their faces, a few completely, and the rest with various types of *niqab* (veils or masks) leaving only their eyes exposed. I find it disconcerting not to see my students' faces. I see only eyes, heavily mascaraed, nervous, and frightened.

"Good morn..." I begin. My voice cracks. "Excuse me." I clear my throat. "Good morning." I smile and position myself strategically between the blackboard and the teacher's desk. I wonder if my smile is being returned, and, if so, by whom.

"Good morning, sir," the students respond in unison as though they had practiced.

I write my last name on the blackboard and pronounce it for them. I have them repeat it. I pick up my class roster and begin roll call. The students' family names are so long that they run off the side of the printout. I stick with first names. I am pleased when the first few students recognize my pronunciation of their names. Each student responds by raising her right hand and saying, "Here, sir." But when I call out "Fatima," many hands shoot up. I scan the upraised hands.

"You are all Fatimas?" I say.

"Yes," says one of them. "We are eight Fatimas, sir." I laugh. The students look at each other. I hear stifled laughter from behind the veils of two or three students, enough to tell me they have a sense of humor.

I use the second name on the printout to distinguish Fatimas. When I finish roll call, one student tentatively raises her hand.

"Sir," she says. "What is your first name?" I recall that in some Middle Eastern countries, it is acceptable to call a teacher by his or her first name.

"You will like my first name," I say. "It is an EXCELLENT first name." The students lean forward in their chairs expectantly.

I pick up the chalk and slowly write F-A-T-I-M-A.

Even before I finish writing the name, laughter begins. It grows until it fills the room. The ice has broken. I replace "Fatima" with "David" and present my lesson, which goes smoothly.

By the end of the week, I settle into a routine. I learn to distinguish my Fatimas by the number of gold bangles on their wrists and the intricate henna markings on their hands. Identification becomes easier when one Fatima comes to class with her face uncovered. I am elated. I have won her trust.

In the weeks ahead, I measure my progress one veil at a time. By mid-semester, all but two students have uncovered their faces. Both students are religiously conservative women from small villages. One is shy but participates in class activities. The other is angry and disrupts class to the point that I refer her to an advisor who transfers her to another class. I fear I have endangered the experiment. The advisor informs me that the student's objection is not that I am a man, but that I am a non-Muslim.

My students and I are happy she has been reassigned. We continue to build a positive relationship throughout the semester (while having a little fun along the way). A few students even brave meeting with me in my office to receive additional help. I check with the other three men in the experiment who tell me that their classes are also going smoothly.

At the end of the term, the English Department chair evaluates the four classes taught by men and deems the experiment a success. From that day forward, men are allowed to teach on the women's campus. In the process, I have moved from anxiety and uncertainty to confidence and comfort in my interactions with women students on the women's campus of the United Arab Emirates University and beyond.

~D.E. Brigham

71

Role Models

*Being a mother is learning about the strengths you
didn't know you had... and dealing with
fears you didn't know existed.*
~Linda Wooten

was living in a fog of grief. My daughters and mother took turns
spending the night with me after my husband died in a bicycle
accident. My daughters had lost their dad. My mother lost a man
she considered her son for more than forty years. They were hurting too, but my pain was so deep I wasn't able to comfort them.

That first month seemed to go on without end, yet I felt as if Tom
had just walked out the door moments before. As December drew
near, my youngest daughter and her family came by with dinner. I'm
not sure I was fully engaged in the conversation. Kendall was talking
about a mission trip her church was sponsoring.

"I've always wanted to go, Mom, but it seems every other time
they've done this trip, I was pregnant with one of the girls."

I tried to listen. I nodded here and there as if the fog surrounding
me had cleared.

"They send a team to work with young women who've been
rescued from human trafficking situations," Kendall went on to say.
It sounded scary. I hoped she wasn't thinking about joining them this
year. She was a wife and mother. Her family needed her. *I* needed her.

"The trip's in April," she said. "I thought you and I could go together."

What? Me? Go on a mission trip? Where did she say this was? I searched my brain for a clue tucked away from her earlier comments. *India. That was it. Was she suggesting I travel halfway around the world? I could barely make it out of bed in the morning.*

"This will be the last week to apply." Kendall looked at me. Waiting. She had that same expectant look she had as a little girl pleading with me to take her for a milkshake. This was so much more than a trip to McDonald's.

April was five months away. Next year.

Next year sounded distant. What could I say or do to help these girls? I was spent. I had nothing to offer. I studied my daughter's face.

"Okay." My voice was weak and lacked enthusiasm.

Kendall spent the next week getting our application forms ready. I spent the next week wondering why I had agreed to the trip. I hadn't prayed about the experience. I hadn't weighed all the pros and cons. Did my daughter know something I didn't know? Perhaps helping others was good for grieving widows.

Serving others was always a good thing to do, but couldn't I find a community project closer to my home in Ohio? Did I need to travel to a place where I didn't know the language? A place that served foods I couldn't pronounce? What could I possibly do for these young women who had suffered unimaginable and often torturous circumstances?

I decided to attend the first meeting in January with Kendall. It would give me time to pray for a way out.

I looked around the large meeting room. Yes, there were people younger than me, but I wasn't the oldest, either. Several young women and a few young men were anxious to make a difference in the world. An older couple sat at the table next to me. That was hard. Where did I fit? I wasn't young, but I wasn't old. I was no longer part of a couple, but I didn't feel single either. The leader had an activity for us to complete and a video to watch. There was a question-and-answer period and more forms to fill out. No one looked at me and said, "What in the world are you doing here?" I decided to read the booklet they provided.

I studied the booklet. Kendall and I brainstormed ideas to raise funds for the trip. Perhaps I wouldn't be able to raise the needed monies. That would be a sign from God that I should stay home, wouldn't it? Stay home and... stay home and do what? By the third meeting, I knew I was going to India for ten days in April. I was entering a world so far from the life I knew and understood, I could hardly breathe. And to get there I had to fly.

I had always been afraid of flying. Each time my husband and I flew somewhere, I prayed we'd make it home. This time proved different. As the plane took off, I realized I had no fear of flying. When we finally made it to Dubai, I realized I had no fear of the work ahead. Living without fear and serving side by side with my daughter? Breathing came easier.

Here I was in a strange land, eating strange foods, and working with girls once kidnapped or sold into the sex-trafficking business. One girl revealed she had been sold into slavery by her uncle at age nine. She was rescued when she was seventeen. But most of the girls didn't speak of the past. They were looking to the future. They were going to school. They had dreams and plans.

All I could offer was the "mom" in me — the woman who could smile with them, laugh at their jokes, and laugh with them when I mispronounced a word or a name. We sang familiar songs in different languages, did crafts together, and shared meals.

One evening, I sat on the floor working a puzzle with five of the girls. I leaned back on my elbows. A voice seemed to wash over me. *You are exactly where you need to be.*

I've had to face many situations that challenged me since that trip to India. I learned how to change the filter in my furnace. I learned how to start my lawnmower and take care of the yard. I had to negotiate the purchase of a new car. To most people, those tasks seem small, but to me they were huge. Before India, I would cry when I had to open my late husband's toolbox for a screwdriver.

India stretched me. Through that experience, I found an inner strength. Those brave, resilient girls I was sent to serve taught me a greater lesson than I could ever have imparted to them. After everything they had been through, *they* showed *me* how to look to the future.

~Rebecca Waters

Chapter 8

STEP OUTSIDE YOUR COMFORT ZONE

☑ Find Love

72

Leaving the Swamp

Inaction breeds doubt and fear. Action breeds
confidence and courage. If you want to
conquer fear, do not sit home and think
about it. Go out and get busy.
~Dale Carnegie

When my wife died of kidney failure in 2006, I withdrew socially. Other than dealing with people at my job as a newspaper reporter, I spent most of my time alone at my Arkansas home. I had been married for eleven-and-a-half years and had settled comfortably into the role of married life. I didn't want to meet new people. I feared any connection I might make with someone new would only end again.

The grieving process was a lonely journey. I adopted a shelter cat, and I was content spending my evenings watching television or reading books while the cat vied for my attention.

That contentment was reinforced when I tried dating. Two old girlfriends found me within a year or two after my wife's passing. Each relationship was dysfunctional, mostly because of my fear of losing again. These relationships ended amicably, and I returned to my lone ways.

Then my cat died. I was tired of loss. Venturing out was pointless because it would only result in meeting someone, becoming attached emotionally, and then experiencing more abandonment. So I accepted my solitary lifestyle.

The only social connections I really made were with "friends" on

Facebook. It was the perfect medium. It was a fitting way to get a hint of personal socialization without getting too close.

But the very medium I used to avoid the outside world led me to an entirely new world. And my concept of infrequent contact was shattered when I found myself craving more interaction with one person.

One of my "friends" was a Boston law professor who had another friend, Holly, who lived north of Chicago. She would join in during some of our posted "conversations" about sports or news or just life in general. One of us would come up with some spirited, fun discussion that the others would join in on. Holly and I began sending chat messages on occasion. The frequency increased, and we would spend several hours in the evening chatting back and forth. Surprisingly, I found myself looking forward to the evenings so I could resume chatting with Holly.

Our chats were deep at times; we'd talk about our childhoods and family lives. At other times, they were light and jovial. We developed our own inside jokes and referred to them often.

The chats evolved into a phone call one evening that lasted over three hours. The more I talked with Holly, the more I realized she was a special person.

I learned she was selling her home, and I blurted out one evening that I would help her with cleaning her yard in preparation for the sale if she wanted. It was totally out of character for me. Since my wife died, the furthest venture I had made was a 250-mile round trip to St. Louis to watch a Cardinals baseball game alone. Now, I was offering to drive 554 miles to northern Illinois to rake leaves.

Weird.

I think Holly thought it was weird as well. A guy offering to drive that far to do yard work sounded more like the makings of a murder story that appears on *Dateline NBC*. Reporter Keith Morrison would stroll down the street, saying pensively, "If only she hadn't worried about those leaves...."

Holly told me she'd think about it. When I looked at it from her point of view, I realized how odd my offer was and understood her hesitancy.

But a few days later, she messaged me, saying if I really wanted to come up and help, she'd appreciate it.

That led me to gassing up the car and driving the 554 miles to meet her in September 2015. Seeing her in person, obviously, was much better than talking on the phone. As the week progressed, I found that getting to know her was rekindling feelings I hadn't experienced since my wife passed away. I was fifty-five then, but this had me bumbling around like a seventeen-year-old kid on prom night.

On the second night of my visit, we watched for a lunar eclipse that most of the country was waiting for. It was cloudy, and we never saw it, but that didn't matter to me. I was star-struck just being in her presence. And later, when I drove her home and made the four-mile trek back to my hotel, I got lost both in bliss and along the road. The trip was a straight line from her house to the hotel. A three-year-old who could do dot-to-dot puzzles could easily figure out the path. But I failed and forgot where the turn was. When I did find it, I pulled into the wrong lane and, when seeing a car headed for me, I drove over the median helter-skelter, thumping over curbs and drawing the wrath of those who knew how to drive. I embarrassed myself all while wearing a goofy grin.

I stayed there a week, and it was blissful. We visited a lighthouse and beach park on Lake Michigan. We bought groceries like a married couple and walked her dog in her neighborhood at nights. I raked her yard and bagged the leaves. We also hooked up a DVD player in the hotel and watched movies.

The last night I was there, we watched *Shrek*. Those of you who have kids know the film; I had never seen it. The premise of the 2001 movie is an ogre who lives alone in a swamp and enjoys his reclusiveness. His solitude is interrupted when he and a talking donkey are enlisted to rescue a princess. In the end, Shrek wins the princess and finds friends, all by leaving his swamp.

Later, as we talked about the week we had, Holly noted that I, like Shrek, had "left my swamp" after I told her I broke from the routine of my own world and ventured out.

Six weeks later, I returned to see Holly. Then in January, she took a train to visit me in Arkansas. I made seventeen more trips to see her in 2016. Sixteen times, I drove back alone. On my seventeenth trip back, I wasn't alone. Holly had sold her house, and she, her two cats and a dog came back with me.

She's been with me now for eleven months, and we've created a life of our own. Two years ago, I was afraid to step out of the box I had created, the protective shell I developed so I would no longer feel loss. One Internet message, one phone call, and one trip changed all that. I shed the shackles of loneliness and despair, and found true love by leaving my swamp.

~Kenneth Heard

73

Making Miracles

*A journey is best measured in
friends, rather than miles.*
~Tim Cahill

M any years ago, I was living in Los Angeles and pursuing a career in television. I was a page at CBS, where I did audience coordinating for shows like *The Price Is Right*, *Dancing with the Stars* and *American Idol*. Then I became a Production Assistant at *Entertainment Tonight* and *The Insider*, where I worked crazy hours and did grunt work until I worked my way up to be an Online Producer and write for the website. My big break came when a Producer brought me on as an Associate Producer for a new show. It was a co-production with China, so we wrote and filmed all the segments in L.A., and then translated everything into Mandarin and aired the show in China.

Since we were a small production, I got to do everything: coordinating, writing, and producing. I even got to attend red carpet premieres and do interviews with celebrities like George Clooney, Angelina Jolie, Zac Efron and The Rock. It was fun and exciting, and a fantastic professional opportunity. I loved my job, and it seemed like I was on my way to a long, successful career in TV production.

Less than two years later, our humble startup lost its funding. One by one, our employees were let go. I scrambled to find a new job, knowing my own doomsday wasn't far away. Little did I know that the day I was let go would be the last day I would work in Hollywood.

Since I was a freelance producer, I wasn't eligible to collect unemployment. I applied for every job I could find, not just in production, but in food service, retail, sales, etc. Although I found a few freelance gigs and temp jobs, it wasn't enough to cover my expenses. I stuck it out for eight months before I realized my savings were running out. My only option, if I didn't want to couch surf or burden my friends, was to move back in with my parents. For a hardworking, ambitious, stubborn twenty-nine-year-old, it felt like I was stamping a big "Loser" sign on my back and letting everyone know I couldn't make it on my own. I cried during the entire drive to San Diego and vowed that as soon as I found a job, I'd move back to L.A.

During the initial months at my parents' house, I was too ashamed to go out, fearing I'd run into people from my past. I figured the first thing anyone would ask me was, "Where are you living?" and "Where are you working?" I didn't want to hear these questions because I was ashamed of the answers. Looking back, although my feelings and depression were very real, I sentenced myself to that prison because of my own definitions of success and failure. I had no idea how many people would sympathize with my circumstance, and perhaps it would have helped to find some people like me who could have been my allies.

Despite my feelings of shame, I knew I had to do something to pull myself out of my self-inflicted misery. I joined a San Diego hiking group on Meetup.com, where they have common-interest groups and social events. I figured hiking would be a fun way to go out and get some exercise. Although there were tons of different events, I talked myself out of going for weeks.

Finally, on the Fourth of July, I had no plans to party, barbecue or watch fireworks, and decided I didn't want to stay at home and be lonely. When I got to the meetup location, I saw close to thirty people lined up with their hiking packs. I looked around and noticed everyone was much older than me. Sure, I had gotten out of the house, but I didn't want to hike with all of these older people. I questioned if I could make it back to my car without anyone noticing, but when everyone started introducing themselves, I knew it was too late.

As the hike went on, the big mass began to break up into smaller groups. I noticed three young girls and a guy. They looked about my age, so I decided to hike with them. It turned out that none of them had ever met before that hike. I don't remember what we talked about, but the conversation just seemed to flow naturally. It was like we had known each other for years. When we got to the bottom of the trail, our small group decided to go out for coffee. While we were making our post-hike plans, another younger guy walked up and asked if he could join us.

That day at Starbucks, the six of us talked and laughed for hours. Before we parted ways, we exchanged phone numbers and e-mails and made plans to coordinate another hike. I knew from the start that this was a special group of people, and I wanted to get to know them better. I wasn't optimistic this would turn into anything more than a single random encounter, but thank goodness I was wrong. We hiked all the popular trails in San Diego, but we didn't just hike. We got together to celebrate birthdays, attended plays, and went to holiday-themed events. The six of us had a special connection, something I'd never experienced before. My newfound friends didn't care that I was unemployed or lived with my mom and dad. They made me feel like a normal person despite my circumstances. They shared their positive energy and made me feel like a part of something special, instead of the outcast I imagined I was.

Although the six of us remained close, we brought mutual friends and significant others into our group. Almost four years after that first hike, we've hiked Mt. Whitney, attended weddings, celebrated babies, and have been there for each other through the good times and the bad.

A few years later, when I was finally working full-time and living on my own in San Diego, I decided to put myself out there once more. The experience with my hiking friends gave me the confidence to try new things and meet new people. I decided to join an adult coed kickball team. After I registered for the league, I jokingly told one of my friends, "Hey, maybe I'll meet my future husband."

The first day of kickball, we went out for pre-game drinks (this obviously wasn't a competitive league). I joined the team as a free agent, so I didn't know a single one of my teammates. I met Drew for the first time at that pre-game happy hour. From the moment I met him, I knew there was something special about him. He had an amazing smile, he was upbeat and positive, and we could joke with each other from the start. After that first kickball game, I texted my friend and said, "I met this really cool guy on my kickball team. I know we just met, but I really do think there's something special about him."

It turns out that Drew felt the same instant connection. He had just moved to San Diego for work and joined the kickball team to meet new people. As the weeks went on, there was no denying our chemistry. We started dating, and it was like nothing I had ever experienced before. We could make each other laugh and had a great time together, but we could also be open and honest with each other. I've always heard people say, "When you know, you know," but I never thought it would happen to me.

After we had been dating for a few months, I brought Drew to one of our group hikes. Of course, my hiking friends had already heard all about him, but he passed the litmus test with flying colors. At this point, the group had become more like family than friends, so the fact that they loved Drew just made everything better.

A year later, Drew asked if we could plan a sunset hike. We sent a text to the group and planned to meet at Cowles Mountain, hike to the top and enjoy the sunset from the peak. Little did I know, Drew and the group had a surprise waiting for me at the summit. As the sun began to set, Drew got down on one knee and proposed to me in front of our closest friends. After I said "yes," our friends pulled out champagne and snacks from their hiking packs. They had been in on the plan and helped Drew pull off the best proposal I could have asked for. Not only did I get to marry the man of my dreams, he asked me in front of the people who had seen me at my lowest and decided to love me anyway.

Drew and I got married this past spring, and our hiking friends were all there to celebrate with us. One was by my side as a bridesmaid, and another actually performed the ceremony. Having them there as a part of our special day meant the world to us.

My life didn't work out the way I thought it would. I'm not a big-time Hollywood producer with millions of dollars, but I have more blessings than I can count, and it seems to me like I got the better end of the deal. To Drew and my hiking friends (we still need a better group name, by the way), thank you for loving me and making me a better person than I could ever have been on my own.

~Maile Timon

74

Leap of Faith

*Every great move forward in your life begins with
a leap of faith, a step into the unknown.*
~Brian Tracy

I sat at my desk and poised my fingers to type. Another cardiology report, and for it I was thankful, but something had been missing in my life for a while. I'd been a medical transcriptionist for four years. It was a wonderful opportunity to work from home so I could be an active and present part of our three daughters' lives. That morning, I dropped our eldest at kindergarten and returned home to let our two younger children play while I worked. But it hit me like a tall wave slamming into my body — my career wasn't really making a difference in anyone's life. I wanted to help someone. I needed a job that would help change the world for the better — something that would stretch my limits and push me to grow. I bowed my head and prayed, "Lord, please show me what you want me to do."

Something began to stir within me, like a soft wind. I didn't have a clue where it would carry our family in the months to come, but I followed it. I was carried along with it like a seed venturing out to find fertile ground.

Softly and gently, I began to see what God wanted for us. We had a loving home, stable jobs, and room in our hearts to spare. I didn't need a different career. This career was perfect, as it provided me with the ability to work from home. What I wanted to do was become a foster mother. I could keep this job, work from home, and provide safety for a child who needed it desperately.

Two nervous days passed during which I wrestled my heart against my practical side. *This is too much. You can't be a parent to a stranger's child. But that child isn't a burden or a problem. It will be a blessing.* My husband and I had a conversation on Sunday afternoon and agreed: Foster parenting was in our future.

On Monday morning, my heart pounded as I picked up the phone and dialed the number I had Googled for the nearest Department of Children's Services. The man on the other end was receptive to my questions and explained the next step: Parents as Tender Healers training. It involved eight weeks of once-a-week classes designed to prepare and educate prospective foster parents. We put our names on the list and headed to our first class a few weeks later.

Intense. That was my one word to describe those classes. My second was *scary*. The children in foster care had experienced such terrible trauma. How in the world could one little set of good parents help alleviate the fear and negativity these poor babies had already seen? Each night after class, I asked myself, my husband, and the Lord, "Can we really do this?" "What if we take in a child and our own children suffer in some way?" "What if we are terrible at this?" "What if we can't keep up with the continuing education training, the endless paperwork, or the appointments?" So many questions, and all we had to walk on was faith. But each night we prayed and received confirmation that this was what God wanted for us. So we continued through all the classes, the horrifying statistics, home visits, background checks, and seemingly endless steps.

In August 2013, with our one-year-old, five-year-old, and seven-year-old daughters, we finally became approved foster parents. Now, we waited.

And waited.

And waited for the phone call that would ask, "Would you like to take a placement?" Every time the phone rang, my heart skipped a beat. *This call could be it! Our chance to help a child.* But the call didn't come for months, and I agonized over why. *Did we make a mistake? Did we misinterpret God's plan for us?* I was ready to give up. It was a terrible idea, a horrible plan.

When we least expected it, the phone rang. I answered, and before I knew what was happening, a car pulled in the driveway with a beautiful five-year-old girl. My heart filled when I saw her. *We were doing it. We were helping.*

The very next day, she went home to family.

This was not what I expected. I barely knew her, but I sobbed nonetheless — not because I was already attached, but because I was attached to the idea of being a foster mom. A carrot was dangled in front of my face and yanked away. And I was back to longing for the next opportunity.

Five long months after we were approved, the phone rang again. In the middle of the night, I woke my husband, dressed hurriedly, and rushed to East Tennessee Children's Hospital. Our next placement was wating for us in the emergency room. I met a Department worker at the entrance, quickly signed papers, and was directed to a room where she was waiting. She was sick, malnourished and filthy, but she was beautiful.

It didn't take long for us to realize the full depth of her trauma. It was greater than I could've imagined. Even though I had training, seeing it in person was still shocking. And heartbreaking.

Six months later, she went home to family in another state. She was safe, and we had a breather. It was time to re-group before our next placement. Time to heal ourselves from the emotional roller coaster we'd been on.

A worker arrived in our driveway with our third placement in September. She was sleeping, but woke when we entered my home. I stared into her large, scared eyes, and my heart melted. This one was different. I felt it instantly. This child, this seven-month-old miracle, was the one.

In August 2015, almost one year after we received our third foster child, her half-brother came to us by our request. We now had five children under our care, and finally had a boy in our home! He weighed a tiny four pounds, thirteen ounces. I'd never held a child this small or cared for a baby straight out of the Neonatal Intensive

Care Unit, but somehow I knew what to do. We all did. We loved and cuddled him and thanked God for him every day.

On August 12, 2016, our family of seven walked into a small courtroom. The children's lawyer and social worker were there. There was no pomp and circumstance. No balloons or fireworks. No streamers. With just a few words, our adoption was finalized. These two amazing children weren't going home, because they were already home. We are their forever family, and they are our forever children. God added two new blessings to our lives because we stepped out of our comfort zones and took a leap of faith. We may not be able to change the entire world, but we have changed the world entirely for our new children.

~Sara L. Foust

75

Stepping Over Logs

*One of the secrets of life is to make stepping
stones out of stumbling blocks.*
~Jack Penn

I used to work in the Gold Coast neighborhood of Chicago as a VP of Marketing and Public Relations. When I was first diagnosed with Parkinson's disease, my neurologist told me that walking would be good for me, so every day at lunch I tried to take a walk around the neighborhood. One day, as I was working my way down Michigan Avenue not far from the Hancock Building, I just stopped for no reason. I stood on the sidewalk, blinking, staring, and wondering what was happening.

My office was not far from Northwestern Memorial Hospital, so there were always a lot of medical people out and about at lunchtime. A woman in scrubs came up to me. "Are you alright, sir?" she asked. I nodded. "Do you think you might be having a stroke?"

"No, I'm fine," I said. "I just seem to have forgotten how to walk." Later I would learn that "freezing" in place is not uncommon for Parkinson's patients. Sometimes we just need to find a way to restart our legs.

The nurse got me to sit down on the edge of one of the planters on the street. I told her that I had Parkinson's, and she smiled. She asked me, "How long?" I told her it had been only about a month. She assured me that I hadn't been on the medicine long enough, and I was still adjusting. She took me by both hands and pulled me up. She said, "I'm going to teach you a trick. If this happens again, just focus on a crack in the sidewalk ahead of you. Pretend it is a log, and that you must step over it. Once you do, then keep going forward." She had me do it, and she was right. She gave me a hug and then went on her way. I wish I had had the presence of mind to get that woman's number so I could thank her.

One night, I was Facebook messaging with my good friend, Marko. He sent me a much-needed virtual "man-hug." We talked about challenges and obstacles we both were facing in our lives related to health, family, and work. He told me about how he had to put down his dog and how sad it made his wife. He also told me about how an old injury was bothering him, and that he thought he might need surgery to repair it. Despite his pain, he asked me, "How are you doing?" I told him that it was always a journey, and that logs sometimes get in our path. I said, "I think we figure out quickly how to step over logs, which is maybe why God put them there in the first place."

That spring, shortly after I was diagnosed, a ferocious storm went through the town where I live. So much water fell from the sky in such a short time that the gutters and drains could not keep up. There was a large drain in our back yard and a small one on the curb in front of the house, but they were no use.

Slowly but surely, the water crept up to the house, and a lot of mud came with it. Eventually, there was so much that it broke into the window wells of the basement and, because of the muck, it also clogged the drains. Both the sump and ejector pumps, which I neglected to maintain, burned out, so there was nothing we could do but hope the rain would stop falling.

I had always been handy, so I should have had that project finished in no time, but I didn't. For some reason, when I contemplated what needed to be done, I froze. The magnitude was not so huge or the complexity of the project all that hard, but I just couldn't get motivated.

My neighbor John suggested that maybe it was because doing projects like this was a reminder of things that were once easy for me but now were very hard, if not impossible. He said, "T.S., you might have to accept that you will need help and do things differently than you used to." That is very hard for me — another log I need to step over. While working in business, I was very tolerant of ambiguity and change, but in my personal life I am not.

Recently, I stood on a bridge that crosses the river near my house and started thinking a lot about the changes — the logs — that have come into my life through the natural passage of time and as my disease has progressed. Some have been for the worse, but some very much for the better. I had to stop working at a job I loved because I couldn't keep up with the pace. My two sons and my daughter grew up and moved out. My marriage of nearly thirty years collapsed, and I found myself living alone. I lost the ability to drive or to walk without a cane. In response, I started to isolate myself. I came to be known as The Hermit on Bailey Road.

Then one July day, a woman I knew well when I was fifteen called to say she was coming through town on her way back to Iowa. We had a nice lunch and talked that night when she got home safely. That call led to more calls and then more visits. Unexpectedly, love emerged. Suddenly, I was flooded not with water but with joy. After eight months, I made the momentous choice to move to Iowa to be close to her and explore all kinds of new places and opportunities.

Big changes can fill us with doubt, uncertainty and fear, but sometimes a new path is required. We need to break away and find a new, comfortable normal. The important thing is not to freeze up. We need to keep moving forward in whatever new and positive direction that means for our lives… stepping over one log at a time.

~Thomas G.M. Sharpe

76

Dream Come True

*There is no greater reward than working from your
heart, and making a difference in the world.*
~Carlos Santana

I was born and raised in Czechoslovakia, now the Czech Republic, under the Communist government. Ever since my teenage years, I dreamt about going somewhere in the world and helping others. However, I was an idealist with no self-confidence — I thought I was ugly and stupid, and I was afraid of making any changes. Because of this, I could not imagine leaving Czechoslovakia.

I did competitive ballroom dancing for fifteen years. In 1979, after I was divorced and changed dance partners, I met a wonderful dancer. We danced, practiced, traveled, competed, fell in love, and planned to get married in 1981. However, he went to Yugoslavia on vacation and never came back. I was heartbroken for a long time. Then in 1985, he bought a vacation for me in Greece, and we met there for three days. He wanted me to stay with him permanently right then and go with him to the United States, but I needed time to adjust to the idea of leaving family and friends.

One year later, I was finally ready to leave. He promised he would be waiting for me in Yugoslavia, but when I arrived, he called me from the United States and told me that he could not come.

The following day, I met a young man also from Czechoslovakia at a café. He asked me to dance with him. Even though it was dangerous to tell anyone, we admitted to each other that we both wanted to escape

Communism. Together, we tried to cross the border to Austria, but we got caught and ended up in a Zagreb prison for one night. We were caught one more time, but were released and experienced a homeless weekend on the streets. Finally, we got transit visas through Austria. We spent six months in a beautiful Austrian village near the Alps, waiting for our visas and airplane tickets. During that time, I learned a lot about opera (the young man was an opera singer), fell in love, got pregnant and lost the baby. Finally, on December 17, 1986, we arrived in Boston, where my ex-fiancé waited for us. He had agreed to sponsor us.

The next several years were spent learning the English language, and then I went back to school. I enjoyed school tremendously and did very well. I worked two, and sometimes three, jobs to pay for my living and education. I earned my associate's degree at a community college and then received a scholarship as a Davis Scholar at Wellesley College, where I lived on campus for two-and-a-half years until I graduated in 1995. I loved every class I took there, had wonderfully dedicated professors and enjoyed the most beautiful campus to walk through each day. I felt like I was in heaven.

When I thought about what to do next, I remembered my dream to travel and help others. I had no boyfriend at the time, so I decided to join the Peace Corps. I applied in January 1995, and in December I received an invitation to teach science in Cameroon. Even though I was afraid of teaching, I decided to try it.

I arrived in Cameroon in June 1996. After three months of intense training, I was posted in Tatum, a small village in the Northwest Province, where I taught biology at a secondary school. I discovered that the teachers were punishing the students physically by beating them with a stick or assigning them heavy manual labor. I knew I could never do anything like that, so I decided to use unconditional love.

It took several months of hard times before the students realized how much I loved and cared for them. From then on, everything changed. I had never experienced so much unconditional love flowing from me to them and from them to me. Before this time, I would never have thought it possible for a human being to experience so much love because I did not have a chance to give or receive love in Czechoslovakia, where I was often left alone.

The Northwest Province is the most beautiful part of Cameroon, with high mountains, beautiful waterfalls, forests, farms and streams. I felt I was in paradise. I loved every minute of every day preparing for my classes. Since we had no science lab or equipment, I took the students on many field trips, and they loved it. I also taught them a few ballroom dances after I learned that they loved to dance. I also started the Joy & Success Club after I realized that many of the students wanted to share their deeply felt spiritual beliefs. This club continues to this day and has been a model for other schools and universities in Cameroon.

I met my future husband shortly before I left for Cameroon, and we were married in the village of Tatum in 1998. I served one more year with the Peace Corps and then joined my husband in Oregon. I could not forget the many students who wished to attend school, but I could not help them all because of limited finances. Therefore, in 2000, I founded Educare-Africa, a non-profit organization dedicated to improving the living and learning conditions of students in Cameroon. I am a full-time volunteer, president, and executive director, and I travel to Cameroon annually to assist them personally.

My teenage dream came true, but it was quite a journey.

~Pavla Žáková-Laney

77

Risk and Reward

Curiosity will conquer fear even
more than bravery will.
~James Stephens

My hands were shaking. I was alone inside a Starbucks in the middle of Chicago, and I was about to take the biggest risk of my life.

You see, I was adopted at birth. Through my own investigation during adolescence, I learned that I had three full-biological siblings who were older than me. I found out their names and had been secretly keeping tabs on them via Facebook for nearly a decade. I was always waiting for the "right" time to make my move until that chilly, rainy December afternoon when I realized after years and years of pondering that there is no such thing as a "right" time.

I had recently come across a quote by Jack Kornfield in *Buddha's Little Instruction Book* that kept circling around my brain: "The trouble is, you think you have time." To me, he was saying that humankind delays taking action either because of fear or because of the fairytale idea that if we wait long enough, what we are hoping for will fall neatly in front of our feet. But what if it doesn't? Not only was I getting older, but my birth parents and siblings were getting older, too.

As I sat drinking a piping-hot Americano at a tiny wooden table and reading a book on twins separated at birth who reunited, the quote once again forced itself to the forefront of my brain. This time, it propelled me forward. I gently closed the book, grabbed my phone, and found the paragraph of text I had saved in my phone's note section for over a year. It contained what I would want my first words to my birth family to be. I clicked on that text, selected "copy," and carefully opened the Facebook application. I typed in the name of a sibling and went to her profile, and then I pressed the "message" icon for the first time. There it was: a blank page with a flashing cursor. I tapped the cursor and clicked "paste." The string of words I had once mulled over were now one button away from serving their purpose. My head was spinning, and there was only one way to make it stop. I closed my eyes, took a deep breath, and hit "send." Not even a minute later, I got a message back that read: "Wait. Huh? Lol"

With those three words, my body felt like it was on fire, and I began pacing back and forth so fast, it was as though I was running in circles.

She didn't know.

Five minutes later, after realizing I was the real deal, she called me in hysterics. I thought she was mad and apologized profusely for dropping this bombshell on her, but she kept telling me she loves me already, and she would have searched for me if she had known. After our short phone call, I immediately messaged her and asked how to refer to her. Not even two seconds later, she said, "You are my sister if you are comfortable with it."

And that I am. A shoe has never fit so perfectly.

~Alyssa Kamensky

78

A Salvage-Yard Romance

Just do it.
~Nike slogan

My old car wasn't worth the price of a new tire, so when I got a flat, I decided to check out Don's salvage yard for a used one. As I drove into his driveway one early spring afternoon, I saw a small woman bent over a flowerbed next to the house. At the same time, a man came outside chewing on a carrot. Hmm. This guy was health-conscious. Or his wife wanted to keep him on the straight and narrow road to good health.

I parked by the shop in his neat yard and got out of my old car to meet him. After introducing myself, I asked about buying a used tire. Don greeted me pleasantly and then checked my tires for size. Yes, he had one that would fit. It would cost only ten dollars, and he would change the tire for me.

I was impressed with his business manner. He treated me with respect and courtesy. I liked his soft-spoken manner.

We made small talk while he changed my tire, and then I left. But I couldn't get him out of my mind. Vaguely remembering him from our school days, I wanted more information about this gentle businessman, so I sought the advice of a friend who had been in Don's class. Was the woman Don's wife? No, my friend told me, Don had never married. She couldn't remember ever seeing him out on a date with anyone. He was shy. But he was well-liked, she added, and had a good reputation as a businessman. The woman was probably his mother.

My interest grew.

I wasn't actually looking for anyone to date. I'd been divorced for thirteen years, had my share of dates and romances since then, and was well past that stage in my life. With my children raised and gone, my single life of living with my elderly parents fit me fine. Except when my car broke down or I got a flat tire.

If I asked him out, would he accept? Or was he too shy? Or was I? I'd never asked a man out. Did I have the courage to step out of the comfortable place I'd enjoyed for the past five years? The only way I could find out was to ask. But how?

I came up with a scheme. I planned a return trip to Don's salvage yard, prepared with a long, mental script. I'd ask him if he remembered the tire he'd sold me. Then I'd say I wanted another tire just like it to use as a flower planter. What a crock! I couldn't grow a plant to save my life.

Then I'd ask him if he wanted to go on a picnic — the perfect date for a shy guy. Our picnic had to be at a quiet, isolated place. Nonthreatening.

It was time to take action. On my way back to Don's, my legs became rubber, and my mouth dried up. I felt like a silly teenager. When we settled the tire transaction (this one was free, he said with a smile) and he had loaded it into the trunk of my car, I lingered. We made small talk until… it was now or never.

"Um, how would you…" I started. "Um, would you like to go on a picnic with me next Sunday?" This was Monday. If he agreed, I'd have a whole week to control the butterflies in my stomach.

"That sounds like fun," he said, surprising me. "I haven't been on a picnic for a long time."

I told him I'd pick him up at 3:00 on Sunday, and then went home to sweat and stew over my bold actions. I was out of practice. This would be no ordinary date, for there was something special about this gentle, soft-spoken man. All week, I scolded myself for being so impetuous. Every time I pictured him in my mind, my heart pounded.

My mom chuckled while I planned my picnic-date menu, shopped and cooked. I prepared a feast. A hard-working man should have a good meal, I reasoned. I filled a tray with cheeses and cold cuts, and wrapped slices of buttered bread and filled jars with mustards, mayo, and pickles. I made coleslaw, and I baked cookies and wrapped them carefully. Then I baked a bean and ham casserole, too, and surrounded it with towels for warmth. For our healthy dessert, I included slices of out-of-season, high-priced fruit. Mom laughed. Men don't like fruit, she told me.

Then I drove over to pick up my date. We had a lovely time during a perfect day in early May. No mosquitoes yet, and long daylight hours. We watched a pair of trumpeter swans on the pond and enjoyed the antics of other birds and animals. We hiked for miles, it seemed, and I quickly learned that Don was not shy. He talked and talked. And, it turned out, his favorite food was fresh fruit.

I could tell he was as reluctant as I was to end our date. Back at his house, he introduced me to his mother — and to his cow, his calf, and his mother's chickens. You get the rural picture.

"This has been fun," he said finally. "I'll have to take *you* next time. I'll call you when you get back from your trip." I had told him of my plans to visit my sister in Arizona the following week.

Not one to leave things to chance, I bought a picture postcard of the Grand Canyon in Arizona and sent it to him.

"Having a great time," I wrote. "Wish you were here to enjoy it with me." I sealed the card in a white envelope so the postal carrier or Don's mother couldn't read it. This card was for Don's eyes only. How bold of me! But I didn't care. I'd fallen in love.

He called me after I returned home. We enjoyed a second date... and a third... and a fourth. Six weeks later, we married and lived happily ever after for the thirteen more years of his life.

Two salvage-yard romantics had leaped out of one comfort zone into another.

~Sally Bair

79

Family Day

Being a family means you are a part of something very
wonderful. It means you will love and be loved
for the rest of your life.
~Lisa Weedn

love Family Day. It's a Canadian holiday that occurs during the
same weekend as President's Day in the U.S. It was created to
give people a chance to spend more time with those they cherish
most, and that's exactly what we do. I plan something every year
to celebrate it. It's become one of my favorite days of the year, a blissful time with my two boys and my amazing husband, Mike.

It also always reminds me of the day I learned the true meaning
of family.

Right after finishing university, I got married and enrolled in a
college to get some more hands-on education. While going to school,
I also worked in a group home for adults with mental and physical
disabilities. It was there that I met Terry, a thirty-eight-year-old man
with Down syndrome. Terry had the mental capacity of a small child…
but one of the biggest hearts of anyone I've ever met.

Unlike many of the other residents, Terry hadn't grown up in
facility housing. He'd always lived with his mom and dad, until they
passed away. I could see that the drastic change in lifestyle was a difficult adjustment for him. Terry and I quickly formed a bond. I'd look
forward to seeing him every day. We'd often have coffee and donuts

together, or dance in the living room, two of Terry's favorite activities. He was funny, caring, and loved the *Three Stooges*. He was my friend.

Two years flew by. During the week of my college graduation, my first husband and I learned that we were expecting a baby. As the months passed and my delivery date grew closer, I felt both happy and sad. Though thrilled that I would soon be a mother, I knew that once I was on maternity leave, I wouldn't get to see Terry regularly anymore. Then it hit me. *I should just take Terry home to live with me.*

I know it sounds crazy, maybe just a result of all the pregnancy hormones. All I knew was it was the right decision. After countless conversations and a towering stack of paperwork, a forty-year-old, five-foot tall, stocky Ukrainian man with Down syndrome moved into my house. When Terry first moved in with me, his skills and vocabulary weren't the best. His parents had done pretty much everything for him, and even in the group home it had been largely the same.

I knew that with a baby on the way I had to start teaching Terry more life skills. It was a slow process, but he was gradually catching on to the basics, day by day. I never felt frustrated, because it just felt right to have his beautiful energy in the house. When Michael was born, Terry immediately fell in love with him, and affectionately nicknamed him Bugaboo — a funny name that stuck for years.

Michael's first year was wonderful, and Terry was right by his side for everything. To my surprise, Terry was absorbing everything I was teaching Michael. As the years passed, Michael and Terry became inseparable. They were the very best of friends. And as Michael's abilities increased, so did Terry's. They learned a lot from each other. We never really discussed who Terry was in our lives, and Michael never thought to ask. Terry had just always been there, eternal and beloved.

When strangers would ask Michael if he had any siblings, he would respond, "No, but I have a Terry!" It was cute.

Then one day, when we were out getting Michael's hair cut, something happened that forever changed the way I thought about family.

While the stylist cut his hair, she asked him questions like, "Are you in school?" "What grade are you in?" "Do you like your teacher?"

He confidently answered all her questions with his adorable little voice. And then she asked him if he had any brothers and sisters. Michael responded, "Yes I do. I have a brother named Terry and he's forty-five years old!"

"Forty-five!" the hairstylist responded, confused. "Don't you mean four or five years old?"

"Nope, he's forty-five!"

I looked up from the magazine I was reading. I laughed, but as I thought about his answer, I realized the significance of what he'd just said. On the drive home I asked Michael why he told the hairstylist that Terry was his brother. In a very matter-of-fact way, he said, "Because he is and I love him." I was dumbfounded by his incredibly profound answer. I drove home speechless, tears rolling down my face.

Without being taught or told, my five-year-old had figured out that we were a family.

From that day forward I introduced Terry as Michael's brother. Some of the looks and questions I received over the years were hilarious. Terry lived with us for more than thirteen amazing years, until his health deteriorated and he needed to move into a nursing home. In that time I watched Michael quickly evolve into the role of big brother, even though Terry was forty years his senior. Michael read to him, protected him, cared for him, and watched him grow older. They were truly brothers.

We all miss Terry a lot, but what he brought to our family can never be replaced. He taught us that family doesn't just exist in the DNA. Family is a feeling. Family is love. Since Terry left us, we continued growing our family unconventionally. Many of Michael's friends have lived in our house at times, and all of them are considered close family members. Though they've left the nest and moved on, they're still in our lives and still in our hearts.

For Family Day this year, I arranged for my family to celebrate at a new restaurant that had just opened. To my great surprise, as the afternoon progressed, all the friends who have called our house a home stopped by, one by one, to celebrate this day with us. As I sat there listening to everyone joke and share stories, I thought about Terry and the gift he brought our family.

In reality, I only have a small family, but to me it's larger than life. And what a life it is.

~Heidi Allen

80

Take a Chance

Why not go out on a limb? Isn't that where the fruit is?
~Frank Scully

"**M**om, just give it a try."

"I don't know, Danny. I'm fifty-five. Fifty-five-year-olds don't do Internet dating. We meet people the old-fashioned way."

My son snorted. "Of course, they do! Besides, how's the old-fashioned way working for you so far?"

"Ummmm…," I mumbled.

"Exactly. Alexa's mom met Rich on the Internet, and now they're engaged." Alexa is my daughter-in-law. Her father had passed away from cancer seven years after I lost my husband to the same disease.

Danny continued, "They met on an 'Over 50' website. You would be meeting men who have some of the same life experiences and values you do."

"I have Walter. We share the same values." Walter is my rescue dog.

"Sure, Mom," he chuckled. "It's just something to think about. Dad's been gone almost twelve years. It would be nice if you weren't alone."

After hanging up, I did think about it. I thought about the life I had built over the four years I had lived in Taos, New Mexico, since moving from Colorado. I was teaching at a local charter school, going out with friends, and meeting with my book group every month. My younger son, Ben, had recently moved to Taos from Colorado to help start a new CrossFit gym, so I even had family nearby. Danny and his family were only about five hours away in Denver, so I was able to see my granddaughters pretty often. For the first time since losing my husband, I was feeling stable and happy in my "aloneness." Why should I mess with something that didn't feel broken? Other dating experiences had not been exactly successful. Sure, "alone" morphed into "lonely" from time to time, but much less often than before. I decided to pass on Danny's suggestion.

Not long after my conversation with Danny, my stable, comfortable life began unraveling at an alarming rate. My landlord of three years called to tell me she wanted to sell the condo I was renting. Did I want to buy it? If not, my lease would not be renewed, and I should consider this my forty-five-day notice to vacate so she could get it ready to put on the market. While looking into my finances to see if purchasing was an option, my principal called me into her office to tell me my position was being cut and my contract would not be renewed the following year. My head swimming, I called my landlord to tell her I wouldn't be buying the condo and set about searching for new employment and a place to live.

While searching online for jobs and housing one day, an advertisement popped up for the "Over 50" dating site Danny had told me about. Thinking it might be a sign, I decided to fill out the profile and check it out. Everything else in my life was off-kilter; why not add one more thing?

Over the next couple of weeks, I ran around packing up my classroom and condo, putting things into storage, and moving into an efficiency condo I had leased for the summer. While updating my résumé and looking for teaching positions, I would get notices from the dating site telling me someone had looked at my profile and sent me a "flirt" or a message. The site would also send suggestions for profiles I might want to look at. Curiosity always got the better of me, and I couldn't help looking at the notices.

One day, a notice popped up telling me that someone had checked my profile, but had not sent any notice of interest. I opened up his profile to take a look. Steve was my age, recently widowed, and had lived in the Denver area for about twenty years. He was in the process of selling his Denver home and moving to a mountain home he owned about an hour north of Taos. One of the photos in his profile was of a vintage Volkswagen bus — the kind with the pop-up camper top. On a whim, I commented, "This looks fun!" on that photo and went back to my job search, a little disappointed that he wasn't interested in even chatting in the website's chat room. A couple of days later, a notice popped up that I had an e-mail from a potential date. Surprisingly, it was from the man with the VW bus. He liked that I had responded to his picture of the bus and decided to take another look.

We began writing back and forth, sharing more about our lives and experiences as we got more comfortable. Both being widowed was something that mattered very much. It was so nice to be able to talk to someone about that kind of loss and have him understand. Because his loss was much more recent than mine, he had a lot of questions about the grieving process. As I shared my story with him, I felt even more healing myself.

Finally, we decided to take the big step of meeting. We agreed to meet for lunch at Orlando's, a New Mexican food restaurant in Taos. I was so nervous about meeting him. I would stop and laugh at how worried I was about what to wear, what I would say, and how it would go. When I got to the restaurant, I looked around, but didn't see anyone who matched the pictures in the profile.

Oh, no! What if he stands me up? I worried.

Not long after I sat down, I saw Steve walk into the outdoor seating area. As I stood up to greet him, I felt a rush of recognition beyond just matching a face to a photo. I felt like I knew him, even though we had never met before and had only talked online.

After we ordered, he told me how nervous he had been getting ready for our date. We laughed about feeling like teens and how strange it was to be dating at this time of our lives. As lunch was winding down, we were both wondering what came next.

Suddenly, Steve grinned and said, "I drove the bus here. Would you like to go for a ride?"

"Of course!" I answered. "Can Walter come, too? He's waiting in the car."

That first ride in the bus called Buttercup was the first of many adventures Steve, Walter, and I have shared.

Sure enough, Danny had been right. As dating quickly evolved into an exclusive relationship, followed by an engagement and plans to marry, our common experiences and shared values have formed the foundation of a surprising and wonderful second chance that neither one of us expected, but are so grateful for. Sometimes, it's a good idea to listen to our kids.

~Lynne Nichols

81

The Glory of Love

Friendship involves many things but, above all the
power of going outside oneself and appreciating
what is noble and loving in another.
~Thomas Huxley

am an introvert. I have a small circle of friends, and I generally do not make friends easily because being with most people takes so much energy.

Twenty-nine years ago, I started working at a new school. The English Department had an empty classroom that we used as a lounge. We gathered there every morning and afternoon, and I really enjoyed the people I worked with. I thought one woman in particular, Cheryl, was fascinating. I really enjoyed talking to her and looked forward to seeing her every day.

What I didn't know was that Cheryl was even more of an introvert than I was. I don't know what possessed me, but one day I announced to her, "You and I are going to be friends." She later told me that my forwardness had startled her. I could see she was reticent, so I said a few weeks later, "You can try to hide, but it won't work. We are going to be friends." And as the year went on, we did become friends. The more time we spent together, the more we discovered how much we liked one another.

My husband had a very close friend named Jerry. Jerry was more like a brother than a friend to us. In fact, to this day we refer to each other as brother and sister. My husband was not much of a handyman, so Jerry did most of the small projects around our house, and he ate dinner with us three to four times a week. He is my oldest son's godfather. Whenever I needed him, he was only a phone call and ten minutes away.

Jerry very much wanted a special lady in his life, but he worked in a male-dominated field and was shy around women. Previously, I had set him up on a date with a friend, and although the date went fairly well, it took him so far out of his comfort zone that he did not ask her out again. He was intimidated by the fact that she had a master's degree, and he only had a high-school education. After the date, he told me, "You are trying to make a silk purse out of a sow's ear."

Jerry would talk about his idea of the perfect woman. He wanted a woman who had the poise and bearing of a lady, but who was zaftig and high-spirited. I realized that I knew that woman: Cheryl. But, like my other friend, she had an advanced degree, and Jerry would immediately feel uncomfortable around her. Also, she is nine years older than he is, and I worried that they would see the age difference as an impediment. Similarly, when Cheryl would describe her perfect man, I knew who he was. She wanted a big, strong, affectionate, teddy bear of a man, one whom she could lean on, and who would take care of her and her house. Jerry fit that image perfectly. But I knew if I tried to set them up on a date, they would both freeze, and it would be a disaster. I was afraid that if I invited them both to dinner at the same time, they would see through what I was trying to do. I resigned myself to the notion that although they were ideal for each other, there was no way to bring them together.

But it was meant to be, so karma intervened for me. One day, Cheryl asked me if I knew a handyman who could do some small repairs around her house. Immediately, I thought of Jerry, but I knew I had to tread cautiously. I told her I knew someone, but I would have to get his permission to give her his number. That night when I got home from school, I called Jerry and explained the situation. I asked him if he was interested in helping her out. He said "yes," so I gave her his number.

The first time he went to her house, he worked for four hours.

The second time, he worked for two hours, and they sat on her couch and talked for an additional two hours. The third time, no work was accomplished, but much talking took place. Soon, every time I called him, he was with Cheryl. One night, my husband and I were headed for Denny's, and I called Jerry and asked if he wanted to join us. He came and brought Cheryl along. They were so comfortable with each other, sharing private jokes and just glowing. I looked at them and asked, "So, when are you two getting married?"

Cheryl looked at Jerry and said, "I don't know. Are we in love?"

Jerry replied, "I think so."

The wedding was wonderful, and my oldest, who was only four or five at the time, was Jerry's best man, although my husband was at the altar, too.

Now, they have been married for twenty-six years. All three of my boys call them Aunt Cheryl and Uncle Jerry. They truly are my brother and sister. After my divorce, they helped me raise my sons. We spend nearly every holiday together. We cook together and for each other. The family joke is that it is not a true family celebration without Aunt Cheryl's Jell-O, so she made spider and ghost Jell-O Jigglers for my middle son's rehearsal dinner before his Halloween wedding. We have cleaned each other's houses in emergencies. When my nineteen-year-old cat died, we were all there together in the vet's office crying and holding him. We share a lifetime of memories together. In recent years, both Jerry and Cheryl have had serious health issues, and now my sons try to rotate on a weekly basis, checking on them and doing small repairs for them.

All of this happened because I somehow found the courage to step out of my comfort zone and try to make a new friend. In doing so, I found a new family.

~Sandy A. Reid

Chapter 9

STEP OUTSIDE YOUR COMFORT ZONE

☑ Take a Risk

82

The Moonlit Kayak

*There's nothing more addictive or incredible in life
than reinventing yourself and allowing yourself
to be different every day.*
~Thalia

A few months ago, I met a handsome doctor on a business trip. He was visiting Miami and wanted a tropical, outdoorsy date. I am a chunky, short redhead who considers shopping at a bargain store to be exercise. If I'm feeling exceptionally motivated, I park far away from the entrance.

"You have to do something exciting. Get out of your comfort zone. He wants a tropical outdoors adventure. *Bienvenido a Miami, baby!*" my sister said when asked for advice.

"How about going to Pollo Tropical for dinner? We can sit on the patio with a bowl of *tostones*," I replied. "In this heat, I think that is tropical enough."

Ignoring me, she went on. "Go camping or play beach volleyball or hiking or… kayaking! That's it! Kayaking! My co-worker just went full-moon kayaking and says it was very romantic. I can get you the information." Sis reached for her phone.

"Let's see — outdoors, exercise, water, mosquitoes, alligators — it is so *not* going to happen," I declared with certainty.

The next day, my sister and I were wandering in a gigantic mall trying to locate a sporty outfit that would make me look like I kayaked all the time. Apparently, I also needed (pretty) waterproof shoes. Isn't *pretty waterproof* shoes an oxymoron?

I picked up Dr. Jack at his hotel. I was wearing some kind of elastic black sport shirt with cranberry-colored shorts. On my feet were ridiculously expensive, pink plastic Mary Janes that my sister and I found at the Crocs store. *Fifty dollars for plastic shoes. This guy better be an awesome date,* I thought.

The drive out to the bay was wonderful. My companion was charming. The conversation flowed with ease. We arrived at Oleta River State Park and found a parking spot near the full-moon kayaking hut. I placed car keys, iPhone, and a lipstick in Ziploc bags inside a small, plastic purse. Of course, I needed lipstick! I *was* on a date after all. We got paddles and life vests, and watched a kayaking safety demonstration. The guide explained the correct way to get in and out of a kayak and how to paddle. The taller you are, he told us, the greater the chance of tipping.

Jack is 6'5". I was starting to lose my cool composure.

About fifty kayaks were bumping into each other as we slowly left the mangroves and paddled toward Biscayne Bay. Every time someone gently hit us, I thought my heart would dive into the water. Orange paddles seemed to miss my face by inches. Alligators probably lurked just below us.

Once in open water, the ride became smooth. I loosened the death grip on my paddle. This was when I first looked around. The moon was breathtaking. Its reflection on the bay reminded me of a poem in Spanish that I heard in high school. The breeze was warm and made my red curls dance around my face. The lights on the tall buildings in the distance twinkled like faraway stars. And a lovely man was sharing a yellow kayak with *me.* Guides everywhere watched over our group. I stopped worrying about tipping over, or being an alligator's Happy Meal, or getting paddled in the face. I was alive and blessed. I was doing something totally uncharacteristic, and I loved every minute of it.

We arrived at a beach with a campfire. Dr. Jack pulled me out of the kayak, smiled and kissed me. It was a fairy tale and, like Cinderella, I was wearing awesome (albeit plastic) shoes. Leaving our kayak and life vests on shore with the others, we sat on the wet sand. Jack and I kissed, sipped wine, munched on s'mores, and listened to a guitar-playing guide sing "Margaritaville" and "Brown-Eyed Girl" under the light of the full moon. We stayed until the end, and there were only a few kayaks left. Someone took ours, so we grabbed another.

I ended up with a diminutive life vest. I was only able to hook the bottom part of the vest — the one that belonged around my waist — under my breasts. Forget about latching the top. Who needed it to fit anyway? I was not going swimming.

While gliding over the water with the satisfaction that I was now an accomplished outdoors athlete, Jack got cute and rocked the kayak. Someone screamed. Swallowing water, I realized I was the one making the Banshee-like noise. Slow motion. Thoughts crossed my mind. The small life vest could not hold my weight since I was definitely not floating. I was grateful for the Lasik surgery that I had that allowed my eyes to open underwater. I was regretful for the Lasik that made me clearly see the darkness, algae, and muck. I kicked my feet. I felt my fifty-dollar Crocs slipping. I felt for the purse I attached to the life vest. Car keys, lipstick, and my loyal Siri were still with me. I sent God a "please let the Ziploc bags work so there is no water damage" prayer. I spotted Jack at a surprising distance, holding on to the back of our kayak and calling my name. One of the tour guides was with him, her kayak parallel to ours.

The sound of me coughing out murky water made them look my way. Slowly, I reached the kayaks. We were alone. It was very dark. I was scared. The jig was up. Words came out at once. "I will not be able to get back in this thing. I am a wimp. I have never been kayaking in my life. I have never done anything remotely athletic at all. My shoes are new and slipping off my feet. I bought them yesterday with the outfit so I could look cute and sporty. If I lose the shoes, my sister will make fun of me forever!"

The guide smiled. She was totally calm. What was wrong with her? Couldn't she see this was a crisis? "Hand me the shoes." Her voice was a sweet lullaby. I handed them over. "They are pretty. I will not lose them, I promise." She placed them inside her own one-person kayak.

"Hold onto the side of your kayak, and I will pull you up from the top latch of your vest. I will have you sitting in the kayak in minutes."

She reached for the vest's top latch and grabbed a handful of my breasts.

"Your life vest is too small!" She was surprised. The lullaby voice and Zen-like peace were gone.

Panic. More words. "Someone took our kayak and our life vests. We had to take one left behind. This vest obviously belongs to a girl who does not eat and has no breasts. I could not hook it over mine because I *love* donuts."

She was calm again. "No worries. Let's try this. Pull yourself up while your friend and I steady the kayak. Once you are halfway, I will grab the bottom latch and get you in."

I pulled so hard that the Incredible Hulk had nothing on me.

And yet, I was still in the water.

I am never leaving Biscayne Bay. I should arrange for my mail to be delivered and call my pet sitter.

Jack chuckled and swam behind me. "I will push you up."

I was mortified. Jack was grunting loudly near my left ear from the effort of trying to lift me out of the water. He had one hand on my butt, the other, who knows where. *I am going to die of embarrassment.* When there was movement because my date was, undoubtedly, Ironman, the guide instructed me to quickly lift my right leg over the kayak and push. It was not easy or pretty. My grunts were now harmonizing with Jack's. It worked. Between the pushing, grunting and pulling, I was straddling the front of the kayak.

I am a beached whale in cranberry-colored shorts, I thought.

It was over. I breathed. I was safe.

"You have to let go of the kayak and get inside the seat." *Oh, God, it is not over.*

"Why can't I just stay hugging the kayak? I love it so much," I asked in a Minnie Mouse squeak. Both Jack and the guide patiently convinced me to let go of my new love. After earthquake-like movements, I was, once again, sitting in a kayak.

Jack got in like the flutter of a butterfly's wing.

We slowly started on our way back. "You know, Jack, if you had wanted to grab me, all you had to do was ask." We laughed. I relaxed. The three of us fell into pleasant conversation.

On dry land, I hugged and thanked our guide, and was reunited with my pink Crocs. Jack and I — dripping water, holding hands, laughing, and listening to the squishy sounds of our shoes — walked back to the car.

In life, people stay away from experiences that might end up in the disasters we build inside our heads. Sometimes we are right — what we fear most, actually happens. We take a risk and end up falling out of a kayak into a dark bay. Isn't that just fantastic?

~Marta A. Oppenheimer

83

A Fish Out of Water

I am not afraid of tomorrow, for I have
seen yesterday and I love today.
~William Allen White

was never a tough guy, a hard case. My world was twelve years of public-school education, four years of engineering in college, and one year in an air-conditioned office at a California aircraft company. Three good meals a day, a roof over my head and the comforts of home were all I ever knew or expected to know. But this wasn't the 1950s. This was the late 1960s, a time of radical change — disruptive on a good day, chaotic on a bad one. It was a time for stepping out of the expected, the ordinary, the comfort zone, in a dramatic way.

My job came with a critical-occupation draft deferment, a good thing since the Vietnam War was going full bore. I thought, albeit naïvely, I would be doing important work. In the back of my mind, though, was the knowledge that young men my age were being drafted for no other reason than they had not had the privilege of going to college. However, it didn't take long to realize that my job, while interesting, was not critical to the efforts of the U.S. government, the basis for the deferment. Maybe it was too many terribly graphic TV reports, or maybe a nagging conscience, but I realized the deferment was not for me — not something I had earned or deserved.

A few weeks later, I found myself in Marine Corps boot camp, the first leg of a trip to Vietnam. To go from working for people who spoke in a polite, thoughtful manner to taking unquestioned orders from someone with all the sensitivity of a wounded rhino was stunning. If I had any vestige of a civilian comfort zone left, it disappeared the first night of training with my introduction to the drill instructors.

"I'll give any of you one free punch. If you can knock me down, I'll graduate you from boot camp tomorrow," Sergeant Winborne roared at us at 3:30 a.m. our first night. There were no takers.

"You're going to find out you can do a lot more than you ever thought. We'll show you," Sergeant Davis bellowed at us menacingly a day later. He was right.

Surprisingly, despite the intense difficulty, training went fairly fast as we drove headlong toward the real thing. There was boot camp, infantry training, jungle warfare training, and suddenly I was getting off a 707 at the giant U.S. airbase in Da Nang in April 1969.

Everyone has moments of truth that define their existence. Mine was the first day in Vietnam. To be issued equipment that would serve me throughout my tour of duty, I went to the battalion armory. The corporal put an M16 rifle and several empty magazines on the counter, and then went into a side room. He came back and casually dropped about 150 rounds of live ammunition next to the rifle. The hot sweat I was covered in from the infernal heat was nothing compared to the terrible feeling in my stomach, the weakness in my knees, and the cold sweat of fear that came over me. The wait was over, and the truth had arrived. The fish was all the way out of the water with no chance of diving back in anytime soon.

Would it be an understatement to say Vietnam was entirely different from southern California? The daily 110-degree heat; the suffocating humidity; the deadly poisonous snake slithering through the grass five feet from my left foot; the leeches that had to be burned off my leg with a cigarette. Colleagues at the aircraft company would never have tolerated me going without a bath for a month or wearing the same clothes for three, but that was routine and unavoidable in Vietnam. Clinging to a river bank at 11:00 one night, waiting desperately for the rescue helicopters to finally arrive; listening to the bullets snap over my head and the sickening thud of the ones that hit the trees behind; the rockets screaming in with a roar like a freight train coming through the sky; and the frightening *whump, whump, whump* of warheads exploding around us. Vietnam was so different that my previous life had nothing at all for comparison.

No matter how bad it was, no one could keep the sun from coming up in the morning and going down at night. Finally, that happened enough times for me to go home to a life that had changed indelibly. The fish was back in its water, but its comfort zone had been changed forever.

~Tom Lockhart

84

The Blue Jacket

Just being there for someone can sometimes
bring hope when all seems hopeless.
~Dave G. Llewelyn

From the prison visitors' station, I looked outside and saw the pouring rain. Pouring was an understatement; it was more like a giant swimming pool had been turned upside-down, the water hitting what had recently been a dirt yard. Mud splashed up a foot or more before it settled on the ground, only to be disturbed again. I wasn't thrilled about walking through that downpour, so I pleaded with the guard who was confiscating my only raincoat, which was bright blue.

"Could I just wear my jacket to the next guard station and give it to the guard there?"

The young male guard looked like he might be convinced, but the female correctional officer who was about my age cut him off. "Ma'am," she said, "blue is not permitted."

There was no arguing with her. She also confiscated a cough drop and a scarf. If it were up to her, I don't think she would have let me in at all. However, I finally made it through the metal detector and set off across the yard.

By the time I arrived at the next checkpoint, I looked like I had showered with my clothes on, but this guard was kind as well as very young. He asked if it was my first time visiting the prison, and when I said it was, he carefully explained the rules to me. I had trouble listening because I was so nervous that I was shaking slightly. I told him I was visiting an old student, and I wasn't even sure I'd recognize him. He reassured me by telling me there would be correctional officers in the reception room if I needed them.

That wasn't what I was worried about.

It turns out that when you tell your third-grade students that they'll always be "your kids" no matter what, you may end up visiting one of them in prison.

I had taught in the most violent part of Oakland, and Jorge was one of my students who had the least going for him. His mother loved him very much, but had her own demons she was fighting. She was only fourteen years older than him. His grandmother who was raising him did her best, but she didn't speak English and didn't read or write in Spanish.

Jorge saw more tragedy up close and personal by the time he was fourteen than most people do in a lifetime. Although he was a thoughtful, compassionate, caring person, the street offered him security that he couldn't find anywhere else. He was now twenty-one and facing nineteen years in prison.

This was not at all what I had in mind when I had envisioned keeping in touch with former students, but when Jorge asked me to visit, I remembered saying that I would always be there if I could. So I made the two-hour drive, wore the colors allowed, except for that blue raincoat, and walked through the pouring rain to see him.

I was nervous for so many reasons, none of which the correctional officers could help me with. The little boy I knew was now considered by society to be a hardened criminal. I didn't know if I'd recognize him or if he'd be the same person. In addition, I had written a book about my experience teaching and told his story in a very honest manner. I wasn't sure how he'd take it.

As I had feared, I didn't recognize him at first. But when he saw me and came over, I could see that his eyes were the same. They were sadder, and maybe wiser, but they were still the eyes of that boy I had known.

Jorge came straight up to me and said, "I read your book. I liked it." I let out a sigh of relief, and we started chatting. He told me with pride that the first thing he did when he received my book was to walk it around the prison, showing off the dedication (to him) and asking the other inmates if any of them had been in the dedication of a book before.

We sat in uncomfortable plastic chairs, careful to always face the guards. As we kept talking, I forgot how frightened I had been. A state prison was possibly the furthest I could get from my comfort zone, but in a way I felt like we were just having coffee... at least temporarily. We tried to catch up on eight years during our two-hour visit.

Before Jorge had to be escorted back to his cell, I asked him if there was anything surprising about what I had written about him. He thought for a minute and said, "I never knew there were people who didn't know how hard life is for people like me. They should know that."

Driving away from the prison was both easier and more melancholy than driving there. I wasn't afraid anymore. I knew that it was filled with sad, broken people, but there are plenty of hurting people on the outside, too. Many people make their own prisons; they just don't come with razor wire and handcuffs.

Jorge was the same person he had been in third grade. He was more experienced, had less freedom, and had much more grief, but he was the same person. He wrote to me later to thank me for coming, but I felt like I should thank him. In this longhaired inmate who couldn't even wear his own clothes, I was able to see the little boy whom I had promised would always be one of my kids — and I was able to keep that promise.

~Bronwyn Harris

85

Disembarking

Once we accept our limits, we go beyond them.
~Albert Einstein

Ever since I can remember, I've been fascinated by skydiving. And even though jumping from a perfectly good plane seems like an act of pure insanity, I couldn't help but get a twinkle in my eye when I thought about it. I was so obsessed with the idea that when people asked why I was in a wheelchair, I joked and said, "Because the parachute didn't open!"

A few close friends knew of my desire, but it wasn't something I usually talked about. That is, until opportunity literally moved in next door. His name was Zack, and he was taking classes at my college while training to be a paratrooper in the Army. Of course, I didn't know this at first, but in no time at all, Zack was coming over to borrow toilet paper and share stories of his weekend retreats. One weekend, he came home limping, and when I asked him about it, he said he had landed a jump wrong.

"A jump?"

Seeing my interest, he proceeded to tell me all about his jumping adventures. I knew I had found a kindred spirit, so I shared with him my enthusiasm for the sport. He didn't laugh or tell me it was absurd, but instead encouraged me to do it and assured me it was very safe.

A few months before our college graduation, Zack approached

me on campus and sat down on the bench next to me. "Got any plans this weekend?"

"No," I replied.

"Well, you do now!" he said with a smirk. I knew this smirk all too well, so it was obvious he had something up his sleeve. I asked him what he meant, and he proceeded to explain that he and a few friends were going skydiving. He wanted me to tag along. He said that he had already talked with the owners of the shop, and they were experienced in jumping with people with disabilities. He said I didn't have to make my mind up yet, but to consider it.

"Are you kidding me?" I exclaimed. "I am so doing this!"

Zack smiled and said, "I figured you'd say that."

I didn't know all the details yet, but I knew I couldn't let this opportunity pass me by. I decided not to tell my family because I didn't want them talking me out of it, but I did, however, let a few close friends in on the secret. I guess news like this travels fast because, before I knew it, a half-dozen friends and acquaintances were asking directions to the jump site so they could watch me take the plunge!

Zack picked me up, and we headed to the jump site. When we got there, my van was swarmed with about fifteen of my friends, whom I later nicknamed my fan club. I was embarrassed by all this attention, but deep down I was eating it up. We made our way to the sign-in office, and the owner came out. Following close behind him was Erik, the guy I would jump with. For the next twenty minutes, they explained how they used a technique called tandem jumping. They would attach me to Erik with a harness, and I'd basically go along for the ride while he did all the work.

That was all the info I needed. I forked over the $100 and signed my life away on the dotted line. As the plane pulled up, Erik went over any last-minute concerns I had. I was pretty confident about things and too excited to really think at this point, so he said, "All right, let's head to the plane!"

It was all starting to seem surreal. Before I knew it, they had lifted me into the plane and set me on the floor right beside the door. Soon the plane was full, so the engines started, and we took off.

It took about eight minutes to ascend to 12,000 feet. They used that time to get me hooked up to Erik. Basically, he sat behind me, scooted close, and then latched our harnesses together. We were approaching 10,000 feet, so it was time to get into position. They slowly opened the door right next to me, and a gust of freezing air rushed in. The sound was deafening. By the time Erik scooted us to the edge of the plane, my heart was nearly beating out of my chest! The sky was the brightest of blues that I've ever seen, and the earth below looked like a beautiful patchwork quilt.

All of a sudden, I heard Erik yell, "READY… ONE… TWO… JUMP!" and we tumbled out of the plane. I must admit my first reaction was panic. It goes against every natural instinct we have to leap into thin air. But that initial feeling of panic only lasted a second or two, and then my other senses went on sensory overload. Contrary to popular belief, it didn't actually feel like falling. Instead, it felt like I was hovering in front of a huge and powerful fan. The wind enveloped my entire body, and I could literally feel it infusing every pore. My cheeks were flapping in their own rhythmic dance, while my teeth chattered in pure exhilaration. I had the perspective of a bird and felt the insignificance of an ant.

With a pull of the chute and a jolt that caught me off-guard, the freefall came to an end. We were still up pretty high, but the rest of the ride would be tranquil. I felt more alive than I'd ever felt before. I was humbled by the sheer brilliance of Mother Nature, but at the same time the enormity of what I had just accomplished was beginning to set in.

All of my life, I had been proving to people that their doubts in me had no merit, and now I had just proved it to my biggest critic… myself. I realized I could do anything I put my mind to, despite my disability, or perhaps *because* of my disability. My perspective had changed in an instant. I have never walked, but that day I learned to fly.

Erik regained my attention when he said we were coming in for the landing, and I saw the fan club cheering as they ran toward me.

The next few minutes were a bit fuzzy. Once they got me back into my chair, I saw Zack heading toward me. He bent down and gave me a hug.

"What'd ya think?" he asked.

All I could manage to say was "Thank you…"

~Dana Carpenter

86

A Bolt from the Blue

Move out of your comfort zone. You can only grow if
you are willing to feel awkward and uncomfortable
when you try something new.
~Brian Tracy

"The boss wants to see you," our TV newsroom secretary told me.

"Right now?" I asked. It was only Monday, so I couldn't have done anything wrong yet.

"Don't worry," she laughed, "but now would be good."

I knocked on the open door of the boss's office, and he waved me in. "Sit down for a second," he said. "I have a favor to ask you."

He got right to the point. "Our weekend meteorologist has left us suddenly, and I need you to fill in on the Saturday and Sunday newscasts until we find a replacement. Will you do it?"

I was dumbfounded. "You sure you have the right guy?" I asked suspiciously. I was a news reporter, not a meteorologist. I didn't know a cumulus cloud from a kumquat.

"I think you can do it," he said. "Besides, you have all week to get ready."

Five days? I couldn't believe he actually said that with a straight face. But I had learned years before there was no arguing with the boss. I decided instead to put him off. "Can I have some time to think about it?" I asked.

"Sure," he said, "no problem."

I walked back to my desk feeling bewildered. Working in television newsrooms for almost fourteen years, I knew how to speak on camera. But I probably knew less about meteorology than a fifth grader. "Evaporation, condensation, precipitation," I muttered. That was about it. What's more, I had no idea how our weather guys got their information, or how to operate the computers that generated the maps to show on-air. And how was I supposed to interpret the clouds on those weather satellite photos? *No,* I thought, *there is no way I can do this, not in five days, not in five years.*

I looked at my watch. I had scheduled an interview for a story I was working on, and it was time to link up with my photographer and head out. I would break the bad news to my boss when I got back.

Upon returning to the TV station a couple of hours later, I was greeted by the assignment editor. "Going to do weekend weather, huh?" he smiled.

"What?" I howled.

"Yeah, I saw the memo," he said, pointing to the bulletin board across the hallway. "Good luck!"

I marched over to the wall and read the words typed on my boss's stationery: "Nick has agreed to fill in on the weekend newscast, taking over weather duties until a permanent weather anchor is found. I want to thank him for his dedication to teamwork."

So, I guess that was that. There was no arguing with the boss.

Just then, Larry, the weather guy on the morning show, stepped up. "Come by my desk when you finish writing your story," he said. "I'll show you what we do."

"Thanks. I'd like that," I told him, though I didn't sound convincing.

That week, Larry spent hours patiently showing me how to create computer-generated weather maps. "What is this big red L?" I asked him.

"An area of low pressure," he explained. "You know, rising air, so clouds and precipitation can form." I stared at him blankly. "Don't worry about that now," he said. "It'll come." He almost sounded confident in me. That made one of us.

Both he and the weeknight meteorologist didn't rely solely on information from the National Weather Service; they made their own forecasts. But they weren't taking any chances with me. "Say it word for word just like the official Weather Service forecast," Larry insisted. *No problem,* I thought. *I don't know any other way.*

Saturday came too soon. I spent the afternoon painstakingly following the detailed instructions Larry had given about accessing the official government forecast and how to ingest satellite photos into the computer to use on air. As I was finishing up, he called to see if I had any questions. I asked him, "What should I point out on the satellite photos?" I thought I heard a sigh on the other end of the line.

"Those clouds to the west of us will eventually bring rain tomorrow," he explained. "Just say that."

I had no idea how that was going to fill my three-minute time slot, but I acquiesced, "Okay."

"Break a leg," Larry chimed, and hung up.

Prior to that evening, I had considered myself an experienced TV newsman, speaking authoritatively about politics, crime or the economy, and interviewing hundreds of newsmakers in all manner of stories. But suddenly I felt like a rookie on his first day out of college. Here I was, in the fourteenth largest television market in the nation, preparing to talk, allegedly with some semblance of expertise, about something I had little knowledge of. I sensed disaster.

And with good reason. I wish I could say that everything went surprisingly well, that I spoke clearly, effortlessly and even cleverly about the forecast, and that afterward everyone gave me a high-five. But frankly I have tried to blot that first experience out of my memory. It was a train wreck. I managed a stumbling explanation that the clouds to the west would bring rain the next day, but there was nothing effortless or clever about it, and there were no high-fives when it was over. My friends later consoled me with, "It wasn't that bad." My friends were too kind.

Even so, I did the weather segment the following evening, and despite my expectations that I would be called into the boss's office on Monday and relieved of my weather duties, it didn't happen. I worked the weather shift the next weekend, and the one after that. I started filling in on the morning show and the noon newscast when Larry took vacation. I even did the weeknight show a few times. People on the street began to engage me in conversations about the weather. I threw myself into the job and began to enjoy it in a way I had never enjoyed news reporting. Reading books about air masses and fronts and how topography and oceans affected our weather, I continually discovered new wonders about our atmosphere and found a growing appreciation of the role and responsibility of meteorologists. My boss never did find a permanent weather replacement. I don't know if he ever looked.

In time, I took classes in atmospheric science, completing a three-and-a-half-year university program. I soon met the stringent requirements to be certified by the American Meteorological Society and the National Weather Association, eventually serving in leadership positions with the latter and often mentoring college students.

Now, as I enter my twenty-seventh year of television weather forecasting, I remind students that they need not be afraid when challenges come from out of the blue. "Life will take you places you never dreamed of going," I tell them. "So when an opportunity arises, go for it. You'll find that you are capable of much more than you think."

And don't forget, if you see clouds to the west on the satellite photo, it might rain tomorrow.

~Nick Walker

87

We Call That Bait

You don't need a silver fork to eat good food.
~Paul Prudhomme

I was a brand-new lieutenant in the Air Force, fresh out of training, and had been assigned to California. For a small-town girl who'd grown up in the heart of Texas hill country, California was a mystical land of sun, beach and surfing.

My phone chirped with a new text message. I shivered once I read it. My handsome and charming new boyfriend had just invited me to have dinner with him that evening. Of course, it would be sushi.

One of my new friends saw me cringe and asked what was wrong. I simply showed her the text message. She beamed. "That's wonderful!"

On the other hand, I was genuinely terrified. I asked her, "How on earth am I supposed to eat this stuff? Back home, we call that bait!"

She howled and asked where I grew up.

"Texas."

"Now I know they have sushi in Texas," she said. I shook my head adamantly and assured her that no self-respecting Texan would be caught dead eating a mouthful of bait.

It took the entire afternoon, but she finally convinced me to give it a try — saying that I might surprise myself and actually love it. After another hour of asking me what I had to lose and why shouldn't I try something new, I was officially out of excuses.

"Surprise yourself. Say 'yes,'" she said.

She grinned ear to ear when I finally accepted the dinner invitation.

On the drive to the restaurant, I was a mess. I stuffed my hands between my knees in an attempt to keep them from knocking together and was threatening to break out into a cold sweat.

But opening the door to the restaurant was like opening a door that led to a completely new world. Several sets of lovely printed canvas murals hung like flags from the entryway ceiling as we walked into the restaurant. The murals were covered in stunning Japanese art, and the women in them wore intricately detailed kimonos, bursting with a rainbow of colors. Delicate cherry blossoms floated down from the sky around them like snow. And to my genuine surprise, my stomach rumbled at a rich, savory smell that I could not yet name.

We were seated front and center at the sushi bar, where a glass deli-like case showcased a kaleidoscopic array of fish and seafood. There were brilliant hues of orange salmon, pink shrimp, crimson fillets of tuna, and even octopus in pearly white and indigo. I began to find myself cautiously intrigued. I was also pleasantly surprised to learn that we didn't have to order everything raw!

In a sea of foreign words like *sashimi, nigiri,* and *maki rolls*, I realized that some of these things actually featured cooked shrimp and crab, even salmon.

I put my faith in my boyfriend (a great call as he is now my husband of eleven years) to order for us.

He selected a colorful mix of sushi rolls that contained both cooked and raw seafood. Just knowing there would be something that had seen the inside of a frying pan or oven was enough for me.

After we put in our order, I realized that our dishes would be prepared right in front of us by a white-robed sushi chef. I had never experienced anything like it. It was as if we had front-row seats to an orchestra, only one that would be performed with knives instead of instruments.

A row of gleaming steel blades hung on the wall behind the chef, containing all manner and shape of knives — some long, some very small and curved. I watched as he panned his hand across them before grabbing the perfect one. I sat mesmerized as his hands flew with the speed and grace that could only come from years of expertise.

It was pure amazement watching the sushi chef work, his knives flicking this way and that, to create the most unique food I had ever seen. And I found myself smiling with wonder as our dinner was presented to us—each roll carefully arranged within a wooden boat.

Once I actually worked up the courage to try a piece, I realized I had a new problem: There wasn't a fork in sight. Only chopsticks.

My boyfriend saw me pause and asked so sweetly if I knew how to use the chopsticks. My face flushed, and I had to admit that I had never picked up a pair in my life.

He took my hand in his, placed the chopsticks between my fingers, and then curled his other hand over mine and showed me how to use them. It was incredibly romantic. So romantic, in fact, that I kept "forgetting" how to use the chopsticks all night, and needed repeated handholding lessons. He happily obliged.

I went with the safe pieces first: shrimp and grilled salmon. But I had never tasted either one prepared like this. There was a deep complexity in flavor, a sweetness, but also a wonderful savory taste that I had never experienced. That's when I learned that rich, savory taste actually had a name: *umami*. It's known as the "fifth taste"—after salty, sweet, sour and bitter. I realized I liked *umami*. A lot!

Chopsticks shaking, I went for it, and carefully ate a piece that contained raw tuna. The flavor was new… different… and stunningly delicious.

And with that realization, an evening that had started out full of fear melted into one of the most memorable nights of my life.

My boyfriend told me later that the fact I was willing to try something so foreign and new left a wonderful impression on him. Our relationship was young, but he had seen a hint of an adventurous streak in me (even if I hadn't yet), and he loved it.

The next morning when I came to work, my girlfriend was already there, ready and waiting for a full report on how dinner went. I looked sheepishly at my feet.

"You did like it, didn't you!" she screeched with laughter.

The rest of the morning flew by in a blur, and it was finally time for lunch. When my girlfriend asked what sounded good, I grinned. "Wanna go get some bait?"

~Kristi Adams

88

Stand-Up

*You can't be that kid standing at the top of the water
slide overthinking it. You have to go down the chute.*
~Tina Fey

Before the debut of *America's Got Talent*, Ed McMahon hosted
Star Search, seeking talent from across the country. Our popular hometown radio station decided to hold a local contest
offering the winner a trip to Hollywood to audition for the
real show.

"We need singers," the disc jockey said. "We want to hear from
our local musicians, dancers, and magicians." It sounded like a lot of
fun, but of course, I had none of those talents. "And I know we have
some comedians," he added.

I'll never know why, but I couldn't get that idea out of my head.
Comedians. Granted, I had a lot of funny stories, and certainly our
adventures throughout my husband's Navy career provided plenty
of bizarre tales. But stand up and do a monologue? What made me
think I could do that?

Nevertheless, my mind kept replaying those words despite the
memories conjured up of grade school, where I'd been petrified of
reading aloud in class. Somehow, a week later, the phone jumped
right into my hand, and before I could regain control, my fingers had
punched in the radio station's number.

A voice sounding exactly like mine said, "I want to sign up for
the *Star Search* competition."

"Great! And what is your talent?" asked the cheery male voice.

The still functioning part of my brain posed the same question. *Yes, what exactly is my talent?*

I don't have a talent, came the response from the working part of my brain. But I heard that other Barbara Bennett say, "I'm going to do stand-up."

"Wonderful! We haven't had anybody sign up to do comedy yet." The man collected the necessary information and went over the rules with me. When he gave me a choice of several show dates. I took the last one offered, hoping I'd be able to coax the crazy side of myself off the ledge of lunacy.

I spent every minute of my lunch hour for the next few weeks trying to write material for a two-minute performance. My rogue brain cells had at least created a somewhat feasible story line focused on having recently lost over sixty pounds. My naysaying brain cells continued to ask how I was going to do this without throwing up or passing out. But I kept going.

After writing out the basic idea of the routine, it was time to practice. Professional humor requires perfect timing. Fortunately, we owned a video camera, and my office was only two miles from the house. Every day, I sped home to record myself doing the material, play it back while sipping soup, then recorded again to adjust that all-important timing. But the idea was to take it out of the solitude of my living room and onto a stage as a monologue — *mono* meaning one. Solo. All by myself. Musicians and singers typically perform with others, or at least musical accompaniment. Bands and dancers perform in groups. Even a magician has a rabbit or two! But a comedian is alone. Center stage. All eyes on him or, in this case, her.

A week before the competition began, the radio station began announcing who would be performing at the first show. The second week, the contestant list included a comedian.

"We have to go," I told my husband Bob.

It might have been better if we hadn't. The guy simply wasn't funny, and the audience was brutal. They booed and even threw ice cubes at him. Making it worse, he kept going — actually reading the one-liners from a sheet of paper. The host of the show tried to gently end the act.

"I'm supposed to have two full minutes," Mr. Humorless insisted indignantly, apparently oblivious to the jeers of the crowd. I would have been more embarrassed for the guy, but he was just so very bad.

"Well, that was cruel," I said to Bob as we headed to the car after the show. "And scary."

"Hon, you could tell a knock-knock joke and be funnier than that guy. Don't worry. You'll do great."

The night of my debut, I felt pretty confident. It probably helped that the event took place in a bar. Hopefully by show time, major critics would be softened by Happy Hour.

I watched as the first violinist from the Philharmonic Orchestra played, followed by an opera singer who'd performed on Broadway. Next up came the lead singer of a popular local band. That's when the overwhelming doubt and paralysis hit.

Are you crazy? I yelled at myself. *You don't have to do this,* I assured myself. True enough. And yet I *needed* to. While I hadn't figured out why, I'd chosen to volunteer and needed to go through with it.

I was next. Picturing my big fan base of family and friends waiting out there, I released my death grip on the stair railing. I was still hidden by the curtain, but had made it up the steps onto the stage and walked shakily toward the emcee.

"How are you tonight, Barbara?" The host greeted me with the confidence of a pro.

"Fine, thank you," I lied.

"So how long have you been doing stand-up?" he asked.

My mind shifted into comedic mode. I paused, ticked off a few fingers and said, "Counting tonight," with a thoughtful, timely pause, "about eight seconds." The laughter blew away my fear, proving I could do this.

The goal had never been about winning, just finishing. I did that, taking fifth place to boot! All without a stumble, to startling applause, and cheers sufficient to fully banish my fear of public speaking. A few years later, I began a career I loved, providing educational seminars to large groups about avoiding scams — quite an ironic result of having scammed myself, then an audience, into thinking I was a "real" comedian!

~Barbara Bennett

89

One Simple Word

Life begins at the end of your comfort zone.
~Neale Donald Walsch

was sitting in the bleachers at the Ontario Motor Speedway in California. How did I happen to be there? My daughter Deb had just been chosen as their Race Queen for that year.

She'd asked me to go and take photos of her with the drivers. My cheap little camera took good photos, so I agreed. However, I knew absolutely nothing about racing, and these were the same racecars that competed in the prestigious Indianapolis 500.

When not taking photos of her, I'd sit in the bleachers, questioning those seated around me, who apparently knew about racing.

"Why are these racecars so long and slender?" I asked. Patiently, race fans would give me the answers, like, "That shape is more aerodynamic."

"Oh! Thank you." I'd jot that down in my notebook, eager to learn something about the race before it took place.

One day, while I was busily jotting notes, Jim Bryant, the sports editor of our local newspaper, stopped by. Deb had introduced me to him earlier.

"What're you writing there, Kay?"

"Just trying to learn something about the race, Jim."

His next comment caught me completely off-guard.

"Write about it for our paper," he said, "and I'll pay you."

Surely, he was joking. "But, Jim, I know absolutely nothing about this sport." But he said it again. Somehow, that time, I uttered one simple word: "Okay."

The next thing I knew, Jim told me how many words to write, with instructions to give my typed articles to him. Then he left.

Yikes! What had I just done? I'd agreed to write about a sport I knew nothing about! I wanted to run and hide. But I'd just made him a promise, and now I had to make good.

Little did I know that one simple word had just thrust me into the amazing — and intense — world of high-speed motorsports.

My first story was about blind children who had been brought to the track. They could not see the racecars, but were thrilled to hear the engines, smell the fuel, and feel the vibration.

Article No. 2 was about my daughter's hectic schedule as the Race Queen.

Then I realized I had better start writing about the actual sport of auto racing.

I bought a tape recorder. As I walked toward the race garages, my heart was pounding wildly inside my chest. Approaching a driver, I blurted out, "Hi! I have to write something about racing for our local paper, and I know nothing about it!"

Luck was with me that day. That driver was Indianapolis 500 winner Al Unser, Sr. Realizing my plight, he explained some simple racing facts to me. That became Article No. 3.

I was now a sportswriter!

As my knowledge began to grow slowly, so did my love for the sport. But I was a woman trying to excel in a man's domain. I often ran into roadblocks. I was severely harassed by some racing officials, and occasionally a reporter or two. That made me even more determined to succeed.

One race weekend, I saw a photo op to go with my article, but no newspaper photographer was there. I bought a 35mm camera; the camera shop taught me how to load the film. After many blurred shots, I managed to improve, and my photos began to be published. I was now a published photojournalist!

Month after month, despite learning my job the hard way, my confidence grew. Pushing myself harder, I called a racing magazine and applied to do photo-articles for them. To my amazement, I was hired as a freelancer.

And then I learned there was a small radio station in town—KSOM. I dialed their number. "Would you like to buy some interviews with race drivers to air on your station?" They asked me to quote a price. Calling an out-of-town station to see what they paid, I put some numbers together and sent them to KSOM. They hired me to do twelve one-minute interviews at every race, with a sponsor opener and closer on each one.

It was awkward at first, but the drivers helped. My reports were soon aired at every racing event. Then a call came into KSOM from the national Mutual Network: "Who's doing your radio reports?" KSOM gave them my name; I was soon broadcasting "live" hourly from the track for Mutual.

When ESPN's *SpeedWeek* came into town, I was thrilled. This racing was now covered by their television network! As a newlywed, I'd co-hosted a "live" morning TV talk show. Mustering my courage, I applied to work for ESPN.

"Women are not allowed to be pit reporters."

I was crushed. But they did hire me to create short TV reports from the races.

That's when I hired my own TV camera crew—as producer, on-camera reporter, directing the editing, then driving frantically to our local airport to put each report on a plane to ESPN to make the Eastern-time deadline.

To learn what the drivers went through behind the wheel, I took racing classes—NASCAR stock cars, road-racing cars, even a high-speed NHRA Super Comp dragster. Their jobs are really tough!

There were legendary drivers to interview: Mario Andretti, Richard Petty, Jeff Gordon, John Force, Janet Guthrie, Danica Patrick, and dozens more.

When a few teams asked me to do their public relations, I agreed; I now knew the sport very well. When race magazines began to fold, it was time to create my own racing website: www.carsandcompetition.com.

It's now forty-five years later. I've covered almost every kind of motorsport there is, from motocross bikes to Formula One. I've broadcast the Baja 1000 off-road race "live" on radio from Mexico, and taken photos in the pits at the Indianapolis 500. If it's racing, I've had my work in it somewhere...

It's often been brutally hard work, with long hours and constant learning. Each day, I learn new racing info, and have been honored with 103 national and state awards for my coverage in motorsports television, radio, journalism, photography, public relations, books, and websites.

Sometimes, I ponder how I was suddenly propelled into this fabulous role. It was pure serendipity. Once I uttered that one word, "Okay," to Jim Bryant, it was off to the races!

~Kay Presto

90

A Story from My Heart

Sharing a bit of yourself, opening a window into
your own world, is a good place to begin.
~Jeff Greenwald

I s there something you always wanted to do, but it was just too "out there" to even consider? My "out there" thing was writing for Chicken Soup for the Soul, and actually submitting my story. I had tried before, and even gotten as far as choosing the topic and sitting down at the computer, typing a couple of paragraphs and then stopping to look them over. It was terrible. The writing was too tight, too newsy, nothing even near the story I wanted to tell—the story that was in my heart.

My comfort zone was writing news, straightforward, to the point. It was answering the five "W questions": Who, what, when, where, and why, with a how thrown in for good measure. I knew how to get an interview, ask the right questions, assemble the information and write the story. I was a journalist from the time I was in high school and through college. After raising my kids to school age, I took my first job as a stringer for *The Buffalo News*, covering everything from town board meetings to school board meetings. I wrote features that included a look at a local expert on elephants, an unusual spelling for a local hamlet, and the annual strawberry yield. I loved it, but it wasn't exactly inspirational, and I wanted to inspire.

I went on to design and implement my own community outreach

service through a state agency that served local school districts. The work was tailor-made for me. My mission was to build support for public schools within the community. I believed in what I was doing. When a school budget got passed, or a story about kids helping a local homeless shelter got published on page one of the local newspaper, I felt accomplished and proud. I knew I could do this job forever. It was made for me, and it was definitely in my comfort zone! But it wasn't Chicken Soup for the Soul.

I had stories inside me to inspire, amuse, thrill and delight readers. Stories about real life experiences — sad, deep, joyous and beautiful — but writing them was definitely not comfortable. I couldn't just bang them out and shoot them off to the local editor. I had to think about my own personal experience and lay bare my angst, my fears and my deepest feelings. It felt like the most exciting, exhilarating thing I could ever do, but also the scariest. I didn't know if I could write about the most frightening, serious, personal subject I had ever tackled... myself.

Finally, I settled on a subject, something that came from my heart and profound loss. I happened to belong to that awful "club" that no one would ever willingly join: I was a mother who had lost a child. He was a beautiful, lively fourteen-year-old and had been hit and killed on a sunny August day by a drunk driver. He was my baby, the youngest of three, a football player who on that very day had made the team at the high school he was going to attend that year. His name was Andy, and his was my Chicken Soup for the Soul story.

Andy was on life support for two days after he was hit, and we were faced with all the agonizing decisions that face parents whose kids die like this, one of which was donating his organs. It turned out to be an easier decision than most of the others that were forced upon us, such as which casket to buy or what to do with his things. It was also the decision that eventually offered us a source of comfort, even joy, as we connected with one of the kidney recipients who survived because of Andy's gift.

So that was my story, and I was determined to find a way to turn on the tap and let it flow from my soul onto the pages of a *Chicken Soup for the Soul* book. The theme of the edition was "The Power of Gratitude," and it was appropriate since gratitude was one of the very few bright spots in the sorrowful landscape of losing Andy.

I stared at the computer screen and bit back the tears that threatened to flow. I put my fingers on the keyboard. I wasn't afraid of the tears; they were part of my daily routine now, and every bereaved parent can relate. I wasn't even afraid of baring my most intimate agony. It had been twenty years, and I was a regular speaker in my community about the dangers of drunk driving. I was afraid of not being able to *write* it in a way that would touch the hearts of whoever ended up reading it. The process was anything but comfortable, and I used the delete key a lot more than I ever did when I was crafting a quick story about school kids making strawberry shortcakes for senior citizens' breakfasts or school boards passing new programs.

It was an amazing, excruciating experience. I finally stopped deleting and just wrote, letting the story take shape, arranging the facts and embellishing them with the emotions, raw as they were. When I finished, it was like waking up from a dream, looking down at the screen and seeing me and Andy, the hospital, the doctor, my husband and the kidney recipient come to life as I read.

"Wow," I breathed, "I think it's pretty good." I proofed and edited, polished and rephrased, and then swallowed hard and sent it off. I knew these things take a while, so I went back to my life and mostly forgot about it until the wonderful day when I heard from Chicken Soup for the Soul and learned they were including it in *Chicken Soup for the Soul: The Power of Gratitude*.

Of course, I was beyond thrilled, but I didn't react as one might think I would. I didn't say, "Hooray, I've done it!" I was very happy that someone, an expert, had agreed that the story had merit and was good enough to be included. And I was delighted that I was going to have something special to share with my friends and family. I realized, however, that the day I sat down with the laptop, even before I started writing or hit the send button and shot the file off to the Chicken Soup for the Soul website, I had already succeeded. I had climbed out on the proverbial limb, and it had turned out to be a pretty exciting place to be — a place that allowed me a new view, a different perspective and a great amount of satisfaction.

~Luanne Tovey Zuccari

91

Moving

The vision must be followed by the venture.
It is not enough to stare up the steps —
we must step up the stairs.
~Vance Havner

oving, moving, moving, fifteen times in forty-two years of marriage. The family joke was that I had a baby whenever we moved. That wasn't exactly accurate, but I sold all my baby equipment in moving sales four different times. My eight children were born in five different cities. For move number 12, my husband had accepted a job at a church in a quaint community nestled in the North Georgia foothills. I was skeptical. Would I have another baby?

One Sunday, I was telling my new church friend, Jan, about a recent teahouse visit.

Jan listened bug-eyed. At the end of my description, she said, "Clarkesville is the perfect place. We should open a teahouse here."

"I'll pray about it," I said. That response always bought some time.

"I'll talk with my husband about it," she said.

I began to seriously consider it. I had always been fascinated by teahouses and wanted to open my own business, but I had never before admitted this, even to myself.

When we got together again, Jan reported that she got a "no." "But you should do it!"

How would I do it? I was a stay-at-home mom, a carpooling

taxi-driver and the classroom snack provider, among 101 other duties.

Over the next few days, my dream kept me awake at night. What would my tearoom look like? I decided on five essentials: shelves filled with interesting books, a guest book for my customers, a very nice powder room, a central location on the downtown square, and a sound system to play soothing, relaxing music. I would envision my dream tearoom every time I closed my eyes, almost smelling the fresh baked scones and the tea steeping in individual pots.

I had no business experience other than making the money stretch to feed many mouths and clothe many bodies. Where would the money come from? What if I failed?

Strolling the downtown square, I passed strangers who smiled and waved. "Would a tearoom work in Clarkesville?" I asked local storeowners. When I stepped into Julia's Gift Shop near the square, I heard soothing, relaxing music. That would be perfect for a tearoom. A Realtor found an ideal storefront that I thought would work. Add a kitchen and furnishings and the dream could become reality!

I made an appointment with a small business counselor who would review my business plan for free. I shed my mom-clothes and wore my closest approximation of a business outfit. With notes in hand, I shared my five essentials. The counselor listened to me ramble. Then he asked, "How much will a fork or a knife or a tablecloth cost?" "How many cups of tea will you need to sell to make a profit?" "How much does a kitchen cost?"

I slid down in the chair. "But it would be fun."

He shook his head.

I had asked God not to let me make a mistake, so He packed up my dream. I had no working capital. Besides, I was going to Brazil to visit my daughter in a few months. Soon after that my son was getting married. School would start for the children at home.

Three months later, the phone rang.

"Hey, Dea," the Realtor I had dealt with said, "I don't know what you decided to do about that tea café thing you talked about, but I have German friends who renovated a historic building to create a dessert place. They decided they don't want to run it after all, and I wondered if you would be interested."

"Where is it?" I asked.

"Downtown on the square, near that place we saw," he answered. "They already have forks, knives, tablecloths. The kitchen has been approved by the health department and a sign has been ordered."

I froze in disbelief.

"Want to go meet them? See the place?"

"Well," I said, regaining the ability to speak, "I do need to take my daughter to ballet class downtown. I guess I could meet them then." It sounded intriguing, but in my mind I had already moved on. I had my plane ticket for Brazil and a recipe for my son's groom's cake. A business was not part of my plans now.

"I'll stop by," I said.

The handsome German couple greeted me with smiles. They offered me a cup of coffee and slice of coconut crème cake. Around the cloth-covered table, they shared their vision and the history of the 1890 structure. The chandeliers glistened and reflected on the pine floors.

And those essentials for my tearoom? To my left was a tall, wooden bookcase with an assortment of interesting books. Check. To my right, on the table, was a guest book. Check. A glance in the powder room revealed linen hand towels in a decorative basket. Check. The business was on the downtown square. Check.

Music filled the air. "What music is this?" I asked, as it sounded familiar.

"You may have heard this at Julia's Gift Shop?"

"That's where I heard the music."

"When she closed, we bought her sound system and these CDs were in it," he answered.

I sat in silence, as questions bounced in my head. Should I do this? Is this crazy?

What I said out loud was, "This is lovely. When do you want an answer?"

"As soon as possible."

"I've got to talk with my family," I said to them.

I promised to report back the next week, but I knew I wouldn't do it.

I arrived at our meeting the following week prepared to say "no," but for some inexplicable reason armed with all my "business plan notes."

I sat down, but "No" would not come out of my mouth. "How much will it cost to get open?" Surely that answer would kill the dream.

"We'll give you a couple of months free rent to get started," he said.

The dream was resurrected.

Then he said, "We want you to open in four weeks."

I wanted to say "no" but I agreed to come back again with a final answer. If I ever wanted to do this, now was the time.

I did give birth in Move 12, to the Baron York Tearoom Café and Gift Shop. It operated for seven years on the downtown square of Clarkesville, Georgia, serving people from all over the world. I celebrated brides and birthday princesses. I taught dining etiquette and tea education. I provided an elegant escape where women and men found solace and refreshment.

Then Move 13 came along. My husband took a new job in North Carolina. The Baron York closed. At the request of my customers, I published a cookbook. And *A Dollop and A Pinch: Recipes and Stories from The Baron York* was born.

~Dea Irby

Chapter

10

STEP OUTSIDE YOUR COMFORT ZONE

☑ Take Back Your Life

92

Driving Away from Fear

The best piece of advice someone has
ever given me was "do it scared."
~Sherri Shepherd

My knuckles were white and my heart was pounding as I gripped the steering wheel. In less than a mile, I could turn off the four-lane highway onto a quieter country road, but I wasn't sure I would make it. The speedometer barely registered fifty miles per hour, and yet it was taking all my will to keep my foot on the gas pedal instead of slamming the brake. For the hundredth time, I checked the rearview mirror. Cars were whipping past in the left lane, and more vehicles were lined up behind me. I couldn't slow down; I was already impeding traffic. "Please," I prayed, "just let me make it to the exit."

I'd had a number of nerve-wracking experiences as both a driver and a passenger over the years, but my highway phobia remained latent until one late spring day as I was driving my fourteen-year-old daughter and her friends back from the shopping mall. It hadn't been a recreational outing. My daughter's friends, a sister and brother, had moved in with us temporarily to escape a dangerous situation at home. Our trip to the mall's food court had been arranged so they could visit their mother in a neutral space. The new living arrangement was proving stressful for everyone. I thought I was coping with that stress—until I had an acute panic attack on the highway ten miles from home. I had to pull off the road repeatedly in order to make it back to our driveway.

The panic attacks only got worse as the weeks passed. Soon I was avoiding the highway altogether, even if it meant going miles out of my way. It didn't help that I was pregnant with my fourth child. Fluctuating hormones during pregnancy can lead to increased levels of anxiety. Knowing this, I told myself that I'd confront my fears after my child was born, and our home life had settled.

Our temporary guests found a safe, long-term home, and I gave birth to a healthy baby girl. But the panic didn't go away as months and then years went by. My heart would race and my stomach would churn every time I steered onto the highway, no matter how short a distance I was travelling. A counsellor told me that I was reinforcing my terror every time I avoided the highway and took an alternate route instead, but I didn't feel I had an option. I began to depend on my husband and other people to drive me anywhere that couldn't be accessed by a two-lane road. I withdrew from my teenagers' volleyball carpool and asked them to chauffeur me once they got their licenses.

My phobia was a source of shame, a secret that I did my best to hide from my youngest child as she grew from a baby into a young girl. But when she turned seven, she started commenting on the fact that I always took the back roads whenever I was behind the wheel. I was devastated when I realised that she would soon know my secret: I wasn't the strong, brave woman I pretended to be.

I did some soul-searching and reached a disheartening conclusion: It was too late. After seven years of negative reinforcement, my neural pathways were set. I was permanently conditioned for a panic response. As much as it grieved me, it was time to throw in the towel and accept the consequences.

But just when I'd made this decision, a friend told me an extraordinary story. She'd stepped out on a limb financially in an act of faith and had been rewarded with an unexpected gift that exactly met her needs — right to the very penny.

I was humbled by this story. I was also a person of faith, and yet I'd reached the conclusion that overcoming my highway phobia was impossible. But was it truly impossible, or was the obstacle only in my mind? Over the years, I'd made several attempts to overcome my fear, all without success. I resolved to try once more — but this time I wouldn't give up.

I started at the library where I found the book that would change everything. The author of *Freedom from Fear* was no stranger to phobias. For thirty-one years, Dr. Howard Liebgold hid a crippling case of claustrophobia, at the expense of some of his closest relationships. But just when he was ready to take his own life out of despair, he discovered an organization that was having astounding success treating phobias. The workshop he took transformed his life, and he made it his mission to pass on all the secrets of that transformation.

I devoured Dr. Liebgold's book. I was inspired by his personal testimony, encouraged by his corny sense of humor, and empowered by the practical details of his step-by-step program. Most important, I was in the right frame of mind to receive his wisdom. I committed myself to following his program, with its combination of knowledge, gradual desensitization, positive reinforcement, and relaxation techniques.

The first step was the hardest: getting back out on the asphalt. I waited until late evening, when traffic on the nearest stretch of highway would be light, and it would be dark enough that no one could identify me. I pulled off to the side of the road until there was a gap in the traffic. I could barely go forty miles per hour at first, and I had to signal and pull off every time I saw someone approaching in my rearview mirror. My heart raced, but I persisted, doing loop after loop of that same two-mile stretch. Night after night, I repeated this exercise, rewarding myself with little treats for every victory, no matter how small. Gradually, my speed and confidence increased, and I was able to expand my territory.

I wept the first time I drove all the way to the far edge of the next community without stopping — a distance of only twenty miles. And when I made it over a mountain pass and into the heart of the nearest large city, the tears really streamed down my face. I drove back home in a rainstorm the same night, as proud of myself as I have ever been.

I'm still a cautious driver by nature, but I can get anywhere I need to go without hesitation. I have no trouble keeping up with the flow of traffic, and the urge to slam my foot on the brakes is gone. When conditions are good, I even find myself enjoying the open road!

Fear is a greedy thief: The more territory we concede, the more it takes. But with the right tools, that territory can be reclaimed, as I've discovered to my immense gratitude.

~Rachel Dunstan Muller

93

Choosing Hope

*It is hope that gives life meaning. And hope is based on
the prospect of being able one day to turn the actual
world into a possible one that looks better.*
~François Jacob

My parents never kept my adoption a secret, speaking openly
about what they knew of my birth family and even taking
me to the adoption agency to let me see where they picked
me up. My parents encouraged my quest to find my birth
parents, and I requested my original birth certificate when I turned
nineteen. When it came in the mail, I could barely speak. I was holding the key to my past in my hand. There it was, the name of my
mother, the address where she grew up—everything I needed to
find her.

I sat on it for months while trying to gain the courage to begin
my search. We adopted kids are told to never get our hopes up about
our birth family. We are told to realize that there were reasons we were
given up, and that those reasons might be painful to discover. We are
told our parents might be drug addicts, dead, or (the most painful)
may want nothing to do with us.

That was the one that frightened me most. If my mom was a drug
addict... whatever. If she was dead, well, I didn't know her to begin
with, so I would grieve her passing and mourn that I would never
know her. But if she didn't want me... Well, that was different. You

see, my adopted mom had kicked me out a couple of years before. We were both going through a lot emotionally. My parents had divorced years before, and she was raising me on her own. That was when the abandonment hit home. If my own mother who raised me couldn't accept me, what did that say about me? A mother is supposed to love her child no matter what. What kind of monster was I that my own mom couldn't stand to be around me?

I didn't think I could handle that level of rejection again. I knew it would destroy me to not be wanted by two mothers in one lifetime. One might ask, "Your birth mom already gave you up. Did you not already feel abandoned by her?" My birth mother was fourteen years old when she had me. She was a child herself. I couldn't imagine being faced with pregnancy at that age, especially in her case, where she didn't know she was pregnant until the day I was born.

I didn't resent her for giving me up, but I just couldn't bring myself to try to find her. The rift between my adopted mother and me had compounded the trust issues I already had. I also had a stepmom in the picture, which only confused matters further for me as my dad became more and more involved with a family that I didn't consider to be my own.

Eventually, though, my curiosity won out over my fear. I just had to know, for better or worse. So, I began searching Internet databases. Numerous Google and Facebook searches brought many women to my attention, but none of them looked like me or matched all of the descriptions I had of my birth mom.

Then one day, I was absentmindedly searching Facebook for her name, and a new face appeared. It was a woman in her thirties, with a medium complexion, big blue eyes, and a smile I knew. A grin that showed almost all of her teeth. A grin that made her eyes sparkle and crinkle up just a little bit. A smile that I had seen so many times in photographs of myself.

I checked the name. Her last name had changed, but her maiden name was in parentheses beside it. There it was: my birth mother's full name next to a beautiful, smiling face. I sent her a message. I don't even remember what it said now, but it was heartfelt and excited. Then I waited, trying not to check my Facebook every hour. I waited, and waited, and waited.

I waited for two years. It didn't hurt me, not really. Like I said, we adopted kids are told not to get our hopes up.

Then one night I got a message from a friend of mine. It's a message no one ever wants to receive. One of my closest friends had killed himself. I stared down at my phone in shock and then began looking up news articles to figure out exactly what had happened. I left my phone on the charger and went back to sit on the couch. My phone buzzed again and I sighed, not really wanting to check it but knowing it could be more information about my friend. So, I went and picked it up.

A Facebook notification appeared saying I had a new message. I was too preoccupied to even consider who it could be from. I opened it, and for the second time in an hour, I stared at my phone in shock. It was from *her*. Since we weren't friends on Facebook, the message I had sent her had been moved to an alternative box. She had just found it.

I read it and burst into tears. She spoke of her love for me, and how she had thought about me every day since making the decision to give me up. She told me the whole story and welcomed me to come and meet her family. My family. Within hours, I had a message from the oldest of my younger brothers. We are only a few years apart, and we speak with startling similarity. All three of us, in fact, speak with the same cadence. We have the same gestures, the same high-strung, bright-eyed excitement for life. Nature versus nurture is a fascinating study.

Within days, my grandmother had also messaged me to welcome me home. Never in my wildest dreams did I imagine the amount of love I have received from them. I moved in with my brother to get to know him. We argued and fought and loved each other just as siblings should.

I live apart from all of my families now, but I feel their love daily. I have three families: my birth family, my adopted family, and my step-family. I worked up the courage to reach out, to look fear in the face and say, "I am going to do this anyway." And now I feel like one of the most loved and adored children on the planet.

~Clara Ember

The Joy of a Mortal Body

*Yoga is the perfect opportunity to be
curious about who you are.*
~Jason Crandell

I started doing yoga in college. I was naturally flexible, so it felt like an easy form of exercise. I could already touch my toes, balance on one leg, and twist myself into eagle pose. Usually, I wouldn't even break a sweat. I wasn't particularly committed or regular in my practice, though. I didn't even own a mat. Since I went so rarely, it just made sense to rent one at the studio each time.

Fast-forward a few decades. I graduated, started working, got married, and moved to Montreal. My husband Derek and I had three kids: two girls and one boy. My third pregnancy especially took its toll. My hips hurt, my legs cramped, my back ached, and my neck felt stiff. My obstetrician tracked my weight on the same chart she'd used for my previous pregnancy, so I could see month by month how I was gaining weight more quickly this time around.

Fast-forward a couple more years. Our kids — Sonya, Leena, and Arjun — were now seven, five, and two. The hurting, cramping, aching, stiffness, and discomfort from my third pregnancy had never completely gone away. My birthday is at the end of March. I had always used it as a time of self-reflection, and this year I realized I was feeling worn down. If I didn't do something, I'd probably break.

Right around that time, the yoga studio around the corner advertised a thirty-day hot yoga challenge for the month of April, which sounded appealing in the chilly springtime. But thirty days straight? I wasn't so sure.

But I wanted my kids to know the version of me that used to be full of energy and stamina. I kept thinking about how I could make it work—sixty minutes for each class, plus ten minutes to the studio, five minutes to shower, ten minutes home—ninety minutes minimum per class every single day for an entire month. Was that realistic? When would I do this? The mornings were already jam-packed trying to get us ready and out the door. Fitting in exercise during the workday had never panned out. That only left the evenings, but I didn't want to miss out on dinners and bedtime snuggles. And I couldn't imagine doing yoga after the kids were asleep, when I was bone-tired and didn't want to leave the house.

Hot yoga is intense. The theory behind the heat is that it makes the heart work harder, the body sweat more, and the joints and muscles loosen, allowing a deeper expression of each posture. The first time I tried it in my twenties, I had to lie down on my mat for the second half of class so I wouldn't throw up or pass out.

I told Derek, "I haven't worked out twice in a row since…" I really couldn't remember.

On April Fool's Day, which was a Saturday, the kids and I went out for breakfast. The yoga studio was on our walk home.

"Mom, why are we stopping?" Leena asked.

"I need to do something," I said.

Sonya wrote my name on the wall chart where I'd eventually put a sticker each day I showed up for class. I paid the non-refundable fee for the 30-Day Hot Yoga Challenge. That night, after Sonya, Leena, and Arjun were all asleep, I went back to the studio for Day One.

Turns out I could no longer reach my toes—or even my ankles. I lost my balance on Warrior One when I tried to reach my arms overhead. My spine did not want to twist or backbend or forward fold. I was no longer made of rubber, but rigid plastic that might crack in half if I wasn't careful. But I felt proud of myself anyway and excited that I was in the studio, finally doing something for my body and myself.

I texted Derek: "Signed up for 30-Day Yoga Challenge. Want to do it with me? Laura can babysit every night after kids asleep."

Laura was a college student, our go-to babysitter. She'd agreed to a discount rate for the month.

"Sure. Let's do it," he texted back. Derek had recently recovered from a bout of sciatic nerve pain. His physiotherapist told him he had very tight hips and needed to work on his flexibility. Both of us were gradually falling apart, and we needed to take drastic action.

The second class felt more brutal. I was still sore from the first class. I did not want to go back, but I did. On Yoga Challenge Day 4, Derek came with me. At first, I was a little worried about how much I'd be sweating and how ridiculous I'd look in my tight workout clothes. Then we started the practice, and I got too busy with my steady yoga breathing and trying not to fall over. I only had time to focus on what my body was doing, not how it was looking. I swapped one kind of self-consciousness for another.

"I had trouble with the balance poses," I said on our walk home — in case he'd missed me toppling out of standing bow pulling pose.

"Pigeon felt great," he said. "My hip was really open."

Taking on 30 Days of Yoga had a big ripple effect throughout my life. It became a key habit that created other habits. I drank more water. I became more mindful about what I ate. Heavy, greasy food did not feel good during class. I did laundry more regularly to deal with my sweaty workout clothes. I made sure the living room was tidy for Laura every night. I focused better at work. I started feeling more in control, less helpless about change, more open to challenges even outside of yoga. I found I was more patient, kind, and thoughtful.

Day in, day out, even when I didn't feel like it, I kept showing up for myself on the mat. I did miss a few days in April, but overall I was consistent. Yoga is now a crucial part of my life. And even as I get better, I find new ways to express each pose, even ones I think I know already. This same practice echoes throughout my life — from trying new recipes to seeking new experiences or accepting bigger challenges at work.

There are people in my class who can do headstands and crow pose and double pigeon. Their bodies are supple, lithe, and graceful.

But instead of feeling defeated, I feel inspired.

For a long time, without really acknowledging it, I'd lost the joy of being in my body. By ignoring and masking the pain I'd allowed myself to live with on a daily basis, I'd numbed myself to other feelings as well. Now, through yoga, I've found my way back to that joy again, to appreciate the here and now, to connect with myself, to access the fullness of human experience. It isn't always comfortable or easy, but it is full of revelation and opportunity for second, third, and fourth chances — as many as we are willing to give ourselves.

~Mitali Ruths

Life Guard

*Love yourself first and everything else falls into
line. You really have to love yourself to get
anything done in this world.*
~Lucille Ball

Not many people choose to become a lifeguard for the first time at age thirty-five, but I did, and it was one of the best experiences of my life. The decision began while I was pounding away on a treadmill that overlooked the pool at my health club. The treadmill was a perfect analogy for my life: I was running, but getting nowhere. I was in a rut physically and emotionally, and I knew it.

As I ran, I watched the lifeguards work. Most of them were teenagers or college students. I had always wanted to be a lifeguard. Both my parents and my younger sister were lifeguards when they were teens. I grew up around water and was a strong swimmer.

What was not strong, however, was my self-esteem. In my teens and college years, I had an eating disorder that made me loathe my body. Even though I was thin, I would wear T-shirts over my bathing suit and avert my eyes from others — certainly not traits compatible with lifeguarding.

I recovered from my eating disorder in my mid-twenties when I became a mom, and I forgot about lifeguarding until I found myself on that treadmill at age thirty-five.

A stay-at-home mother of two boys, my body was finally healthy, but my marriage to a dentist (who had complete control of our finances) was not. As I ran on the treadmill, I thought not only about lifeguarding, but the need to change my life.

After one of my treadmill runs, I went down to the pool and nervously approached the pool director (who was much younger than me). "Will you be holding lifeguard classes soon?" I asked her.

As fate would have it, she said a new class was starting the following week, and she would be hiring many people who passed the class. "Are you interested for yourself?" she asked.

"Yes," I said. "I've always wanted to be a lifeguard."

I held my breath expecting her to laugh, but she told me how awesome she thought it was and encouraged me to sign up. "We could use some lifeguards with more life experience," she said kindly.

That night, when I told my husband I had signed up for a lifeguard certification program, he looked at me like I had lost my mind. I hadn't. I realized I had just taken the first step to reclaiming myself.

The lifeguard certification program was not easy!

The hardest part was walking onto the pool deck for the first time in my bathing suit with twenty other candidates — none more than twenty-five years old! With my little tummy pooch from two C-sections, I knew I looked like I could be the mother of some of them, but they didn't seem to care.

In the pool, our age didn't matter. What mattered was how quickly we could pull a drowning "victim" up from twelve feet under, or give CPR to a choking child.

I passed the class and was hired as a lifeguard and swimming instructor at the fitness club. Working at the pool gave me an amazing surge of self-esteem, confidence and inner strength. I felt the strongest I had in my entire life.

Every time I blew my whistle or helped a child, I helped myself, too. I filed for divorce — something I should have done years prior. Having my own paycheck and earning power — even though it was peanuts compared to my husband's — was a huge motivator.

I worked as a lifeguard for almost two years until I transitioned back into the career I had before I got married. They were truly two of the most important and amazing years of my life.

As lifeguards, we're emboldened that we can save someone else's life, but I saved my own, too.

~Caurie Putnam

96

Body Liberation

You are allowed to be both a masterpiece
and a work in progress, simultaneously.
~Sophia Bush

"Come on, Marie, we want to see your pretty bathing suit. Take off your shirt." My suit had a pink lace overlay and a little flounce around the waist. I loved it, but I was a big girl and embarrassed. Even at eight years old, I was very self-conscious about my weight, so the shirt stayed on.

As I got older, I covered up my bathing suit with shorts. My thighs, butt, and belly were the bane of my existence. I would try to diet or have brief ambitions of exercise, but the truth was I was a big girl who preferred drawing to sports, and pretzels to carrots. I was most comfortable wearing baggy clothes that would hide my full figure. Overalls were a favorite. Thank goodness for the baggy, grunge fashions of the 1990s.

When I went off to college, my lifestyle changed dramatically. Without even trying too hard, the weight fell off. My body confidence improved, but I still wouldn't walk around in a bathing suit.

Fast-forward twenty years, three kids and various body changes, and I'm still not completely comfortable with my body. I'm actually in the best shape of my life. On the one hand, I know I look good. My jeans are "skinny," and my ample glutes look good in them. On the other hand, I can think of many reasons I would love to sit down with a plastic surgeon. Each morning I look in the mirror and think, *I really wish I could lift these a bit and smooth out this and... I AM SO SICK OF IT!*

This year, I will turn forty years old, and it's time to begin a new chapter. So here I stand in a room full of strangers without a stitch of clothing on my body. In order to force myself to completely accept my body, I am posing nude. I am standing here while artists draw what they see before them. On full display are my breasts that nursed three babies, my stomach that cradled my unborn children, my belly button that flipped inside out three times and never quite recovered, my wide hips, my big butt, my stretch marks and cellulite. They will draw me and help me see beyond the imperfections.

The room is warm, even though it's quite cold outside. They have the heat turned up for me, which is very considerate. It's a spacious room on the second floor of the art school with tall windows letting in plenty of natural light. There is also a large lamp shining down and casting shadows and highlights on my body. I am standing with one hand on my hip and the other resting on a pedestal. One knee is slightly bent, and I am completely naked. My flaws are on display. I'm avoiding all eye contact and just staring at the light switch on the wall. The instructor is walking around the room speaking with the artists about their work, and offering suggestions and constructive criticisms. I could be a piece of furniture as far as they're concerned. A sofa or a wingback chair. This is just another day in art class for them. Meanwhile, in my mind a war between self-doubt and liberation is taking place. For the most part, I feel confident and secure, excited by what I'm doing. But there is also that small, nagging voice in the back of my head saying, *I can't believe I'm doing this. What was I thinking?*

Time moves surprisingly fast considering I've just been standing in place. It is time for a break. I don my robe, and the instructor calls me over to one of the artist's easels. The artist is an older woman with a very soft voice and a kind face. She tells me with a smile, "Look how beautiful." I turn toward her easel and see a sketch of a woman. She is tall. Her thighs are thick. Her belly tells a story of motherhood, and her breasts appear soft. She looks beautiful and proud. And she is me!

~Marie Petrarch

97

Mascara First

There are some things one can only achieve by a
deliberate leap in the opposite direction.
~Franz Kafka

I turned the wipers on high as I sprayed squirt after squirt of fluid to clear the snow off my windshield. The harder I tried to clear it, the worse it got. The snow kept freezing into layers of mush so thick I couldn't see the road. Convinced I had a serious issue with my car's heating system, I headed to the nearest service station.

"Give 'er another squirt," the mechanic hollered, as he stood poised to observe. A minute later, he pronounced his diagnosis. "Lady, you filled 'er with summer fluid. Don't you know you need the blue stuff, not the pink, in December?"

No, I did not, and that was not the only thing I didn't know when I ended up alone after twenty-eight years of marriage!

After being a stay-at-home mom for years, raising four children from breastfeeding to bridal feasts, diapers to driver's licenses, I was on my own. Those who knew me best knew what I had endured, but the concept of "security" always came up. Even the minister, after counseling, had swept his arms around the grand rooms of the house and asked, "Are you willing to give up all this?" I had already figured out that, despite what we are led to believe, most of us cannot "have it all." I made the choice. I took the risk to let go of my "security" in order to save myself, my health, and my sanity.

I needed an income. Despite having been a nurse, I was afraid to go back into the profession after so many years out of it. I was afraid of harming someone. My solution was to seek a job where this could never be an issue. I called a local undertaker and asked how soon I could begin training to become an embalmer! He talked me out of it immediately, explaining that undertakers are also responsible for picking up bodies, like maybe a three-hundred-pound man from a fifth-floor apartment, and carrying him out.

I went to Plan B. I enrolled in the Registered Nurses Refresher Course, and for many months buried my head in thick textbooks with thin pages and fine print. (I only noticed this when a friend, who was studying for her MBA, pointed out that her books had thick glossy pages, large print and lots of pie charts!) I completed all the requirements, wrote twenty-four exams, and discovered that I actually loved studying. I was eager to go back to the profession I had enjoyed in my earlier life.

Having a job, a paycheck, and structure in my life gradually built up my previously battered self-confidence. But holidays are not easy when one is solo, so I happily volunteered to work Christmas, Easter, and Thanksgiving so young nurses with children could be home with their families.

I lived in much more humble accommodations, but I discovered the joy of not cleaning four bathrooms and vacuuming Oriental rugs. I had to be careful not to indulge in luxuries, but I did take the advice of a friend I admired. She was a woman who managed to look elegant even while cleaning up after her dog in the park. She took care of herself. We were discussing budgets one day when she looked me in the eye and said, "Even if you are hard up, buy the mascara first, not the lawn fertilizer."

It's been twenty years now, and my life has slowly and gradually returned to some state of equilibrium. One thing I learned that I valued above all else was the difference a single day can make. Through many lonely, stressful and painful days, it took only one day of something good happening to make it all bearable. I had many lessons to learn besides which washer fluid to put in my car. But my friends were wonderful teachers, helpers, comrades in joy and loyal supporters in trials.

When I moved two thousand miles away from home and the security and comfort of close friends, I knew my survival would depend on new friends. But sometimes even finding a new friend involves taking a risk. I was checking out of a hotel in Jacksonville, having spent two weeks there prior to finding accommodations in the big city where my new life had taken me.

Suddenly, the impact of not knowing one soul in the city, with a metropolitan area population of over one-and-a-half million, weighed heavily on me. In a weak voice, I muttered to the checkout clerk — who had been kind to me during my stay, helping me fax documents and such — that I knew not a soul in the city. She was a rather reserved lady, approximately my age, and she peered over her glasses at me. "Here," she said. "Here's my phone number. If you'd like to call, we could meet somewhere for coffee." A total stranger, a woman whom I later learned lived alone, was reaching out to me, giving me her contact information, and I was touched.

I called a couple weeks later. We met at a nearby coffee shop. During the conversation, we both acknowledged that it is difficult to meet friends as one gets older, and we both could use a friend in our lives. I suggested some guidelines that went something like this. We have coffee. If we like the time together, great. We can do it again. If, for any reason, either of us dislikes it or is uncomfortable, we cease. No questions asked. No badgering. No coercion. End of story. Period!

I received an e-mail shortly after we had our first coffee. "Enjoyed it. Love to do it again."

I wrote back, "Me, too!"

We started having lunches. We are from totally different backgrounds, different religions, different political views, and different regions of the country. We have fun and laugh a lot every time we meet. She is a witty and wise woman, and I admire her immensely. I no longer live in Jacksonville, but Lyn and I are still close friends. She has been there for me during some significant crises, and we look forward to becoming closer as the years go on. She dared to risk giving her phone number to a stranger from Canada, and I dared call a stranger and meet her for coffee.

Since leaving Canada twelve years ago to establish a new life in Florida, I have met many wonderful new friends and enjoyed experiences I would have felt were impossible years ago. I have stumbled, fallen, picked myself up, put on my mascara and started all over again. Am I out of my comfort zone? You bet. That's where I live! But it's actually more fun and much richer than living with mahogany furniture, chandeliers, and Oriental rugs!

~Phyllis McKinley

98

From Restriction to Open Spaces

I can't imagine a person becoming a success who doesn't give this game of life everything he's got.
~Walter Cronkite

took a look at the calendar — exactly thirty-nine days until moving day. I was terrified!

The children were so happy, they handmade a countdown sheet so they could began marking off the days. I didn't sleep much during those thirty-nine days. The "what-ifs" kept me up at night and almost scared me into changing my mind and staying right where I was.

I had lived in the projects (federal, public housing) all of my life. I was born and raised there. And when my great-grandmother died, she was living there; it was all that I knew. To others, it was poverty, but to me it was my life. And here I was getting ready to step out of my normal into an anomaly; I was petrified, to say the least. The rent wasn't adjustable at the place I was moving to. I couldn't sleep at night, worrying. *What if I lose my job? What if I end up homeless? What if I can't afford my light bill?*

Finally, I talked myself into going for it. The worst that could happen is that I wouldn't be able to pay my rent, and my children and I would end up homeless. I decided that it was better to fail than not try at all, so I did it.

On April 15, 2015, I gave away the last few pieces of furniture in my old apartment. I packed up the kids and my clothes and headed to my new, fully furnished luxury apartment. With tears in my eyes, I was mentally stuck somewhere between feeling undeserving of such a beautiful new start and terrified of failing as my entire family watched me take this leap.

I was awestruck by what I walked into. Every piece of furniture, linen, dish, and decorative piece was brand-new and well-placed for my children and me. Friends, family and strangers alike came together to make this transition possible for us, and I had no words that could adequately express the appreciation I felt.

After the excitement wore off, the feeling that I would somehow fail continued to consume my thoughts. Renter's insurance, light bill, gas bill, budget—all of these things were foreign to me, but I was determined to give it my all.

I thought the move would be the scariest part of this transition, but I was wrong. Great new apartment, great high-salary job... what more could I ask for? The more appropriate question would have been, "What's the catch?"

When one lives on government assistance, any change of address or employment must be reported immediately. Since I was still receiving food assistance and medical insurance, I turned in the appropriate documentation and didn't give it a second thought.

A week later, I received a letter from the local Health and Human Services Department that stated I was no longer eligible for food assistance or medical insurance. My new income was too high.

For most people, this would be considered good news, but for me it was scary. I was once again frozen with fear. I went from a sliding-scale rent that fluctuated based on income, free health insurance for myself and my children, and $600 a month in food assistance to $1,065 set rent regardless of income, health insurance that was deducted from my wages, and $0 in food assistance.

I thought about giving it all up and going back on assistance. But after speaking with my boss and other people who made up my support system, I came to my senses. After all, there was nothing to turn back to. I had given it all up. I made the decision again to move forward and give it a try. The worst thing that could happen was failure.

Fast-forward to the present day: It has been more than two years since I moved out of public housing and stopped receiving government assistance. And guess what? I survived. I haven't been evicted, I haven't made a late rent payment, my children have never gone hungry, not even for a day, and I don't have a single regret!

I am living in a new kind of freedom, and my "normal" has a whole different definition. Poverty no longer controls me; instead, I am living in "wide open spaces." It's the best feeling in the world.

Poverty is a hole that consumes everything it touches. It's too deep to climb out of alone, and it's comfortable enough to cradle us until we leave this earth. We have to want out, but the door is heavy. I am dedicated to helping anyone who wants to take that first step and experience those wide-open spaces.

I've committed my life to helping anyone and everyone who decides they want to be free from poverty. Someone helped me, and now it's my turn to pay it forward.

~Yashika R. Smith

99

Cooking Up a New Life

The only thing worse than starting something
and failing... is not starting something.
~Seth Godin

n December 2015, I attended a conference. Five well-established and successful women were on the panel. The topic for their hour-long session was "Bouncing Back after Setbacks." As I sat there listening to their many personal and professional blunders and setbacks, I remember feeling lucky that I hadn't made that many mistakes in my own life.

Those women had lost thousands in investments, started companies that had failed, sold companies that later ended up being worth millions, and lost partners in the name of business. They had passed on wonderful opportunities. Despite knowing that they had, in fact, bounced back and were again doing very well, I was starting to feel sorry for them.

Then, as if someone whispered in my ear, I heard the words: "Don't be so proud of yourself. You haven't made any mistakes because you haven't lived at all. Look how boring your life is." *Whose voice was this, and with what audacity did it speak to me like that?*

I think, for the first time, I heard my own heart speak. It shook me to my core, and it took all I had to keep from crying. I tuned out the rest of the presentation and started thinking of the mistakes I had made in my own life. The voice was right. There weren't many at all. I had followed a straight path for thirty-eight years. I went to school, earned bachelor's and master's degrees with honors, and stayed at every job I'd had far longer than it was professionally beneficial for me to do so. In fact, at thirty-eight, I had only had three jobs. "The devil you know is better than the one you don't" was my motto.

A quick review of my life made me realize that it was the actions I *hadn't* taken that I was suddenly regretting. I *hadn't* studied abroad. I *hadn't* risked love. In fact, I was perpetually single. I *hadn't* started a business. I *hadn't* traveled enough. Even my wardrobe was filled with predictable black clothing. I had said "no" far more than "yes."

The voice that whispered to me lingered into the New Year. It was like it mocked me. The thought of turning forty frightened me. It's one thing to be unhappy and unsettled in your twenties, and perhaps even in one's thirties. But was I going to start a new decade with the same boredom? I lacked any zest for life. I needed something to pick me up, some activity I could look forward to. Something new to do.

I started thinking of activities that I enjoyed and thought about cooking classes. *Perhaps I'll sign up for a few cooking classes at the adult education center,* I thought to myself. Then I thought back to the last baking class I had taken. I had been highly disappointed. *I could teach this!* I thought.

And that's exactly what I did. I contacted several local adult education centers and, despite my lack of teaching experience, the centers took it for granted that being a native Italian was a good enough qualification to teach Italian cooking. As the class approached, I started to get anxious. Imposter syndrome set in. *Who am I to teach cooking?* The reality was that I was, in fact, a darn good cook, and a baker, too. My cooking and baking have always been praised, and I actually enjoyed doing them. I just needed to build my confidence to lead a class.

And it worked! During my first class, my voice shook. My legs felt like they would give out on me. But with each recipe we prepared, the students became more excited. They were actually enjoying it.

Perhaps it was the cooking classes that gave me more confidence, but I started to think of additional ways I could grow and add some zest to my life. I couldn't stop thinking about starting my own business. I had always loved traveling back to Italy and had visions of

bringing people there on culinary tours. We'd take cooking classes, visit wineries, and bond with the locals over meals we'd share. And with that thought in mind, I built a website, formed an LLC, and Lazy Italian Culinary Adventures was born.

I knew I needed visibility for the new business. I started posting all over Facebook, continued teaching my classes, and even started teaching them at home. I contacted a newspaper and told them about my business. They wrote up a full feature on my business, headshot and all. As I read the paper and took calls from my neighbors congratulating me, I wondered, *Who is this person?* I hated having my picture taken, hated the spotlight, and now I was sending my photo to anyone who would consider writing about my business. I appeared on three local TV shows, and while my voice cracked and my heart raced, I kept telling myself, *You got this.*

As I write this, I'm preparing to lead our inaugural culinary trips to Italy. I'm sure I will be nervous and anxious. I'm sure my voice will crack as I embark on this new journey. I'm certain mishaps will happen. However, I have faith in my ability to figure things out. I am no longer sitting on the sidelines of my own life. I'm finally looking forward to waking up every morning.

~Francesca Montillo

100

Conquering My Mountain

Leave the beaten track occasionally and dive into the
woods. Every time you do so you will be certain to find
something that you have never seen before.
~Alexander Graham Bell

At age fifty, I found myself on a rocky path. I had just gone through a divorce, and I lacked self-confidence. I realized that I had consistently put other people's needs and expectations ahead of my own. I remember looking in a mirror one rainy afternoon and seeing a tear-soaked, puffy-eyed shell of a person who no longer recalled who she was, what she loved to do, and what she was capable of doing.

Back when I was in my early twenties, I looked forward to a life of adventure. I thought I might hitchhike across the country like my brothers did, scale mountains and swim in ice-cold streams in the stunning landscapes of the western United States. But when the time came to feed my soul like my brothers did, I shriveled in fear. Instead, I fed myself preemptive rhetoric like, *I'm a girl, and girls shouldn't be so adventurous. Something bad could happen to me.* This went on throughout my adult years, when my adventures were confined to car camping.

Not only did I avoid adventure, but I also held back from pursuing just about anything else I had yearned for in my youth. By age fifty, I still hadn't pursued my interest in art, playing the guitar, and singing. I hadn't become a forest ranger, geologist, or paleontologist. Instead, I played it safe.

Then a new man entered my life. He picked up on my soul's unspoken desires. "How about backpacking for five days in Yosemite National Park?" he asked.

"Sure!" I said, wanting to impress him with who I wanted to be, not who I had become. And then I thought, *Backpacking? I can't go backpacking! I'm a girl. Backpacking's dangerous!*

Because I liked this guy so much, though, I worked through my fears and trained like mad for a month so I could go backpacking with him. I had never felt so full of self-doubt, but I kept reminding myself, *Isn't this what I always wanted? Isn't this supposed to be who I am, or who I think I am, or who I claim I am?*

For an entire month, I scaled local hills with an increasing number of water jugs in my backpack until it matched in pounds what I had to carry on the trip. My heart pounded out of my chest. My legs trembled, even with the aid of trekking poles. My back ached in as many places as there are vertebrae in a spine. And then the day finally came when my Adventure Man shot the deadweight cannonball that was me from its chamber and thrust me out with him into the wilderness at Yosemite.

Day One's hike proved to be the shortest trek, but the biggest reality check. I couldn't have been more relieved to drop the forty-pound backpack to the ground when we got to a clearing that would serve as our campsite for the night. When Adventure Man reminded me we would squeeze in a two-mile satellite hike to the North Dome vista before dinner, I forced a smile and replied, "Wouldn't dream of missing it."

Ill thoughts aside, when I first caught the view from North Dome across to Half Dome, where ants climbing along its uppermost ridge turned out to be people hiking to the top, or the view down into Yosemite Valley where meadows and trees rolled out before me like a lush, emerald green carpet, the views took my breath away... in a very good way.

Day Two proved better than Day One and had me thinking, *Maybe I can do this after all.* The trek was longer, but my body hung in there. At the end of the day, I traversed a long tree trunk that had fallen across a wide stream, so we could camp at a desolate location on the other side. Sweating and shaking, I barely kept my balance with the weight of the backpack nearly tipping me over into the water on several occasions, but I made it and let out a deep sigh of relief when I reached the other side. I turned around, and after realizing what I'd done, smiled broadly and said, "Wow, that was all me. I did that." Soon, as we dumped our backpacks in the clearing of our campsite, we stripped down to nearly nothing and swam in the deep stream, losing the feeling in our bodies after ten seconds in the ice-cold water that had made its way from the snowier elevations upstream.

On the morning of Day Three, just as we settled into a breakfast of reconstituted eggs and sausage, I panicked when a young cinnamon-colored bear came way too close to our campsite in search of food. Adventure Man yelled at the bear, but it wouldn't go away. We waved our trekking poles over our heads to make us look bigger than the bear, but it wouldn't go away. When Adventure Man threw several rocks at the bear, I smacked him in the arm. "Throwing rocks? At a bear? Are you freakin' kidding me?" But Adventure Man knew better than I did. The bear decided it wasn't worth the effort and instead made its way over the stream on the same log we had crossed the night before — the same one we would have to cross within the next hour to get back on the trail. The next several hours, while trekking along heavily forested trails, I looked over my shoulder more than I looked ahead of me.

Later in Day Three, I had a major meltdown, when after eight miles my body decided it'd had enough. I could not walk one more step. As soon as my body decided to shut down, my rational brain decided to shut down with it. The only thing that didn't shut down was the waterworks coming from my eyes. Adventure Man missed the meltdown because he had gotten ahead of me on the trail. Eventually, I thought to blow the whistle that dangled from my backpack, after which he doubled back to find me slumped across a rock, unable to even lift myself or stop crying. He let me have my cry, and then announced, "Well, I guess this is a good time for having lunch." He injected as much humor as he could into the moment. He snapped a photo of me, after which I flipped him the bird. He snapped another photo of me, catching me flipping him the bird. He snapped one more photo of me twenty minutes later, and I managed a smirk.

The rest of the trip was harsh. My feet, full of blisters, stung with every step. When we took a wrong turn somewhere near the end, the final five-mile hike on the highway turned into eight miles — all uphill. It got so I had to take off my hiking boots the last two miles and walk in my socks, which felt marginally better than with the boots. But I made it. When we reached the car and dropped the backpacks to the ground for the last time, I felt an immense weight fall off not only my shoulders, but also my soul. I felt lighter than air.

After Adventure Man loaded my backpack in the car, I sank into the passenger seat and pulled down the sun visor to make use of its mirror. There in the mirror, I saw the reflection of that monumental mountain I once feared now fading like a phantom into the twilight sky. And I also saw someone I hadn't seen in a while — a bright-eyed, glass-full-to-the-brim me. Someone full of adventure, gratitude, and newly found wisdom. And I knew from that moment forward, I'd never lose myself again.

~Susan Maddy Jones

101

An Agoraphobic's International Flight for Love

*Your vision will become clear only when you look
into your heart. Who looks outside, dreams;
who looks inside, awakens.*

~Carl Jung

When two agoraphobics fall in love across an ocean, one is going to have to board a plane. I have agoraphobia, anxiety attacks, and depression, but on January 16, 2016, I found myself at Washington Dulles International Airport with a round-trip ticket to Heathrow Airport to meet a woman I fell in love with two years earlier over the Internet — a woman who loved me just as deeply in return.

Daphne and I met on a website dedicated to helping people with chronic problems. Divorce, anger issues, or anything of the sort were fair game. She suffered from chronic fatigue syndrome, fibromyalgia, and agoraphobia. I lived in California; she lived in England outside of London. And from the moment we decided to video chat with each other, we fell in love and spoke every day for hours. This started in August 2013 when we were both twenty-nine.

Neither of us wanted a long-distance relationship. The days, weeks, and months passed by with talks about how we'd start our lives together.

Daphne was a painter and card maker who lived with her parents after a rough patch. While we awaited a miracle that would bring us together, we would send each other what I called a "Pandora's Box." This was a simple box or container in which we would put knickknacks from around our homes along with notes or small gifts. I received various things from her, such as an earring, a seashell from a beach she had visited in Spain, English coins, and a bag of her favorite tea. I would send her things in kind from the States.

I thought it all ended when I said something unintentionally offensive—something that I didn't realize would be a problem in England. Daphne shut down her chat camera and didn't speak to me for four weeks.

I was dying inside. I knew I'd never hear from her again, so there was only one thing to do after four weeks: let go of the woman I wanted to marry or do something drastic.

Finally, I sent Daphne an e-mail that contained nothing but the song "Take Me Home Tonight" by Eddie Money. Four days later, she responded with a song, "Beetlebum" by Blur. That was all, no words, just the song. This little song duel went back and forth until, after two months, I asked Daphne if she would be willing to speak to me again. She agreed, and by the time our video chats resumed, we were head-over-heels for each other again.

Fast-forward to September 2015. I had moved from California to Virginia and back to my parents' house for financial reasons. I had worked diligently on myself, knowing full well I'd never have a chance with Daphne if I couldn't work up the nerve to fly to England. Then, I surprised her with an e-mail: an itinerary for a visit. We had spoken about this many times before—the possibility of a two-week visit to see if we were both absolutely "bonkers," as she put it.

The day finally came. I had two weeks off from work and my father was nice enough to drive me to the airport. I said my goodbye to him and walked into the airport, worried about whether I would have a panic attack.

I couldn't stop thinking of everything that could possibly go wrong. I wanted so badly to be back at home, in the dark with candles lit. It took all I had not to turn around and walk out. My father was still there in the airport. He would have no sympathy, as U.S. Marines usually do not, but he would understand.

But I managed to get on that plane and fly to England. I took the National Express from Heathrow to Stansted, and this is when it hit me: I was perfectly fine on the bus. Flying is terrifying, but having done that, I didn't see how a bus ride would be challenging — even when I tried to think of ways to *make* it challenging on myself. It was a beautiful epiphany.

I taxied to my hotel, half a mile from Daphne's home. My heart was pounding, and I felt like I could take on the whole world. Here I was, standing in a foreign country, about to see the woman I loved. It was a situation worthy of a Hollywood movie. I settled into my room, invited Daphne over and patiently waited, wondering what my first words to her in person would be after so long.

It was 9:38 p.m. in the United Kingdom when I heard two faint taps on the hotel door. My heart skipped a beat. But I was ready.

~John Esteban

Meet Our Contributors

Devora Adams is a writer and life coach who lives in New Jersey with her husband and four daughters. She is the author of *Amazing Women: Jewish Voices of Inspiration*, published by Menucha Publishers, as well as a proud contributor to the *Chicken Soup for the Soul* series. E-mail her at the_write_direction@yahoo.com.

Kristi Adams is a travel writer for Europe's *Stars and Stripes*, and served as a weapons officer in the U.S. Air Force. She lives in Germany with her husband, who is serving on active duty, and a curmudgeonly rescue cat. This is her fourth story published in the *Chicken Soup for the Soul* series. Reach her on Twitter @KAdamsBooks.

Heidi Allen began her journey as a successful wedding photographer, but knew she was supposed to be doing something bigger. Determined to make her mark, she has had many careers. Yet, it was working as a TV makeover producer where she realized she was meant to motivate and inspire, and the "Positive People Army" movement began.

Adriana Añon received her Bachelor of Arts in English from the University of Ottawa in 1997. Originally from Uruguay, she has lived and taught in Japan, Canada, Brazil, and the U.S., where she published her first short story. She currently lives in Ottawa with her husband and two children, whom she adores.

Colleen M. Arnold is a family physician in Lexington, VA, and holds a Master's degree in Pastoral Ministry. She is a widow and mother of three young adult daughters. She enjoys hanging out with family, writing, reading, walking, and working on her blog, *Living with Loss: Learning Lessons, Finding Joy*, which can be found at colleenarnold.org.

Sally Bair lives near Lake Superior. She received her B.S. degree, with honors, and worked as a journalist. She writes a weekly devotional column and has written three Alaskan adventures for kids and four seasonal devotionals. She has three children, ten grandkids and three great-grandkids. She enjoys nature, teaching Bible, and writing.

Sarah Barnum lives in Northern California with her husband Michael. She runs a freelance business: TrailBlaze Writing & Editing and enjoys riding her Appaloosa horse, Ransom.

Barbara Bartocci is the author of nine books and numerous magazine articles in major women's magazines. She is also a speaker who gives talks and seminars around the country to business, women's and church groups. The mother of three, she no longer skis (knee issues) but loves to do long-distance bicycling.

Barbara Bennett loves writing. She used her natural humor and acquired wit to survive twenty-six moves in seventeen years. Her memoir, *Anchored Nowhere: A Navy Wife's Story*, began as a keepsake of the five foreign countries and four states they temporarily called home. She lives in Raleigh. E-mail her at rbennett9@nc.rr.com.

Jean Bevanmarquez lives in Northern California and spent eighteen years in Kona, HI. Her career as a professional communicator spanned many fields: sales, counseling, marketing, management, administration, and volunteer coordination. She is passionate about helping others better their conditions, and facilitating change.

Arlene S. Bice is an author, speaker, and teacher of poetry and memoir. She is a member of IWWG, and founding member of Warren Artists' Market. She lives in South Hill, VA.

Paula Scott Bicknell got her start working for a daily newspaper. She now writes historical and contemporary fiction under the pen name Paula Scott. To learn more about her, visit her at psbicknell.com.

Micheline Birger is a retired nurse with a Bachelor's in Nursing from the University of Maryland and a Master's in Metaphysics from the University of Metaphysics. Comedy and writing are her true loves. She is a freelance writer and has several books on Amazon. She aspires to sell her screenplays and other works.

Barbara Brady lives in Topeka, KS with Merris, her husband of sixty-two years. She is an active member of the Kansas Authors Club and believes everyone has a story to share.

D.E. Brigham has taught English as a Second Language for several years in Turkey, Saudi Arabia, and the United Arab Emirates. He has retired from teaching and lives and works as a writer in Eastern Tennessee, where he enjoys pickleball, kayaking, and hiking. E-mail him at davidebrigham@gmail.com.

Connie Brown is a professional tourist who enjoys traveling, writing, and spending time with her family.

Michelle Bruce is a wife, mother and two-time breast cancer survivor. She loves to write short stories and children's books. Recently she has been published in *Reader's Digest*, *Chicken Soup for the Soul*, and *Country*. Michelle enjoys family, refinishing antiques, rummage sales with her husband, and playing with their numerous pets.

Terri Bruce has been making up adventure stories for as long as she can remember, though occasionally she tells true stories, too. She produces fantasy and science-fiction stories from a haunted house in New England where she lives with her husband and various cats. Learn more at www.terribruce.net.

Rose Burke writes from the heart, which fuels her primary focus of recreating her mother's life as a Dutch war bride in Canada. She has had success with essays and short stories. Her passions include personal history and photography. Her blog, *Paths Taken*, is a blend of her past, prose and pictures and can be found at roseburkeauthor.com.

Matt Caprioli lives in New York City. His essays have appeared in *Mr. Beller's Neighborhood*, *Cirque*, and *Opossum Magazine*. Matt was a journalist in Alaska for three years and has contributed to the *Huffington Post*, *Worn in New York*, and *The Paris Review Daily*. He holds an MFA in creative writing from Hunter College.

Monica Cardiff homeschooled her three beautiful daughters. Married to the love of her life, she now has an empty nest and is working on writing her second novel. She appreciates all the support she gets from her family, friends, church family, and the ladies in her empty nest group.

Dana Carpenter has always had an adventurous spirit and a love for telling stories. A few years ago she started to combine these two aspects of her life by penning some of her crazy adventures — made even more entertaining when you add living life with a disability into the mix! E-mail her at danac222@yahoo.com.

A.B. Chesler is an award-winning blogger and content creator from Los Angeles, CA. She is a proud six-time contributor to the *Chicken Soup for the Soul* series as well as the author of an illustrated tale for all ages entitled *A Man and His Books*. Contact her at www.facebook.com/ABChesler.

Janet L. Christensen is an inspirational author of children's fiction. She is the mother of two teenage boys and is married to her high school sweetheart. Janet enjoys playing piano, hiking, kayaking, and relaxing with her Cavalier King Charles Spaniel. Contact her via her website at janetlchristensen.com.

Since serving in the Peace Corps, **John Dwyer** has traveled to fifty-eight countries and worked in fifteen. John is a writer specializing in international travel and volunteering for the over fifty age group. He lives on the Olympic Peninsula in Washington State. Learn more at Over50andOverseas.com.

Joanna Dylan lives in Marblehead, MA, with her husband Josh and cat Boss. Despite traveling the world as a former flight attendant, the lure of the sea always beckons her return. She is currently working on a faith-based romantic suspense novel and is excited to see what God's next adventure is for her family.

Clara Ember is a journalist turned poet. She is a yoga practitioner, foodie, and nature junkie with a passion for social issues, health and wellness, and literature. She also loves crafting perfect letters and howling under full moons.

Michelle Emery lives in a small village in northern England. She writes for pleasure in the evenings and enjoys her job as a medical secretary in the National Health Service. She earned a Bachelor of Arts degree (first class) based around English literature and history, and has always had a passion for the written word.

John Esteban is a writer of fiction, nonfiction, science fiction, and several Hollywood screenplays. He lives a very private and secluded life.

Sara L. Foust writes inspirational romantic suspense from a mini-farm in East Tennessee, where she lives with her husband and their five children. She earned her bachelor's degree from the University of Tennessee and is a member of American Christian Fiction Writers and Tennessee Mountain Writers. Learn more at www.saralfoust.com.

Cynthia Graham's award-winning travel blog, *Blue Bag Nomads*, is consistently ranked in the top 200 (and climbing) of the top 1,000 travel blogs. As editorial director, creator, and freelance writer, she enjoys sharing her travel destinations, tips and photos with the hope to inspire you to get out to travel more! You can learn more at www. bluebagnomads.com.

Bronwyn Harris is from Petaluma, CA and now lives in the East Bay. She earned her BS in psychology from UC Davis and her teaching credential from CSU Sacramento. From 2000 to 2007, Harris was a classroom teacher in Oakland and wished to amplify the voices of her students, who deserved so much more.

Kenneth Heard is the Northeast Arkansas bureau reporter for the *Arkansas Democrat-Gazette*. He has also taught English and journalism at two universities, been a television reporter, a golf course greenskeeper, a cable television salesman, a repo man and a romantic dreamer.

Rhonda C. Hensley received her Bachelor of Arts from North Greenville University. She is a pastor's wife, mother of three, and grandmother of five earthlings and one princess in heaven. She enjoys writing, speaking, photography, and spending time with family. E-mail her at frstldy@bellsouth.net.

Georgia A. Hubley retired after twenty years from the money world in Silicon Valley to write about her world. Her stories and essays appear in numerous *Chicken Soup for the Soul* books, magazines and newspapers. Once the nest was empty, Georgia and her husband relocated to the Nevada desert. Learn more at www.georgiahubley.com.

Dea Irby has lived a variety of roles: wife to Tom for forty-three years, mom of eight, grandmom of thirteen (so far), restaurant owner/chef and published author, playwright/director/producer, and world traveler. She currently works as a Realtor with Berkshire Hathaway in the NC Research Triangle area and enjoys being in Toastmasters.

Heidi Johnson graduated with her Master's in Computer Science from BYU in 2004. She lives with her amazing husband and three children in Utah. Heidi has been a stage 4 cancer thriver for the past five years. Although her story is about cancer, her life is not; her dreams are about writing.

Laura Johnson is currently working on her MSc in Psychology at the University of Western Ontario. She loves all things geek and has a soft spot for dragons. When she's not writing, she enjoys playing *Dungeons & Dragons* with her friends and learning new pole moves. Currently, she is working on a fantasy novel.

Susan Maddy Jones is a former computer-science nerd, rewired for creativity and spending time in nature, not cubicles. She blogs about navigating life's ups and downs at www.SwimmingInTheMud. wordpress.com and about her awesome camping, hiking, and DIY adventures at www.TeardropAdventures.com. E-mail her at susan. jones326@gmail.com.

Alyssa Kamensky received her Bachelor of Science degree from Illinois State University in 2013. She majored in Early Childhood Education and currently teaches at a preschool in Chicago. Alyssa enjoys traveling, photography, working with children, and spending time getting to know her newfound family.

Cat Kenwell is a brain injury survivor, writer, mediator, creative artist, compassionist, and all-round cheeky monkey. After thirty years in corporate communications, she returned to school to become a qualified mediator (Q.Med.) and gain certification in post-concussion rehabilitation.

Mary Potter Kenyon graduated from the University of Northern Iowa and is a certified grief counselor. By day, she works as a librarian and by night, she teaches writing at community colleges. She is the author of five books, including the award-winning *Refined by Fire*.

Kelly Kittel is a fish biologist turned author, living in Rhode Island with her husband and three of their five living children. She swims in the ocean year-round, thinking of things to talk or write about. Her first book, *Breathe: A Memoir of Motherhood, Grief, and Family Conflict,* was published in May 2014. Learn more at www.kellykittel.com.

Lindsey A. Knuth was born and raised in Downers Grove, IL. She graduated from Western Michigan University in 2003 and returned to Illinois, which is where she currently lives with her husband, four children, two dogs, and hamster. She hopes to do more acting and writing in the future.

A criminal court reporter by day, **Jody Lebel** writes romantic suspense novels and short stories, which have sold to *Woman's World* and dozens of other publications. She was raised in charming New England, was an only child who had an only child (claiming she didn't breed well in captivity) and lives with her two cats in South Florida.

Arlene Ledbetter holds a Bachelor of Arts in English from Dalton College in Georgia. She has written adult Sunday school curriculum and been published in a number of magazines as well as in four *Chicken Soup for the Soul* books. Learn more at www.arleneledbetter.net.

Ruth Lehrer, a former teacher, retired thirty-three years ago, began writing personal essays, and became an Elderhostel coordinator. Her memoir, *My Book of Ruth: Reflections of a Jewish Girl*, was published in 2010. She conducts a writing workshop at The Bay Club in Bayside, NY.

Tom Lockhart holds a degree in Aerospace Engineering and worked for thirty years developing computer systems for the Department of Defense. He had a pilot's license, served with the Marines in Vietnam and traveled throughout the world and the U.S. He makes recordings of textbooks for distribution to blind and dyslexic students.

Ilana Long is the author of *Ziggy's Big Idea*. Look for her young adult science fiction novel and adult comic fantasy in the future. Ilana is mom to twin teens. Adventure travel and performing stand-up comedy are her not-so-secret passions.

L.M. Lush is a spiritual writer, blogger, and teacher, and is now writing her first book. She enjoys playing piano and cello, photography, and hiking with her dogs, Sadie and Oreo. She plans to open a spiritual center for healing in southern New York in the near future. Connect with her at LMLush.com.

Phyllis McKinley is the author of four books of poetry and one children's book. Her comfort zone is anywhere with family, friends, food, and flowers. She and her husband live in Florida. This is her sixth contribution to the *Chicken Soup for the Soul* series. E-mail her at leafybough@hotmail.com.

Mary Jane Michels earned her Bachelor of Arts in Journalism and Master's of Library Science from the University of South Carolina. She was an elementary school librarian for twenty-six years before retiring to enjoy traveling, reading and working out.

Jamie Leigh Miller received a Bachelor of Arts degree in Journalism from Southern Methodist University. She lives in Dallas, TX with her husband and pets. Jamie Leigh finds joy in sharing the tragically humorous moments in life.

Francesca Montillo is a native Italian currently living in Boston. She is the owner of Lazy Italian Culinary Adventures, which provides culinary and culture trips to Italy as well as Italian cooking classes in the Boston area. She enjoys writing recipes for her blog and is currently working on a cookbook for busy families.

Marya Morin is a freelance writer. Her stories have appeared in publications such as *Woman's World* and Hallmark. Marya also penned a weekly humorous column for an online newsletter, and writes custom poetry on request. She lives in the country with her husband. E-mail her at Akushla514@hotmail.com.

Courtney Lynn Mroch is the Ambassador of Dark and Paranormal Tourism for Haunt Jaunts, a travel site and radio show for restless spirits. When she's not traveling or writing, it's a safe bet you'll find her playing tennis or on a yoga mat. She lives in Nashville, TN with her husband and their cats, Tigger and Tabby.

Rachel Dunstan Muller is a professional storyteller and the author of four children's novels. She and her family live on Vancouver Island on the west coast of Canada. When she's not reading, writing or spending time with her children and grandchildren, you'll likely find her hiking the forest trails near her home.

Dr. Nash holds a Ph.D. in Theology and Ethics from Gloucestershire University and Edinburgh University. As an ordained clergy, she enjoys reading, writing, music, and travel. Dr. Nash is preparing to write inspirational work for churches and academic contributions for use in seminaries and universities.

Randi B. Nelson, MD, MBA, is a general pediatrician, who hails from Brooklyn and Long Island, NY. She is a former investment banking accountant. In her spare time, she enjoys concerts, museums, theater, and traveling. She currently works for a community health center in Brooklyn, NY.

Lynne Nichols is a retired elementary and middle school teacher. She divides her time between Taos, NM and Naples, FL. She enjoys reading, traveling, swimming, and spending time with her family and friends.

V.A. Nirode is a writer, solo traveler, cyclist, and runner based in New York City. In her spare time she works as a tailor and pattern maker for television shows and movies.

Marta A. Oppenheimer, the oldest of four sisters, was born and raised in Puerto Rico. She has degrees from Clark University and Pratt Institute of Art in New York City. She is an art director, freelance writer, and event planner for an animal rescue group. She lives in Miami with her rescued pets in an old house packed with art, books, and Converses.

Ava Pennington is a writer, speaker, and Bible teacher. She writes for nationally circulated magazines and is published in thirty-two anthologies, including twenty-five *Chicken Soup for the Soul* books. She also authored *Daily Reflections on the Names of God: A Devotional*, endorsed by Kay Arthur. Learn more at AvaWrites.com.

Marie Petrarch left a career in fashion to be a stay-at-home mom. She has three amazing kids who keep her busy and amused all day. Marie is blessed to be married to her soul mate, who supports her in every way. She's a happy New Yorker who loves spending time with her family and friends, reading, cooking, art, and working out.

Patty Poet is a PT Assistant, working in home health. She received her degree in physical therapy from Penn State University in 1995. She writes in her spare time and enjoys spontaneous travel, quilting, and piano. Her family is in Pennsylvania and she currently lives in North Carolina. E-mail her at papoet58@gmail.com.

Debi Smith Pouliot attended Central Connecticut State University during the Jurassic Period. She is married, with a grown son, daughter-in-law and two grandcats. She plans to write inspirational books about life in her own unique style to help people be and do their personal best. Debi also enjoys knitting.

Kay Presto's stories have been published in numerous *Chicken Soup for the Soul* books. She recently published a middle grade go-karting mystery novel, *Chasing the Checkered Flag*, which has recently won two national awards. Kay loves writing, and has written ten additional children's books. E-mail her at prestoprod6@yahoo.com.

Rachel Elizabeth Printy is blessed to have grandparents such as Magee and Pagee who have shaped her in countless ways. Both they and her parents, Tom and Debbie Printy, are a huge encouragement to her during the ups and downs of her writing journey. She would also like to wish Shannon and Nick Schell a lifetime of adventures together.

Caurie Putnam lives in a cozy log home outside Rochester, NY with her husband Eric, sons Brice and Brady, and four dogs. This is her third story published in the *Chicken Soup for the Soul* series. She's a graduate of the University of Rochester. Follow her on Twitter @CauriePutnam.

Tim Ramsey has worked in the public school setting since 1983 as a teacher and as a school administrator. He retired in 2013 and then decided to return to the classroom. He currently teaches writing to seventh graders and reading to college freshman. He has been published in five *Chicken Soup for the Soul* books.

Michele Bazan Reed spent forty years working in journalism and higher education before retiring to write travel articles, mystery fiction, and haiku. She enjoys history, books, antiques, dogs, and travel. Michele and her husband have two grown children and divide their time between upstate New York and France.

Sandy A. Reid lives and teaches high school English in St. Louis, MO. Her greatest joy in life is her family, both nuclear and extended.

Mark Rickerby has contributed seventeen stories to the *Chicken Soup for the Soul* series. He is co-creator and head writer of a western TV series in development, co-author of his father's memoir *The Other Belfast: An Irish Youth*, and wrote/sang fifteen songs on *Great Big World*, a CD inspired by and dedicated to his daughters Marli and Emma.

Mitali Ruths lives with her family in Montreal, but she is originally from Texas. She is currently working on balancing in *baddha konāsana* or crow pose.

Isaac Saul is a political reporter and columnist at the positive news website *A Plus*. He was born just north of Philadelphia and went to school at the University of Pittsburgh. He is a national champion ultimate Frisbee player, an avid traveler, and a political junkie. You can find him on Twitter @Ike_Saul.

Thomas G.M. Sharpe received his BA in English/Psychology from the University of Illinois, and his Master's in Business/Law from DePaul University. A long-time Chicago resident, he now lives in Cedar Rapids, IA and is a published author of poetry and nonfiction. He is planning on attempting serious fiction very soon.

Yashika R. Smith was born and raised in the mountains of Western North Carolina. Yashika has been passionate about writing since the age of six. Inspired by the loss of her father to suicide, she began to write as an outlet. She has written poetry, short stories and is currently working on a couple of books.

Jessica Snell is a writer whose short stories have appeared in *Daily Science Fiction* and *Havok*. Her essays have been published by *Christ and Pop Culture*, *Touchstone* magazine, and more. She blogs at jessicasnell. com and you can follow her on Twitter @theJessicaSnell.

Gary Sprague lives in Maine with his wife and two sons. His books, including the humorous *Lettahs From Maine* series and his latest novel, *A Teacher First*, are available online. He can be reached at his blog, middleagedmainah.com, on Facebook @garyspraguewriter, and on twitter @gspraguester.

Brittany L. Stalsburg is a researcher and professional writer based in East Haven, CT. She holds a Ph.D. in political science from Rutgers University.

L.A. Strucke hails from New Jersey and is a graduate of Rowan University. Strucke is a frequent contributor to the *Chicken Soup for the Soul* series as well as *Guideposts*. A mom of four, she loves family, cats and art, writing songs, poems, stories, and screenplays. Learn more at www. lastrucke.com.

Kim Tendland-Frenette is a graduate of the Institute of Children's Literature. She received her Bachelor of Education in 2009 and now works as an elementary teacher in British Columbia where she lives with her husband and two kids. Kim's current projects include kids' books and articles. E-mail her at kimtf.writer@gmail.com.

Jodi Renee Thomas has published stories on many subjects, from relationships to women's rights. She is a featured speaker for the women's movement and an award-winning author of *aMused*. She lives happily in Florida with her teenage daughter, husband, and three dogs that like to bother her while she writes.

Liz Thompson is a former Assistant Secretary General of the United Nations in New York. She was also a Minister and Senator of Barbados. Her new motivational book, *Make Yourself Happy*, will soon be available in the U.S. and online. She is a contributor to the *Huffington Post* and holds LLM, MBA, LLB, and LEC degrees.

Maile Timon is a blogger and content editor. She earned her Bachelor's in Broadcast Journalism from Chapman University. When she's not writing, she enjoys hiking in San Diego, CA.

Pat Wahler is an award-winning writer and proud contributor to fourteen *Chicken Soup for the Soul* books. Her first novel, *I Am Mrs. Jesse James*, will be released in spring 2018. Watch for Pat's first picture book, *Midnight the One-Eyed Cat*, in fall 2018. Learn more at PatWahler.com.

Nick Walker is a TV meteorologist with The Weather Channel in Atlanta, GA, and a songwriter/author of *Sing Along with the Weather Dude*, a CD/book teaching children weather basics, and *Don't Get Scared,*

Just Get Prepared, a CD of songs teaching storm preparedness. Contact Nick at his "Weather Dude" website: www.wxdude.com.

Rebecca Waters is a mother, grandmother, teacher, and author. Rebecca loves to travel and enjoys spending time with her family. Her novel, *Breathing on Her Own*, was released in 2014.

Alice Jones Webb is a freelance writer who holds the rank of second-degree black belt in Isshinryu Karate. She is a freelance writer, part-time karate instructor, and the mother of four children who have also earned the rank of black belt or higher. She currently resides in Tarboro, NC.

Marcia Wells taught middle and high school students for twenty years. After encouraging her students to reach for their dreams, she decided to pursue her own. To date, she has written and published two young adult fantasy novels, and is working on a third. She and her husband currently live in Eastern Washington.

David M. Williamson is an enlisted Air Force aircrew member on Okinawa with over twenty years in the service. He and his phenomenal wife Jami have four awesome children. When not writing fantasy or sci-fi, Dave loves coffee, singing, playing piano, and video games. Learn more at davidmwilliamson.net.

Joey Wootan works as an executive at a local utility company. He enjoys hunting, fishing, and spending time with his wife and son. This is his first story to appear in the *Chicken Soup for the Soul* series.

Following a career in nuclear medicine, **Melissa Wootan** is joyfully exploring her creative side. She enjoys writing and is a regular guest on *San Antonio Living*, an hour-long lifestyle show on San Antonio's NBC affiliate, where she shares all of her best DIY/decorating tips. Contact her at wwww.facebook.com/chicvintique.

Mary Jo Marcellus Wyse is a former English teacher and now a stay-at-home mom to her two young children. She is a graduate of Kansas State University (MA) and Vermont College (MFA Writing). She enjoys running, traveling, reading, and spending time with her family.

Pavla Žáková-Laney received her Bachelor of Science from Wellesley College in 1995. Pavla enjoys ballroom dancing, photography, ice dancing, biking, running, and helping animals. She wrote a book about her spiritual journey and is currently looking for an editor and publisher. She and her husband have four cats and a dog.

Luanne Tovey Zuccari is a retired journalist and community outreach coordinator for public schools. In retirement she is an online copywriter for clients all over the world. She has been married for forty-seven years and has two grown children and eight delightful grandchildren.

Meet Amy Newmark

Amy Newmark is the bestselling author, editor-in-chief, and publisher of the *Chicken Soup for the Soul* book series. Since 2008, she has published more than 150 new books, most of them national bestsellers in the U.S. and Canada, more than doubling the number of Chicken Soup for the Soul titles in print today. She is also the author of *Simply Happy*, a crash course in Chicken Soup for the Soul advice and wisdom that is filled with easy-to-implement, practical tips for enjoying a better life.

Amy is credited with revitalizing the Chicken Soup for the Soul brand, which has been a publishing industry phenomenon since the first book came out in 1993. By compiling inspirational and aspirational true stories curated from ordinary people who have had extraordinary experiences, Amy has kept the twenty-four-year-old Chicken Soup for the Soul brand fresh and relevant.

Amy graduated *magna cum laude* from Harvard University where she majored in Portuguese and minored in French. She then embarked on a three-decade career as a Wall Street analyst, a hedge fund manager, and a corporate executive in the technology field. She is a Chartered Financial Analyst.

Her return to literary pursuits was inevitable, as her honors thesis in college involved traveling throughout Brazil's impoverished northeast region, collecting stories from regular people. She is delighted to have come full circle in her writing career — from collecting stories "from the people" in Brazil as a twenty-year-old to, three decades later, collecting stories "from the people" for Chicken Soup for the Soul.

When Amy and her husband Bill, the CEO of Chicken Soup for the Soul, are not working, they are visiting their four grown children and their first grandchild.

Follow Amy on Twitter @amynewmark. Listen to her free daily podcast, The Chicken Soup for the Soul Podcast, at www.chickensoup. podbean.com, or find it on iTunes, the Podcasts app on iPhone, or on your favorite podcast app on other devices.

Thank You

We owe huge thanks to all of our contributors and fans. We were overwhelmed with fabulous stories about myriad ways that our fans have stepped outside their comfort zones. There were so many excellent stories that we created a second book from the submissions: *Chicken Soup for the Soul: The Power of Yes*, or a similarly titled book, will be published in 2018.

There had to be at least 6,000 submissions on this very popular topic, and our editorial team — Elaine Kimbler, Ronelle Frankel, Susan Heim, Barbara LoMonaco, Mary Fisher, and D'ette Corona — read every single one. Then, Amy Newmark chose 101 stories from a field of 557 finalists, Susan Heim did the first round of editing, D'ette Corona chose the perfect quotations to put at the beginning of each story, and Amy Newmark edited the stories and shaped the final manuscript.

This book was inspirational for all of us — to go even further outside our comfort zones than we already do, and we're a pretty adventurous group. We loved hearing all the different ways that our writers challenged and empowered themselves by trying new things and facing their fears.

As we finished our work, Associate Publisher D'ette Corona continued to be Amy's right-hand woman in creating the final manuscript and working with all our wonderful writers. Barbara LoMonaco and Kristiana Pastir, along with Elaine Kimbler, jumped in at the end to proof, proof, proof. And yes, there will always be typos anyway, so feel free to let us know about them at webmaster@chickensoupforthesoul. com and we will correct them in future printings.

The whole publishing team deserves a hand, including our Senior Director of Marketing Maureen Peltier, our Senior Director of Production Victor Cataldo, and our graphic designer Daniel Zaccari, who turned our manuscript into this beautiful book.

Sharing Happiness, Inspiration, and Hope

Real people sharing real stories, every day, all over the world. In 2007, *USA Today* named *Chicken Soup for the Soul* one of the five most memorable books in the last quarter-century. With over 100 million books sold to date in the U.S. and Canada alone, more than 250 titles in print, and translations into nearly fifty languages, "chicken soup for the soul®" is one of the world's best-known phrases.

Today, twenty-four years after we first began sharing happiness, inspiration and hope through our books, we continue to delight our readers with new titles, but have also evolved beyond the bookstore with super premium pet food, television shows, podcasts, positive journalism from aplus.com, and licensed products, all revolving around true stories, as we continue "changing the world one story at a time®." Thanks for reading!

Share with Us

We all have had Chicken Soup for the Soul moments in our lives. If you would like to share your story or poem with millions of people around the world, go to chickensoup.com and click on "Submit Your Story." You may be able to help another reader and become a published author at the same time. Some of our past contributors have launched writing and speaking careers from the publication of their stories in our books!

We only accept story submissions via our website. They are no longer accepted via mail or fax. Visit our website, www.chickensoup.com, and click on Submit Your Story for our writing guidelines and a list of topics we are working on.

To contact us regarding other matters, please send us an e-mail through webmaster@chickensoupforthesoul.com, or fax or write us at:

Chicken Soup for the Soul
P.O. Box 700
Cos Cob, CT 06807-0700
Fax: 203-861-7194

One more note from your friends at Chicken Soup for the Soul: Occasionally, we receive an unsolicited book manuscript from one of our readers, and we would like to respectfully inform you that we do not accept unsolicited manuscripts and we must discard the ones that appear.

Paperback: 978-1-61159-949-7
eBook: 978-1-61159-254-2

Easy tips to realize your full potential

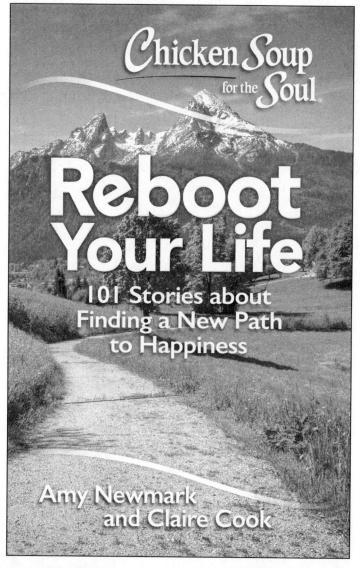

Chicken Soup for the Soul

Reboot Your Life

101 Stories about Finding a New Path to Happiness

Amy Newmark
and Claire Cook

Paperback: 978-1-61159-940-4
eBook: 978-1-61159-241-2

for finding the new you

Changing your life one story at a time ®
www.chickensoup.com